The Disaster Diaries

HOW I LEARNED TO STOP WORRYING
AND LOVE THE APOCALYPSE

SAM SHERIDAN

THE PENGUIN PRESS

New York

2012

THE PENGUIN PRESS
Published by the Penguin Group • Penguin Group (USA) Inc., 375 Hudson
Street, New York, New York 10014, U.S.A. • Penguin Group (Canada), 90 Eglinton
Avenue East, Suite 700, Toronto, Ontario, Canada M4P 2Y3 (a division of Pearson
Penguin Canada Inc.) • Penguin Books Ltd, 80 Strand, London WC2R 0RL,
England • Penguin Ireland, 25 St. Stephen's Green, Dublin 2, Ireland (a division
of Penguin Books Ltd) • Penguin Group (Australia), 707 Collins Street, Melbourne,
Victoria 3008, Australia (a division of Pearson Australia Group Pty Ltd) • Penguin
Books India Pvt Ltd, 11 Community Centre, Panchsheel Park, New Delhi – 110 017,
India • Penguin Group (NZ), 67 Apollo Drive, Rosedale, Auckland 0632, New
Zealand (a division of Pearson New Zealand Ltd) • Penguin Books (South Africa),
Rosebank Office Park, 181 Jan Smuts Avenue, Parktown North 2193, South
Africa • Penguin China, B7 Jiaming Center, 27 East Third Ring Road North,
Chaoyang District, Beijing 100020, China

Penguin Books Ltd, Registered Offices:
80 Strand, London WC2R 0RL, England

First published in 2013 by The Penguin Press,
a member of Penguin Group (USA) Inc.

LIBRARY OF CONGRESS CATALOGING IN PUBLICATION DATA

Sheridan, Sam.
The disaster diaries : how I learned to stop worrying and love the apocalypse /
Sam Sheridan.
pages cm
ISBN 978-1-59420-527-9
1. Sheridan, Sam.   2. Survival—United States.   3. Disasters—United States.
4. Preparedness.   5. Self-reliance—United States.
6. Emergency management—United States.   I. Title.
GF86.S537 2012
613.6'9092—dc23
2012030937

Printed in the United States of America
1   3   5   7   9   10   8   6   4   2

DESIGNED BY AMANDA DEWAY

ALWAYS LEARNING   PEARSON

For Patty and Ace,
from the luckiest guy on Earth

You are responsible, 100 percent, for your outcomes and actions. Keep that in mind as you read this book. This book cannot make you any safer; only you can do that.

The advice and facts presented in this book are presented for fun, to inspire thought, and for the betterment of humanity, whichever is easier. Most of the scenarios imagined are dangerous and horrible. Please don't take anything in here too seriously without verification and your own personal study. Consult a medical professional or local law enforcement. As Lenin used to say, "Trust, but verify."

There's an element of risk to some of the activities in this book. If you try them, that's your lookout.

CONTENTS

The Disaster Diaries

1.

RISE AND SHINE

In the dark room, caught between sleep and dreams, a noise drifts into my consciousness, rushing like the wind in the trees.

I slip from bed, trying to place the sound as it grows louder. My bare feet press against the cold wood floor. A rainstorm? I pull the curtains and touch the cool glass. No rain against the windows.

I stand wondering, squinting into the darkness as the rumble grows, jarring my ankles, shuddering in my knees. The house trembles.

And suddenly, I can hear the sloshing over the pavement, seawater thudding hard into the gate, a terrible authoritative knock. Out the window the streets are vanishing under the white foam, and then the water, torrid and black, nature's true face revealed: indifference. All that water has to go somewhere. Too late for the car, it's hood deep already. I holler at my wife, snatch my infant son from his warm crib, and dash for the stairs. The deafening noise presses us forward, glass exploding and cold seawater rushing in to fill up everything. It's already waist deep as we slog through and pull ourselves up the stairs, gasping. The ocean churns in the living room. I know more water is on the way.

I'm the guy who twists in his bed, snarling into the pillow, during what Nabokov called the "wolf hours" of insomnia. I gnaw at my worries like a dog without a protective cone collar.

I'm sitting on the sand with my family, watching the quiet surf wandering up the beach, with just a hint of onshore breeze building. A gull wheels overhead, cawing.

Then a bright flash, a blinding burst somewhere behind me, over the heart of Los Angeles. The blue sky crackles and turns incandescent white, brighter than the sun; and now it's burning us. I throw myself over my son as the heat rips my back. There's pain, and I can feel the skin bubble. First the hush, then shouts, then screams.

I know what it is, I'm up and running with the child in my arms, before the flash fades and the mushroom cloud stands revealed. We have to get inside, underground, before the blast wave hits and incinerates us, but we don't even have a basement. Where am I running to?

I mutter and turn in bed and punch the pillow helplessly, not quite awake, unwilling to give up.

Another me stands outside in the quiet night streets of my neighborhood, lit with streetlights shrouded in fog. I hear the rumble of distant surf and smell the heady ocean breeze.

A low moan whispers from the darkness, somewhere out of sight.

What was that?

The moan builds, and now it's the throaty hum of a hundred moans, along with breaking glass and a whirling car alarm. Slapping feet. They come at a run: zombies, the living dead, blind and frothing, their bodies flashing staccato through the misty pools of light. I dash inside, but the ground floor of our house is all glass, no barrier to that hunger. Up the stairs we go again, screams and smashing all around.

That does it. When we get to the zombies, I might as well call it a night.

Three thirty in the morning is as good a time as any to start my day. Outside, the night's blacker than an oil slick. Under the harsh kitchen lights, the gurgle of the machine and the bitter smell of coffee reassure me that all is not lost.

Not yet. The world is still turning, life proceeds. The nightmares are, for now, confined to my sleeping hours.

Is it just paranoia? A noisy mind, as the Buddhists say? Too many late-night double features? Or is something radical headed our way; are my dreams premonitions, warnings from my subconscious?

And if so, *if so,* what's to be done about it?

I'm a long way from home, here in the City of Angels. I'm an East Coast boy, and maybe the key to my insomnia lies in my past. Maybe it's obvious.

I grew up in the historic village of Old Deerfield, Massachusetts, famous for the Deerfield Massacre. In the winter of 1704, the French and Indians came over the wall in the dead of night. *They came over the wall, silent, tomahawks in hand.* Children just like me raced through the snow and were caught, scalped, their brains dashed out. Half the town was enslaved or killed.

Many of the houses on my street were preserved as museums, the private fortresses of colonial New England. Their insides were dim and still, frozen in time, available to tour. As a little boy I knew by heart which doors had tomahawk holes hacked in them. I stood guard through the endless summer of childhood, watching for Indians creeping through the cornfields behind my house; listening, amid the burning thrum of cicadas and the frogs peeping in the long grass, for war howls.

Perhaps the simple explanation is correct, that these childhood fears marked me. When I think about the kinds of activities I've engaged with over the years, they do seem to sway toward preparing for danger—and, let's be honest, violence.

I started boxing recreationally in college, indulging an obsession that has yet to truly let me go. I lived in Thailand and studied and fought muay thai, or Thai kickboxing, and from there it was a simple transition to mixed martial arts (MMA). I've traveled around the world training and fighting, and bashed headfirst into my own limitations, physical and mental. I've sailed through gales as a professional sailor and slaved to control burning forests as a wildland firefighter.

What if all this time I thought I was just living my life, I was unconsciously training for something, acquiring the skills needed for a battle yet to come? Was I getting ready for the screams in the night that meant the Indians were piling over the wall? The savage joy of hitting lured me into boxing, but perhaps it cloaked a sense of relief at my growing martial prowess. Why does every little boy (or grown man) want to be Bruce Lee or Mike Tyson? It's not to beat people up; it's because *hey, if I were Mike Tyson I would never feel afraid again.* Bruce

Lee wouldn't be scared if the Indians came over the wall; he'd start kicking ass. And firefighting and sailing maybe weren't just about setting my own schedule and avoiding the dreary office job, but about testing my own limitations, pushing myself against the extreme forces of nature, defusing fear through understanding and practice.

A small part of me has been expecting Armageddon for as long as I can remember. With the onset of adulthood, some of the dark fantasies burned off like fog; but other dreams, darker and more terrible, gathered in their place. And it seems I'm not content to leave them in books or at the movie theater. They come home with me, to be revisited in the hours before dawn.

As student of history, I've accepted that the shit is going to hit the fan someday. Just because life is almost comically good here for us in the United States, that doesn't mean it always will be. If 9/11 happened, if that diabolical plan succeeded, then anything can happen, and we all know it. Anything is possible. Nothing is unthinkable. I'm not saying the dead will rise and feed on the living; I'm saying, keep an eye on them.

The shift of a plate, the raising of the ocean floor, simple tectonics, geothermal dynamics—whenever we start getting the science lessons on CNN, somebody's getting hammered, and one day it will be you and me, friend. Just too much water that needs someplace to go, not even a Category 5 hurricane, not even a perfect storm. You can say what you want about climate change, but do I believe you, or NASA? Stephen Hawking has said that any possible alien contact would be dangerous, as when technologically superior Europeans "discovered" the Americas and the locals ended up getting stomped in every conceivable way—physically, morally, spiritually, genetically. I'm not blurring the line between fact and fiction; that line is already blurry. Stephen King wrote *The Stand* thirty-five years ago about a superflu that wipes out 99 percent of the world's population, and just because the guys at the Centers for Disease Control and Prevention have been wrong twice before (see avian and swine) doesn't mean that smart, knowledgeable people aren't still worried about that very thing. There's got to be a reason they keep standing on the panic button.

I've always been aware of the various potential disasters hanging like icicles over our heads. I never really consciously sweated it—I'm big and reasonably competent, but most important, nothing bad was ever going to happen to me. I'm the hero of this story. If the tsunami comes flooding into Los Angeles, I'll be fine. I swim like a bastard.

But then something changed for me, and it caused a shift in the quality of my nightmares.

Here's the bittersweet truth of having a child: it entails the loss of a kind of narcissism, the end of your own childhood. Maybe you're not the sole reason for the existence of the universe. With the rapid growth of the changeling you care for, his explosive metamorphosis, comes the knowledge that you are changing too, and finite—your perspective is fleeting. You're no longer the one pure reason the sun rises and the heavens wheel above in the night, the moon pulls the oceans, and doves call at dawn. That is the true gift of youth, and some never relinquish it—not a literal feeling of ownership but a deep sense of their own unique perspective, an unreasoning joy in the universe of their senses.

The banal creeps into your life with tiny steps; diapers, formula. The mundanity of child rearing soon becomes impossible to dismiss—I've somehow become the guy juggling a stroller, diaper bags, and a red-faced, surly toddler. In the airport, I push a cart behind my wife and child loaded high with luggage like a Victorian porter. I used to travel light, a pair of socks and a book, and now look at me. I've sailed around the world, I've sparred with world champions, and now I follow my kid around the playground, heckling him to eat a goddamn banana.

In the busyness of caring for an infant, and the subsequent passing months that stream into years, you realize that the self is passing, too—and that this particular road ends in one place. We're all coming to it, the big dirt nap; and when that moves in your consciousness from an acknowledged fact to an intuited *truth*, then the death of narcissism cannot be far behind, because really, how important can you be? By having a child you have shown the universe that you are replaceable.

Some people may process this humbling realization by relaxing and thinking, It's all a big circle of life, but not me. I'm not a fatalist. Blame it on the tomahawk marks. For me, having a kid sharpened the unease to an unbearable point. There's no blasé "It'll be fine, I got it" when you're responsible for the lives of others: Do you have it? Or not?

Having successfully rafted my wife through pregnancy and the first eight months of my son's life, I thought I could step back into my itinerant existence. I took off like a rat for the Peruvian Amazon, as soon as it was even remotely socially acceptable to do so.

Deep in the Tahuayo region, off a tributary of a tributary of the Amazon, I was the sole gringo with three local guides. In the jungle, nearly every living thing is poisonous and stinging. The foliage is so dense that you hack a path through it. You learn quickly not to touch anything with your hands. The machete is the finger with which the local man touches the jungle. My guides had assured me I didn't need a machete, as they had theirs, and I was the *gringo jéfe*. I realized within hours that they had neutered me: a man without a machete is helpless.

It was the dry season, but it still rained every day. First a far-off rushing like a freight train, the wind moving in distant trees, and *viene la tormenta*, here comes the storm. The four of us would huddle under our blue tarp tent, just four dudes relaxing as the jungle went dark. Sleeping on a blue tarp on the forest floor of the Amazon in a thunderstorm is a tough nut for an insomniac.

I lay under my mosquito net and thrashed. I couldn't stop thinking about the Big One or a tsunami hitting Los Angeles—only now I wouldn't be there. They were alone. By making a family, we had sewn our lives together. Cut one thread and destroy them all. Words from *The Godfather* echoed in my head: *"Women and children can afford to be careless, but not men."* Antoine de Saint-Exupéry had written, "Being a man is, precisely, being responsible." That's the secret philosophy of real manhood—a man takes responsibility for *everything* that happens. He never, ever makes excuses. If it's bad, he should have seen it coming, avoided it. He's a master of his fate. For six weeks, I feverishly dreamed of chasing my boy through the maze of the jungle. I could actually hear him cry out amid the cacophony of noises in the dark.

After that first sleepless night, I commandeered a machete—I was paying for this clown-car excursion, after all. With the blade in hand, I felt better, at least during the day. Now I could hack my own path to hopelessly lost.

When I stepped off the plane onto the hot tarmac of Los Angeles, hollow eyed and thirty pounds skinnier, I knew what to do—or, at least, what to *start* doing. It wasn't just "bunker up," or lay in stores of fresh water and canned food (although that was part of it). I had to prepare; I had to learn the skills I might need, not just physically but mentally and philosophically. If something was going to happen, I wanted to be ready.

Was I embarking on this journey in a desperate attempt to prove myself worthy of caring for another life? Maybe. But maybe not. You may think I'm a paranoid pessimist, spouting all this doom and gloom. But after considerable thought on the matter, I believe that's wrong. I'm an optimist. You and me, we're going to make it, at least those first twenty-four hours after the wave hits, the bomb drops, or those corpses start clawing their way out of the dirt. If you are one of the lucky 1 percent who survive the pandemic, it will be a damn shame if you die because you don't know how to start a fire. We're going to make it, and we need to know what we're doing.

2.

THE PRIMARY COMPONENT

Stuck in traffic.

We're driving home from a kid's birthday party in Pasadena. My son is in a sugar-induced near coma in his car seat, my wife next to him in the back. We are listening to classical radio, lost in our own worlds. Los Angeles traffic is nothing new, and we ride in the river of humanity with a kind of inert poise.

Then the radio begins that bleeping, that alarm—the public early-warning system—grinding over the music. Eeehhhnnn, eeehhhnnn Did I miss "This is a test, this is only a test," or is there a thunderstorm brewing? I lean over and glance up; the sky is clear. We inch along in traffic until we are under an overpass, the vast concrete web suspended above us. Then all the red lights flare on bumpers, and even the illusion of movement is gone.

The radio, hissing static now, begins to report snatches of information. "Massive earthquakes striking Japan, China, and Europe . . . Moscow in flames . . . New York rocked . . . earthquakes seem to be traveling around the globe . . ."

I slowly straighten up and make eye contact with my wife in the mirror—she heard that. We stare at the radio, as if there's an answer there. My hand reaches out to turn up the volume, and I feel like I'm moving underwater.

Is there an earthquake on the way? Should we get out of here and run for it? I look to see what other drivers are doing, but nobody seems to move. We all sit like cattle in a cattle car, waiting patiently to get to the slaughterhouse. The radio is warning us now to prepare; it's only a matter of minutes before Southern California is hit . . . could this be a prank? Like Orson Welles and War of the Worlds?

"Should we leave the car and run?" my wife asks. Her voice seems to cut into the dream.

"Uhm . . ." I say, and I glance at my sleeping son. I don't know.

"I guess so?"

My hand reaches down to turn off the car, but then pauses . . . somehow, doing something will make it all real.

Somebody honks, and then a dozen horns start honking. My son starts. I hiss with annoyance. That's really going to help, guys.

And then all hell breaks loose.

I worked as a wildland firefighter for a couple of seasons, and it's an interesting job—sometimes. There's an unusual conflict of needs: gritty manual labor and scientific, high-level risk evaluation. You're digging ditches in an unstable, dangerous environment.

Firefighters study extreme fire behavior and "tragedy fires"— blazes where firefighters burned to death. Even years later, the names of those fires are still etched in my mind with mythic power: *Thirty-mile, Storm King, Mann Gulch*. We walked in the firefighters' shoes and imagined how things unfolded: the timetables, the wrong choices ("At 9:00 a.m., they made their second mistake when they took a break to rest and observe the fire from point C . . .") We noted the missed warning signs. It all seemed perfectly obvious in hindsight. *They let fire get below them on the hill? What a bunch of dummies.*

A grizzled instructor once told me, "Fire applies the test, then the lesson."

He meant that firefighters are thrown into the unknown and forced to make decisions. Some live and some die. Later, in the cold light of day, we analyze their behavior to learn a lesson. And then we make up new rules and regulations. But the test comes first, and it is pass/fail. Life or death.

The apocalypse, whatever form it takes, will test you first; then, if you pass, you might learn something. The only guarantee I can make about the end of the world is that there will be one common factor.

You.

The test will be not only physical but mental. Yes, you may need to be strong and fast and able to run far or climb high, but equally important, if not more, will be your ability to think clearly. In a crisis, your decision-making capacity is the factor that most affects your survival. You'd better make the right choices, and you won't get a lot of time to deliberate.

You already know, to some extent, what fear can do. You've heard stories about guys peeing their pants or people losing control. *That won't happen to me,* you say. You may think, *I'm calm and collected.* You may think, *I'll rise to the occasion.*

You're wrong.

When you are threatened, either consciously or subconsciously, your brain reacts by releasing a flood of chemicals. These chemicals jack up your heart rate and get you ready to rumble—the brain prepares the body for danger. We've all heard of "Fight or Flight." It makes perfect evolutionary sense and provides a huge survival advantage. This response probably goes back to early cell specialization in the primordial ooze.

Our understanding of what happens to your body and mind when you are afraid has increased exponentially over the last few decades. In *Extreme Fear,* Jeff Wise writes that "the science of the fear response [is] in the midst of a golden age." The U.S. Army commissioned the National Academy of Sciences to conduct fear research in 1984, and others have followed suit. Sports psychology, which essentially deals with similar issues—the quality of performance under stress, albeit at much lower levels—has exploded as a field in the last fifty years. Scientists, soldiers, coaches, and athletes now use the latest technology to study the brain under duress. We have a clear, detailed understanding of how the chemicals that your brain releases in response to threat affect your cognitive and physical abilities.

Gross motor skills—pushing and pulling—improve as increased levels of stress hormones and chemicals are released and your heart rate climbs. The faster your heart beats, the more adrenaline enters your system and the harder your muscles work. Great, right?

Wrong. After a certain point, the performance of all other skills—fine motor skills, complex motor skills—shuts down. Supercharging the major muscles makes it harder for you to perform delicate acts. In one study, Navy SEALs ran a rugged obstacle course that incorporated shooting and hand-to-hand combat, and at the end they had to arrest someone using plastic zip-tie handcuffs. The SEALs who had *pre-threaded* the cuffs before the start of the course had no problem. Those who hadn't, struggled to fit the little tabs into the slots, their hands trembling from stress and exertion. They hadn't trained for that particular action, and their course times suffered.

Even remarkably simple fine motor skills can be affected. People under incredible stress have trouble dialing 911: they can't see the numbers, they can't press the buttons. A paramedic I knew said it was common for people dealing with a loved one's emergency to get a neighbor to dial 911 for them. Think about that for a minute—stress and fear can so unnerve you that you might not even be able to operate a phone.

The flood of stress chemicals released by your brain changes your body in hundreds of ways. Even the contour of the lens in your eye changes shape. Blood flows to the major muscles and the fingers get harder to use—your body is preparing to fight and bleed. There's the infamous loss of bladder and bowel control. You may piss your pants not because you're a coward, but because your brain is prepping your body to fight, run, or die, and no longer cares about holding your bladder shut. Your systems run triage.

The same chemicals affect your thinking. Wise writes, "The psychological tools that we normally use to navigate the world—reasoning and planning before we act—get progressively shut down." The part of the brain that makes you a rational human being is overridden by the older brain, the ancient survival system, the primal animal.

I had the good fortune to talk to Charles "Andy" Morgan, a psychiatry professor at Yale and research scientist at the National Center for PTSD. Andy works with Special Forces operatives, studying the effects of stress during their intense training at the SERE (Survival, Evasion, Resistance, Escape) School. This is training for people who might end up stranded behind enemy lines.

He had recently conducted a fascinating study: The participants had to copy a line drawing. They were each given a pen containing two different colors of ink, and halfway through the exercise, they were instructed to flip the pen over and draw using the second color. So he was able to track, in time, what people are drawing (the first thirty seconds in red, the second thirty seconds in blue).

"Adults copy all the big stuff first, and when they flip the pen and the color changes, they start filling in the details. Preadolescent kids start from one end and move across evenly; half the drawing is one color, the other half is in a second color. They move and think in a pure linear fashion.

"We test these adults in survival school about a half hour after they've been interrogated and out of the sixty-four guys, sixty of them copied the picture like prepubescent kids." Just to be clear, these are Navy SEALs, Special Forces operators, and Air Force pilots, not a bunch of civilians on their way home from work. And overwhelmingly, a half hour after being under extreme stress, they were thinking like children. "The norepinephrine is affecting the neurotransmitters," he told me.

I remembered something from my EMT days about trauma and children. Children often regress during trauma, moving backward down the developmental cognitive scale. So a terrified, injured six-year-old may act like a four-year-old; a four-year-old may stop talking and go back to preverbal communication. Andy was telling me that experienced, tough adults did the same thing.

Imagine that you're the flight attendant in charge of evacuating a burning, smoke-filled plane. If you've got a planeful of reasoning adults, the evacuation goes smoothly. But now imagine you've got a planeful of terrified ten-year-olds who need to exit quickly and inflate life rafts. Now you see the problem if they start searching the racks for their carry-ons.

The stress chemicals are mucking up the neurotransmitters in your brain that handle perception. You may dissociate, a clinical term for experiencing distortion in your perceptions of the world around you. You may experience auditory exclusion: Police officers have reported that they thought their gun wasn't working because they didn't hear it. *I didn't hear my gun go off.* I've experienced this myself—when I went elk hunting I was sufficiently nervous (or focused, take your pick) that I didn't hear my first shot. My second shot was so loud it made my ears ring. You might experience tunnel vision: *All I could see was the barrel of his gun pointed at my face, as big as a house.* Colors and brightness can shift, and sometimes people under high stress report seeing things through a fish-eye lens. Or their perception of time changes. *Everything was moving in slow motion.*

Jeff Cooper's color code was one of the earliest attempts to classify the changes that your mind and body experience under stress (he formulated and taught the code during the 1960s but didn't publish it until later). Military and police still use the code today, because it's easy to understand. Cooper was a former marine who fought in World War II and Korea and left the military to become one of the primary innovators of modern gunfighting techniques. What Cooper noticed was that at certain stress levels, marksmanship in his trainees fell off a cliff.

The color code classifies a person's stress level as either White (you're at home, totally relaxed, watching TV), Yellow (you're alert, out on the street), Orange (you're aware of possible threats, taking in your surroundings), or Red (you're fighting). These colors correspond to both the changes in the body and a loss in reasoning ability. If you're a sniper and you need to make a really difficult shot, you have to take deep breaths and pull yourself out of Condition Red and back into Condition Orange. Cooper tied these states to heart rate, as that was the only factor he could really measure. In reality, the correlation is not so direct, but for a simple rule of thumb it isn't bad.

There's a step further, a state in which people devolve into simple, desperate animals. It's called Condition Black (named not by Cooper but by the Marine Corps), where the heart rate is over 175 beats per minute and there's a corresponding catastrophic breakdown of performance. That's not 175 BPM from sprinting on the treadmill, but from natural drugs tearing through your system like a bee-stung bull in a china shop. This is where you start to really dissociate, to have perceptual issues.

Condition Black is what you really want to avoid.

During Condition Black, people might start "behavioral looping," performing the same tasks over and over again, in a frenzy. This explains the guy who gets stuck pushing on a locked fire escape door in a burning building for several precious minutes until he succumbs to smoke inhalation, and the police officer who yells at a suspect to drop the weapon, over and over, while the suspect slowly reloads his shotgun and eventually fires.

Now, looping might be a decent strategy if a wolf is chewing on your arm and you're bashing him with a rock. Keep bashing until you die or he lets go—that's a workable plan. But when even a small amount of critical thinking is required, sometimes people simply can't do it. You just can't step outside yourself long enough to see the fatal flaw in your strategy. Law enforcement officers have been found shot dead with the tendons on their fingers exploded—they were trying to pull the trigger with the safety on and got stuck in the loop. The survival strategy for the caveman can be a death sentence for modern man, who depends on using fancy technology, fine motor skills, and *critical thinking* to survive.

The thing that separates us from animals is the prefrontal cortex, and fear and stress can completely circumvent that part of your brain. The old brain, the one we share with monkeys and fish, takes over and attempts to drive the car. Circumventing the prefrontal cortex can save you or it can kill you. This phenomenon can be explained by something called polyvagal theory. The vagus is the nerve conduit in the brain stem that controls your autonomic nervous system and therefore all those things in your body that you don't consciously control, such as your heart rate and digestion. Polyvagal theory suggests that there is more than one vagus and that they function in a hierarchical system. Like changing states in the Cooper color code, you go from one to the other. Let me explain: There is a point, early on, when a human embryo looks just like a fish embryo. Our lovely modern brain has ancient components, which we sometimes call the reptilian brain. The mammalian vagus is myleinated, which means it reacts quickly as a neurotransmitter, while the reptilian vagus is non-myleinated, and reacts more slowly. But the reptilian vagus can sometimes win out. Under stress, a mammal scoots, while reptiles sometimes hunker down and shut off. The mammalian system can act as a gas pedal for the heart; the reptilian system can act as a brake pedal. Imagine what happens to your car when you stomp on the gas and the brake at the same time, as hard as possible. This superaroused state is what we're calling Condition Black.

You can freeze. There are different instances when this strategy can be successful—for example, freezing when you see a predator, since predators are often drawn to movement. Or it might be your ultimate, last-ditch survival ploy if caught in the jaws of a tiger—play dead, and maybe he will drop you. While this instinctual deep fear reaction *may* save your life, it can come up at the wrong time, and you can end up like the proverbial deer in the headlights.

The Cooper color code is a great tool, and an easy way to think about stress—but it's not quite as simple as all that. For some people, a high heart rate does not indicate Condition Black, while others may start "dissociating" and reach Condition Black at a much lower heart rate.

The new science of stress brought clarity, but humans have been studying fear for eons. Soldiers have been learning how to overcome stress in battle since time began. There are some tried-and-true methods, and if you've ever practiced a sport, you've already utilized them.

Dave Grossman and Loren W. Christensen wrote in *On Combat*: "You do not rise to the occasion in combat, you sink to the level of your training. Do not expect the combat fairy to come bonk you with the combat wand and suddenly make you capable of doing things you never rehearsed before."

Training is the primary way to handle stress hormones and the subsequent loss of cognitive ability. This is how the army operates, and it's something I know from fighting. A famous boxing trainer once said, "I get my fighters to where they can't do it wrong, even if they wanted to." You perform a task a million times so that when the stress hormones shut down your cognition, you can do it on autopilot.

Just because you own a gun doesn't mean you can use it. Unless you train with it, you will fuck it up. And how you train matters immensely. Some police officers working on a quicker draw (called "presentation" in gun language) train by drawing their pistol, firing two shots, and then reholstering. They spend thousands of hours at the range, working on this neuromuscular pattern. What do they do in real fights, under stress? They draw, fire two shots, and reholster while the fight is still going, while the bad guys are still shooting. The quality of your training has a huge effect on performance. If you train wrong, or at half-speed, or sloppily, then when the stress hormones override your system, you'll perform at half-speed or sloppily—you'll do exactly what you've trained to do. If you haven't trained to do anything, guess what you'll do? You'll run around like a chicken with its head cut off.

Unless, of course, this ain't your first rodeo.

Stress inoculation is another way to mitigate the harmful effects of stress, and basically all it means is experience, although I like the idea getting an injection of stress to combat the infection of fear. Training is rehearsal, experience is the real thing.

The best whip against the wild horse of stress is experience; we all know that. The unknown will prey on your worst fears and can drive you into a spiral of panic. If you'd lived through it just *once,* you'd be far more relaxed. The unknown is the killer, the fear multiplier. Just think of the horror movie problem—once you see the monster, the movie really isn't scary anymore.

I was in the tail end of a hurricane in Bermuda, and at its worst it was blowing maybe fifty knots, which is a capful of wind. Fifty knots is a strong gale, but not a full-force hurricane. I listened spellbound on the radio in our boat as a half-dozen pleasure yachts around us were abandoned. Sure, it was rough, a big nasty swell, very unpleasant. I'll bet water was coming in on those yachts, everything was wet, and they were getting bounced around. But they weren't sinking. If the people on board had just *held on* for six more hours, they would have been laughing at how scared they'd been. But they didn't know any better. They hadn't lived through it. To them, it felt like the end of the world. Those boats were eventually salvaged, meaning that they had stayed at least partially afloat; and getting into a Coast Guard helicopter in fifty knots is a riskier proposition than staying with a boat that isn't sinking.

There is crossover for stress inoculation, too, although not evenly across the board. A seasoned firefighter, used to performing in high-risk environments, will probably be less stressed in, say, a kidnapping situation than a person who isn't exposed to stress often. But it doesn't always work—I've seen professional tough guys fall apart in rough seas.

There is a simple technique that can help even an untrained person overcome extreme stress in any situation, and it's sometimes called combat breathing. Basically, the only link between the sympathetic nervous system and the autonomic is breathing. You breathe automatically, but you can also control your breathing with your thoughts, unlike your heart rate or your adrenaline levels. In incredibly stressful situations—if you can't dial 911—you can take four deep breaths, on a four-count (breathe in for four beats, hold, breathe out for four beats), and maybe this will break the spell. But chances are, if you are in Condition Black, you're too far gone to even think of this. That's the whole problem with Condition Black; you don't know you're in it.

Imagine what might happen to you if some science fiction apocalypse actually started. If that rogue wave were actually headed for shore. How you handle the stress hormones, the dissociation, and the cognitive dissonance will be the primary component of survival, at least in the first few minutes. The best way to avoid reverting to your reptilian brain is to train. So let's get started.

3.

WITNESS THE FITNESS

The hammering that I thought would never end finally subsides. Reality reasserts itself; the earth is no longer rippling. The silence is deafening, and then I hear a tinny scream, and I realize it's me who's screaming.

I'm trapped underneath something heavy. I shove and push, exploding with fear and anger.

I'm lucky. I'm alive. I'm just bruised, and I can move. Not much, but I can squirm. I frantically try to create some space around me. Something huge has landed on our car. The world is black, and my mouth is thick with grit.

Claustrophobia drives me, a bubbling terror, a spastic pressure. But the panic is building in my throat, behind my eyes: where are my wife and child? I see a tiny chink of daylight in the dark, and I attack it. Somehow I claw my way out, ripping skin and clothing, snaking and contorting. I tumble to the ground.

Dust swirls in curling serpents; the sunlight blazes in through open spaces. A piece of the concrete overpass, a thunderous weight, has sagged onto the car—not flatly, or I'd be dead, but at an angle. Broken glass glitters and shards lie everywhere. Car alarms blare, people are screaming.

Giant ships of freeway metal have broken free and slid down, the pieces leaning on each other precariously. High overhead, maybe sixty feet up, I can see the overpass, broken off, and a truck—an eighteen-wheeler—lying on edge, poised to slide down right on top of us.

My heart is beating so fast that I can feel it bubbling up into my throat. But there's hope—there's some space still in the car.

"HONEY?" I shout, and I can hear, in a detached way, how ragged my voice is, just on the edge of breaking. I throw myself at at the slab resting on the car, tearing at it, and I have a surreal sense of watching myself from far away.

"We're here," comes a distant voice, muffled, scared. "We're okay. It's tight, but we're okay . . ."

Relief floods my body in an intensely tangible way. I can feel it flow down through my chest and into my limbs, a sweet, intense joy. I collapse, breath coming in ragged gasps.

But now I have to get them out of there, before the next tremor hits and that truck comes down.

All the know-how in the world won't save you if you're not strong enough to pull yourself up onto the roof of your house when the tsunami hits, or if you're not fast enough to outrun the aliens. The one thing that is utterly and completely under your control is your own physical condition—you can get in shape.

Every scenario I run through my head has a massive physical component. Carrying my son in a backpack all day, hiking through a burnt-out Los Angeles. Fighting hand to hand with bandits. But there is another reason to stay fit: The physical is inextricably linked to the mental. The greater the fitness level, the higher the *cognitive* resilience to stress. In-shape athletes handle stress hormones better than out-of-shape people. The adrenaline dumps don't affect their minds as badly.

If you're in shape, you get to hang on to those fine motor skills a little longer.

I've proved it, in the cold light of day. When I was twenty-five I lived for about six months at a muay thai boxing camp in Thailand, training and fighting in the ring. My first fight was against a Japanese guy who was maybe twenty pounds heavier than me and a long time karate stylist—a heavyweight full-contact karate champion (or at least, that's what his manager told me). He was a better fighter than me, and he caught me with a punch in the first round, a punch I never saw. I went out, *donk*, falling stiffly to the ground like a board.

At the time, I was in incredible shape—I'd been training twice a day for five months, running eight miles every morning, and living like a professional fighter. I was getting through ten hard rounds of pad work with legendary muay thai trainers.

I hit the ground and bounced up like a jack-in-the-box. I don't remember it well but I have it on tape. I do remember the referee coming to give me my standing eight count, and I waved him off—because I saw my opponent was breathing harder than I was, even though he'd just knocked me on my ass. I could have had eight full seconds to clear my head, but I didn't want it, because it would have given him time, too. I went after him, didn't let him rest, and caught him with a knee right at the end of the round. He went down from it, but more from exhaustion than the force of the blow. He just wasn't ready for the pace. His techniques, his abilities, and his experience far outstripped mine. I beat him with conditioning.

—

Lawndale, Ca

—I looked up at Sean Waxman, and his flat brown eyes offered no sympathy.

"Let's go, Sam," he said, in a tone that implies I was shirking my duty. I approached the bar, ready for an overhead snatch.

The Olympic snatch is a kind of revelation, an explosive movement—power and strength and flexibility all tied together with timing and grace. Let me tell you something right now: that shit ain't easy. It had taken months of training just to get to this point, to attempt it. In one smooth motion, you lift the weight up off the ground, and then, explosively, you hurl yourself underneath it, bending your body into the overhead squat position, and lift the weight. You've seen those heavy Russian athletes, chalk on their hands and braces on their knees, holding a giant bending bar overhead until the lights go green, then dropping it with an earth-shattering crash. That's the Olympic sport of weight-lifting.

I stood over the bar and bent down, gripping at the extreme ends, as far apart as possible. I controlled my breathing, set my back, and started to lift, first with my legs, keeping the bar close, and then flowing into the surge, bouncing the bar off my hips, somehow transferring the energy through my body. Up came the bar as my body dropped down . . . but I didn't have it. The bar kept traveling, my body exploded like a broken spring underneath the weight, my legs splayed, and the bar smashed down behind me as I sprawled on the wooden platform.

"Well, that was ugly," murmured Sean in the silence that followed. He never moved a muscle. No *Omigodareyouokay,* nothing like that. He sighed, almost imperceptibly. "Let's try that again."

So what the hell was I doing here?

Fitness is a relative term. On its own, it means nothing; only a specific goal gives it meaning. Sure, there is a general sense of being "in shape," but really, that doesn't mean much in the world of kinesiology. What are you fit for? Being in shape to run a marathon doesn't mean you will be in shape to play tennis, although there will certainly be some crossover. A good tennis player will be able to run a long way; a good marathoner won't get exhausted by a tennis match, but he won't be exploding to the net, either. And neither of those would be much good as a powerlifter at a powerlifting competition. Furthermore, all three of those guys would wither in an amateur boxing match. I had a Division 1 soccer player once assure me, "I'm in shape, dude." He "gassed" (as in, his gas tank ran empty) after just a few minutes of wrestling, because he wasn't trained for it. He was way out of his comfort zone, holding his breath and straining. Stress did him in as much as anything. Wrestling isn't soccer. I'm sure if we'd been on the soccer field he would have run circles around me for ninety minutes.

All fitness is sport specific, and should be viewed through the lens of specificity. What are you trying to accomplish?

I grew up in a world ruled by the idea of aerobic fitness: running was the answer to any fitness question. Boxing is still dominated by this idea. Even though boxing is divided into three-minute sprints and one-minute rests, almost all boxers run. If they don't do roadwork they're not training hard enough. The sweet science in this respect is more of a dark art, dominated by turn-of-the-century thinking (that's twentieth, not twenty-first). Pro boxers get up and run six or eight miles every morning. Grizzled old veteran trainers shake their heads at modern science; they know what a fighter needs. Run, then run some more.

The weight lifting I grew up doing, taught by peers in high school gyms and workout magazines, was informed by bodybuilding, although I didn't know it then. Exaggerated muscle size, called hypertrophy, is usually associated with strength. Generally, a bigger muscle is a stronger muscle; that's the visual appeal to bodybuilders. And bodybuilders are pretty strong, compared to me. But that's not the same thing as being *powerful*, which is about being strong and fast.

If you knew the end of the world was coming, if that was a sporting event you were preparing for, what would you do? Well, in the film *Zombieland*, the protagonist mentions that an important survival rule is "cardio," but what he means is sprinting. Most sports are about sprinting, it turns out. Baseball, football, even soccer require less than ten seconds of intense bursts, followed by a lull. Apocalyptic scenarios are about sprinting too—think of Tom Cruise sprinting through the opening of *War of the Worlds*. Fighting, certainly, is about sprinting. What's the difference between sprinting and distance running, in terms of training? I'm glad you asked.

Educating myself in the field of exercise was trickier than I had imagined it would be. There are too many differing opinions, too many workout styles. It's a real maze, a rat's nest of opinions. I tried to find a trainer guru and failed. I picked my way through a half-dozen books, notably *Strength Training*, from the National Strength and Conditioning Association, and *Supertraining*, by Yuri Verkhoshansky and Mel Siff. I spoke to Dr. Ralph Rozenek, a professor of kinesiology at Cal State Long Beach, whose specialty is "physiological responses to exercise." I talked to a bevy of people, some frauds, some half-informed, some crazed conspiracy nuts, some possibly brilliant. A few were all those things at once.

Eventually, I found my way to Sean Waxman, he'd competed at

the national level in Olympic lifting, won California state championships, and trained under Dr. John Garhammer, the preeminent expert in the United States on the biomechanics of weight lifting. When I say "weight lifting" from now on, I mean Olympic weight lifting, not preacher curls.

When I called Sean and introduced myself, his voice was gruff. As I tried to explain the project to him, I wandered off on a tangent: how would I get stronger in a postapocalyptic world without gyms?

There was a pause. "Uh, lift heavy shit," said Sean.

———

Think of human energy as a continuum, a spectrum. Whenever you do something, there's an electric and chemical reaction in the body that makes the muscles work, through a spectrum of systems. The various energy systems fire sequentially: You start off in the nervous system, the neuromuscular system. The brain, the nervous system, sends the electrical signal. Your muscles contain stores of a chemical compound called ATP, which responds to the electrical signal by causing the muscle to contract. Other chemical reactions are involved: read about the Huxley sliding filament theory and myostatin if you feel up to it.

The initial move is anaerobic—it doesn't require air, you're working with what's inherent in the system, the stored electricity and chemical energy in your body. But if motion continues, you begin to metabolize glucose and you start to need air. And now the intensity (or strength) falls off. So during your first few repetitions, your body uses the anaerobic (ATP) system; by the tenth rep (some say thirty seconds of movement, some say two minutes) you move into glycolysis (which is metabolic: you're metabolizing stored glucose); in the higher reps, you're in the aerobic system. You're strongest at first, when all the chemicals are loaded and the chemical receptors are primed to react. Strength falls off slowly, then quickly.

There are many different ways to talk about this: the ATP system, the ATP CP system, glycolysis, the lactic system, and so on. Some charts describe three energy pathways that are in the continuum; some charts have six or seven. But basically, as you move, your muscles use these differing systems in sequence.

The more research I did, the more confusing it got. Some evidence suggests that the aerobic system is actually in use from the beginning. Every time I turned around there was a new study. But the basic idea is sound and unchanging—that you want to train multiple energy systems to make them stronger, not just one. This is a pretty well-known and accepted idea in the sports-science world. Particularly, you have to train your short-term "sprint" system—the anaerobic system—to get better at sprinting. This training also helps your aerobic system: sprinting helps your distance running. But it doesn't work the other way around. (Still, a lot of athletes—especially boxers—have been slow to change their training.)

The one truth I gleaned was that *power* is a function of the neuro-muscular system—you need to train your nervous system as well as your muscles. The electrochemical pathway from the brain through the nervous system to the muscle needs to be fast and efficient. To get big muscles, bodybuilders lift slowly, with the muscle under tension, to tear the fibers. Their primary concern is muscle size. But for almost everyone else, speed is the primary concern. As they say, if you train slow, you'll be slow. So athletes definitely shouldn't be bodybuilding. Or only going on long, slow runs.

Olympic lifting is about the "one-repetition max" (1RM), meaning lifting the absolute maximum weight you can, by giving the absolute effort, *one time*. You have to lift fast, as fast as possible, in order to lift the most weight possible. This is primarily about the nervous system, about training the nerves to fire fast and efficiently. Sean told me that that in a massive experiment conducted at the 1968 Mexico City Olympics, pound for pound, Olympic weightlifters were found to have the greatest level of speed and strength, more than any athletes in any other sport.

So BANG! Olympic lifting demands one big, quick move that's not just about your muscles, it's about how efficiently and powerfully your nervous system works in conjunction with your muscles. The amount of power you can summon is a measure of how well you can get those connections to work.

—

Waxman's Gym in Lawndale is a warehouse, the utilitarian purpose of the gym its own aesthetic. There are no mirrors, just a huge open space with stacks of Olympic weights, lifting platforms, and bars. The cavernous space has a section walled off by bare wood: Sean Waxman's apartment. He lives in the gym. To open for business, Sean rolls up the garage door.

When I met him, Sean looked like he lived in the gym, shaggy and unkempt. He had a rough beard, his hair was shoulder length and curly, and he dressed in sweatpants, flip-flops with socks, and a flannel shirt over his truly massive trunk. His appearance bordered on the ridiculous, but it came from the attitude: *Who cares what I look like, that doesn't matter. How much can I lift?*

His body is a classic of the genre. He looks like a Russian weight lifter from the seventies, thick and beefy, not a sculpted Adonis. The Olympic weight lifter has an almost aggressive disdain for appearance: no six-pack abs, no tricep definition. How much weight can you get up over your head? That's all they care about. The first day we met, Sean wore a T-shirt with a drawing of a set of brass knuckles and

DEFEND THE SQUAT written on it; if somebody was gonna insult the squat, Sean was going to have a problem. I would eventually learn that he had that shirt in about twenty colors.

Sean, in his slightly combative Brooklyn accent, impressed me with the clarity of his thinking.

"What's the best thing I should be doing?" I asked him. He gave me a wry grin.

"Thinking either best, or *better* will get you into trouble. Let's talk about the essence of a lot of sports: it's about getting to the point of attack before your opponent does," Sean said. Working backward from that goal, the way to move the body is to apply force to the ground very quickly.

"I know people say, 'Olympic lifting doesn't resemble my sport, there's no barbells in my sport'; but we're training an attribute. You develop the skill of producing power, and that skill can be applied on the field, in the ring."

Sean talked about how the fitness industry (boo, hiss) had taken the "training pie"—the various elements like mobility, strength, power, agility, and stability—and divided it up in order to focus on and monetize each element separately. Even though some of those things are easy to monetize and easy to train, separating them isn't the best and most efficient way to improve performance.

"*Strength is agility and stability.* If you are filling up a box with rocks, strength is the biggest one—put that rock in first, then put the little ones in," he muttered. It makes sense: the stronger your legs are, the easier it is to balance, to a certain extent.

The movements of the snatch and the clean and jerk take time and training with a decent coach. They can take hours or years to learn, but months is more likely, according to Sean.

For a raw guy like me, a newcomer with a short amount of time, Sean would teach only four exercises: the squat, the dead lift, the overhead press, and the "good-morning" (an old-school lower back strengthener).

"But," he said, "the nervous system is the key to performance, and nothing out there stimulates the nervous system like the snatch, the clean and jerk, and their derivatives."

Sean lent me an ancient, dog-chewed pair of his weight lifting shoes. They were sneakers with hard wooden soles and a slight heel. I clacked around the gym in them and felt ridiculous, like I was wearing dress shoes with shorts, even though everyone had them on.

At the start of our training, we performed another exercise considered old school, the back squat. Ye olde knees-past-ninety-degrees, deep-as-you-can-go back squat. You don't see it that much in the gym these days, because it's hard and considered dangerous. The way to avoid injury is to use the proper form and, most important, to use light weights until you're strong enough to progress. I did the back squat with just the bar, forty-five pounds. I needed to learn an essential skill: how to make my torso into a solid block.

The torso is a wondrous thing. The spine and the ribs and the pelvis have an amazing range of movements. But for lifting heavy shit, you need to turn the torso into a single rod, a conduit of force. The more solid and stable it is, the stronger you'll be and the less likely you are to injure yourself. Weight lifting is a neuromuscular skill that requires training. Neural pathways have to be learned and ingrained, and muscles need to get stronger.

The back has to be arched and locked, which forces you into a structurally sound position. Letting the back round will make you weak and lead to injury—or, worse in Sean's eyes, "you won't make the lift."

Breathing is important for all lifts. For most weight lifting, I had been taught (probably by another kid in junior high) to exhale in a tight manner when doing the hard part of the lift. It relieves pressure and allows you to establish a rhythm for the ten to twelve repetitions you're doing. That's bodybuilding. Curls for the girls, as they say.

In Olympic lifting, you hold your breath. Sean said, "With a big breath, you create a brace of air inside the waist, into the upper back. This is sometimes called the *Valsalva*."

Dr. Rozenek, of Cal Tech, explained, "Valsalva is defined as fixed expiration against closed glottis. The airway is closed, and by contracting musculature surrounding the thoracic cavity, in the chest and abdominals, you increase the intrathoracic pressure. By increasing the intrathoracic pressure you stabilize the spine."

Sean went over the tightening sequence I had to learn to perform before lifting something. You have to practice doing this until it becomes second nature. As well as the Valsalva, you want to "*Kegel*," or squeeze the pelvic muscles as though you're preventing yourself from going to the bathroom.

Sean said, "Think of the pelvis as a bowl, and the spine is a spoon in the bowl, and the muscles radiate off it like spokes. If you set all those muscles tautly, you keep the wheel true."

For the big lift—the 1RM, the maximal effort—you hold your breath. It's anaerobic.

Learning the skill of how to properly set the back and torso, to perform the Valsalva and Kegel and straighten—all at the same time, all as instinct—is a huge survival component. Not only are you stronger, but you are lifting properly and safely. Injury prevention and sustainability have got to be priorities in a long-term grid-down scenario. If you're out hunting, deep in the woods, and a log falls on your buddy, you need to lift it off him quickly and properly. The set of the back and the torso has to become ingrained, natural, instantaneous. If the world is in chaos and there are no emergency rooms or pharmacies, getting back surgery will be a drag.

"It's the essence of the essence," Sean said with a smile. "Whether lifting weights or groceries, a strong stiff torso is the conduit, otherwise it's not only inefficient, it's unsafe. The skill is in absorbing energy, down through the torso. You learn to have the body in harmony, like an orchestra. If one instrument is off, you'll feel it.

"When you get older and you hurt your back, they tell you to stop lifting things," Sean continued. "So you restrict movement, you start limiting your life. You should *lift more*, but in the right way, to rebuild strength and functionality."

Sean's discourse was heavily laden with what I call the UTD, or Universal Trainer's Disease: the unshakable belief that every other trainer out there is a fucking moron, a danger to themselves and others. Nearly every trainer I've ever met has felt this way: at best dismissive, at worst openly contemptuous and *angry*.

Sean was aware of it, and he even knew why it happens: something called the training effect, or the beginner's effect. If a totally out-of-shape person starts training, they will get good results, no matter what they do. If they start running, or lifting weights, or doing kettlebells, or yoga, or Pilates . . . anything will help them. So the universal experience that many people have is they start doing X and *it works*. Now they become experts on and spokesmen for X. Everyone should do it, it can fix everything. The body starts to adjust, and you get less effect— but now you take a few months off, and when you return, the training effect happens again. The vast multitudes of "personal trainers" working in the field don't have the scholastic background, and instead rely on their own experience as a guide. They've seen results with themselves and their clients, and thus they know *what works*. And anybody doing anything else is an idiot.

Sean, at least, had not only walked the walk, and competed, but had also studied. He'd done his undergrad at Cortland State in New York, a school with one of the top physical education programs in the country. Sean was a good athlete who had been invited to two different pro football free agent minicamps, by the Jets and the Panthers, but he'd gotten injured both times. He'd come to Long Beach for grad school in biomechanics.

"I didn't graduate," he said. "I did all my coursework but decided to leave school for my training. I regret it, but I had to create the right environment for myself. Comfort is the killer of will," he said, deadly serious. "I had to create a Soviet Union for myself."

Sean is a tough guy, and he had lived in the gym or in his car in order to train. He'd been homeless to train. He often launched into one of his favorite rants: how a totalitarian state is better for sports science than a democracy. He lamented the lack of money in the United States for weight lifting. In other countries, countries without football, weight lifters are rock stars. But it's not just the professional coaches and athletes; it's the control. In Sean's mind, all of the best sports science, the longitudinal, twenty-to-thirty-year studies, came out of the USSR. Under totalitarianism, coaches could control all the variables. Athletes were fed the same thing, experimented on in the same way, with the same drugs.

"And then there's talent recognition: in China, once a kid is picked for their sport, they live in a dormitory and go home twice a year to see their parents." Sean shook his head in wonderment at how great a system that was.

"Weight lifting is interesting because it's so controlled, and so specific. The weight of the bar is the weight of the bar; everything is measurable," Sean mused.

This brings me to the other really interesting thing about the experience of training with Sean: what I call the *tyranny of weight*. You have to lift the right way. If you don't, if your form is off, if you aren't efficient, then you won't be able to make the lift. You won't lift as much as you're capable of. The fist of the weight, pressing down on you, forces you into the correct position. When you squat with the weight overhead, if you have bad form, or bad shoulder mobility and can't flex enough, you won't be able to do it and you'll fall ass over teakettle—which I did. Often. Olympic weights are made so that they can be dropped. The weights crash, but you don't get hurt. The weight is unequivocal. There is no gray area, just a yes or a no. Weight lifting as a sport is intensely limited, the variables are closed, and there's a long history of these fixed pieces—the most efficient methods are known, refined, perfected. Nobody's going to come along, start doing things totally differently, and win all the medals, like when Dick Fosbury introduced the Fosbury flop to the high jump.

When the form is right, the weight seems much less. Sometimes I'd do an overhead squat with my shoulders in the right position, and the weight I'd been struggling with suddenly felt like nothing. When the snatch went right, when it flowed, the weight seemed 30 percent lighter. It just felt good and rose easily.

Sean is drawn to this purity. There's no judgment, no aesthetic component, just the simple question: did you lift the weight? There is a terrible exactitude to that judgment. To get down and sacrifice at that altar requires a strange meshing of personality and circumstance. It sort of explains the dichotomy of Sean, who looks like a sloppy bum but speaks with precision and watches with a sharp eye to make razor-thin adjustments. "If the lift is off by two millimeters, it will fail," he says.

—

"All this is well and good," you might say, "but I don't have an Olympic trainer, and besides, I'm not going to spend months learning the snatch or the clean. What about sustainability?"

I'm thirty-six years old myself, and I don't have the time to drive to Sean's gym four days a week. I don't have a set of Olympic weights in my garage, although I'd like one. Sean told me a basic level of strength that remains an excellent goal: be able to squat twice your body weight. I found myself much stronger with the ability to brace and set my core, and it even translated into very explosive movements, like hitting a heavy bag. There is a definite health value to learning how to properly lift heavy things.

A very wise boxing trainer once told me, "Get strong doing what you're doing," He wasn't a big fan of lifting weights. A lot of rock climbers will say that the only way to get in shape for climbing is to climb. What does that mean for the end of the world? Well, we already talked about what cardio means: sprints. A vast majority of adults lose contact with the physical, and even those who run rarely sprint. But what are you going to do when you're pursued by zombies? Run sprints now, so that if you ever really need to, you won't blow out a knee in your first three steps.

When it comes to fitness, we're all an experiment of one. There's no "Six-Minute Abs" for the apocalypse.

It's in vogue for trainers today to pooh-pooh running. Everybody is doing the Tabata protocol and CrossFit. Long runs are out of fashion as a method for exercise. I've had a multitude of trainers tell me how stupid distance running is. Sure, I get it; distance running doesn't work the anaerobic systems. "You have to be fit to run, you don't run to get fit," a trainer told me. Long-distance runs only hurt you, they break down the body, and you can get a "better" workout from a nasty set of sprints that tax your nervous system as well.

But read *Born to Run,* by Christopher McDougall, and see if you change your mind. The book explodes the myths and mistakes of running, and perhaps the most interesting is the evolutionary component. I tracked down one of McDougall's sources, Daniel Lieberman, a professor of evolutionary biology at Harvard.

"There are archeological sites in Africa with animals that were clearly hunted that are two million years old. So, we've been hunting for a long time. Yet putting a stone on the end of a stick is only three hundred thousand years old," Professor Lieberman told me.

You see the issue here? How was all that hunting getting done? As Lieberman asks in his book *The Evolution of the Human Head*, "How could small, weaponless hominids hunt or scavenge effectively? Both tasks are, by nature, dangerous, difficult and highly competitive. Meat is an ephemeral, highly valued resource."

All the adaptive features of the hominids that became *Homo sapiens* lead in the direction of distance running. The upright posture, the bipedal gait, the head and neck configuration, and above all the ability to sweat and dump heat meant that these hominids were gaining an advantage when they gave up other traits. Because of the ability to regulate temperature, they could hunt during the hottest part of the day.

Professors Lieberman and Dennis Bramble, of the University of Utah, published a paper in 2004 introducing what has since become the more or less accepted theory—namely, that running and the "persistence hunt" were a critical part of our evolutionary history. The Kalahari Bushmen have been documented doing the persistence hunt. You don't outrun the antelope—you run it to earth. The antelope can outsprint you, but you make it sprint, and make it sprint again, and after hours of relentless pursuit, the antelope overheats. Lieberman's book explains that

> eventually, usually within 10–15 km, the animal collapses from hyperthermia (Liebenberg, 2006). The basis for this kind of hunting lies in human endurance capabilities, which exceed those of other mammals, especially in the heat. Reasonable fit humans are unique in being able to run 10–20 km or more in hot conditions at speeds (2.5–6 m/sec) that exceed the trot-gallop transitions of most quadrupeds (Bramble and Lieberman, 2004). Because

quadrupeds, including hyenas and dogs, cannot simultaneously gallop and pant (Bramble and Jenkins, 1993), a human hunter armed with nothing more lethal than a club or untipped spear can safely run a large mammal such as a kudu into hyperthermia by chasing the prey above its trot-gallop transition speed.

"When we published that paper in 2004, everyone thought we were nutcases," said Professor Lieberman. But when I spoke to him, it had been seven years and not a single rebuttal had been published. The paper was now widely cited, and people were supporting it with other papers.

Watch the incredible variety of body types that participate in a marathon. How many hundreds of thousands, nay, millions, run a marathon every year? How many people run ultramarathons, once thought to be in the realm of the impossible? McDougall mentions Arizona's annual fifty-mile Man Against Horse Race, where at short distances the horses kick ass, but later on humans start to close the gap. In 2011 the fastest man ran 7:33 and the fastest horse ran 6:45. McDougall's argument is persuasive: running is our heritage and we were born to do it.

I hadn't been distance running in years, but as I took back to it, I felt how natural it could be—how healthy, how pure. Running in some way completes us as animals, and the conditioning from long runs is incredibly healthy for a thousand reasons, including the core work and the overall body tension, not to mention the fresh air.

I thought about the training I had planned. Hunting and hiking in the mountains of Colorado were going to require endurance. Moving to cover while shooting guns in the heat of Alabama was sure to require quickness and deftness, at first. But then as the days wore on, surely endurance would once again be the premium. Survival will force you into a shape, if you live long enough. If endurance is always the premium, shouldn't we all be doing long runs and training for triathlons?

Maybe. Being fit for the apocalypse is about surviving not only that first week but those first twenty-four hours, or the first fifteen seconds. You might need that power, that *burst* to get up onto the roof, to pull that beam off your friend. In the weeks that follow, your body will start to adapt to your new environment, whether it be walking all day to scavenge in an urban wasteland, hunting wild pigs with a spear, or sprinting from zombies.

Survival—passing the test—is going to overwhelmingly come down to mental abilities, but the mental is inextricable from the physical. Stay in shape for the cognitive benefits, and get your rest.

You're going need it.

—

I grab the rubble and instantly set my core, concentrate on my Valsalva breathing, and Kegel before I explode, legs straining. The massive slab doesn't shift. It's immovable. It's got to be tons.

"Honey, get us out of here . . ." I hear faintly from inside the crushed car, and my son starts to cry.

My hands uncurl off the concrete slab, white with strain, torn and bleeding. That ain't gonna do it. I look around. I can feel black panic bubbling up inside me. I resist the urge to throw myself at the rubble and blindly dig. I look up, and I swear that tractor-trailer sways.

I hear a distant rumble, thunder that doesn't stop. An aftershock is on the way. I've got a few seconds to get them out. I can feel my heart thundering, and I breathe. In, one-two-three-four, hold, out, one-two-three-four. Now think.

A lever. Give me a long enough lever, and I can move the world. I cast through the rubble, and then I get my first break of the day—a long, thick piece of rebar has snapped loose. I snatch it up, leap on top of the car, and set it deep in the crevasse. It slides in with a steely ring. I can hear the rumble louder now, the wave approaching. I can feel that tractor-trailer overhead, shifting.

"Hold tight, honey!" I yell. I coil in, wind myself in over the bar, set my legs and my whole body, clamp it all down, and then explode against the lever. This is it, this is the one. I can feel, for a second, that I'm stronger than I've ever been.

It gives . . . first a fraction, then an inch, and then, as the ground begins to sway, the concrete slab wobbles like a top, a massive, multiton top, and I bound clear as it comes down. The rebar clatters to the ground. Dust fills my eyes.

Just the car door now, smashed and angled, but it gives way, and I hear the cracking from above. I plunge into the car, grab them both, and explode backward, ripping them out, their eyes wide, lurching and lunging to safety as the world fills up with noise.

4.

PACK YOUR LUNCH

The Big One. Has to be, I think. The earthquake Los Angeles has been waiting for. I become aware of the rising tide of noise around me—sirens, car alarms, screams. A lot of other dazed drivers, some holding bloody heads, cradling bashed ribs. No point in hanging around, no help is on the way, no ambulances can make it through.

We walk miles through the city. My arms ache from carrying my son. His weight increases with the hour. I pass him from arm to arm, using a Gable grip, and even carry him for miles on my shoulders.

"My dogs are barking," I joke for about the seventh time to my wife, who no longer even smiles at me.

The damage actually isn't too bad in most of the places we pass. Broken windows, a few sagging doors, but not the absolute carnage I had feared. The city swells with sirens, and in some places there are collapsed buildings, rubble, bandaged heads and dazed voices. But it's not devastation. For the most part everyone seems okay.

People stand in clusters, talking, even laughing in relief. A few cars crawl along, trying to pick their way home. A shopkeeper is handing out water on a corner; he has cases piled high behind him. This is the friendliest I've ever seen Los Angeles.

It's dark when we finally arrive at our house. The pavement is cracked, and it looks like a corner of the house has settled, but surprisingly, not even all the windows are broken. My neighbor, Greg, had turned off the gas.

We walk up the steps and unlock the door. Inside, I can faintly see the mess, pictures fallen off the walls, glass strewn across the floor.

My wife hits the light switch. Nothing. We pause in the gloom, suddenly reevaluating our whole evening. The whole next week.

"Do we have any flashlights?" asks my wife.

Surviving is often nuts and bolts, food and shelter. On any typical camping trip, with the right ten items, it's fun; without them, you can die. It can be that simple.

What are the immediate dangers you face? What are the probabilities? What's going to happen when the North Koreans detonate an electromagnetic pulse and turn off all electronic devices forever?

For the moment, I live in Los Angeles, and the size of the city is mind scrambling. It's five hundred square miles and nearly eighteen million people. Compared to New York, it's a highly developed suburb that stretches to infinity in every direction.

I have never been through a big earthquake, but of course that's what you think of when you think of California. I called Jonathan Stewart, a professor of civil engineering at UCLA, to discuss the issue.

"Well, if you want to talk about probability, the southern segment of the San Andreas Fault, a big, dirty fault, is well overdue for a large earthquake. That fault, especially in the Salton Sea, is primed and ready to go—it really should have ruptured by now." The professor's voice was calm, clinical. I wanted my prophets a little scarier.

The San Andreas is a slip fault, meaning that the tectonic movement is two plates slipping past each other, as opposed to a subduction zone, where one plate slips underneath another.

"Let me make the math easy," Professor Stewart said. *Please, by all means.* "Say the fault builds up two centimeters a year—meaning that the fault is stuck, it's not moving, but the plates on either side are sliding two centimeters a year. That level of stored energy builds up, in the tension. Over a hundred years, two hundred centimeters, or two meters, of slip is built up, and then that can pop loose, releasing all that built-up movement. That's the earthquake."

I was following this so far. The longer it has been since the last release, the more energy is building up and the bigger the eventual quake will be.

"In 1857 a good chunk of the San Andreas ruptured down south, and of course in 1906 was the big one in San Francisco, when the whole northern part of the fault ruptured," he said. From the academic standpoint, the faults should give way every 150 years. But the southern part of the fault, in the Salton Sea, hasn't ruptured in three hundred years, so it's ready to pop. And if a big event started down there, it would most likely continue up through Los Angeles. It all sounded very ominous.

"The likelihood of that event is pretty good, in our lifetimes," he said.

"How big a quake would it be?" I asked.

"We can infer that 1857 and 1906 are kind of the upper bounds of what we're worried about; the best guess for magnitude is 7.8."

On the Richter scale, in case you forgot, each number is a ten-fold increase—so a quake of eight is ten times bigger than a quake of seven, in terms of magnitude of energy released.

The recent Chilean and Japanese earthquakes were much bigger, but they were from subduction zones (where one plate is going beneath another); that's where you get the truly massive quakes, with the ocean floor going under the continental crust. The United States has those as well, from up in Mendocino through Seattle, and in Alaska—the big quake in 1964 in Alaska was from a subduction zone.

"Of course, 7.8 is the best guess, a low 8 is possible, 8.1, 8.2. Anything bigger is pretty unlikely." Which is big, but not an extinction-level event.

Professor Stewart had taken part in "Shakeout," a giant exercise that started in 2008, the biggest earthquake drill in history. It's now repeated yearly, albeit on a lesser scale. With a 7.8 or an 8.2, the Big One won't necessarily be the catastrophe you thought it was going to be. Of all the agencies involved, and of all the discussions, it became clear that the major casualty was going to be the grid. Utilities. Water and power.

"For most Californians in their one-story houses, there will be a lot of shaking—you'll know about it—but afterward, you'll walk outside and look at your neighbors and say, *'That wasn't so bad.'*"

Some tall buildings will come down, and people will die. But the thing that keeps city managers up at night is that the quake will certainly sever all or most pipes and power lines. Water, power, and sewage will be cut, and it might take months to get them back up. Think about that: a month without the toilets working. Good God, what will happen in some of these apartment complexes?

"The reason it's worrisome is the size of the area affected—the whole of Southern California, all of San Diego up through everything into Los Angeles. That's a lot of people." Like, thirty to forty million?

Think about having no toilets in your house for a month. Think about that happening in your whole city. Think about what that means in terms of disease. Just think of the *smell*. Poor sanitation kills more people around the world than anything else. Estimates suggest that six thousand children *a day* die of diarrheal illness from bad sanitation.

According to Professor Stewart, Los Angeles city planners have been aware of the vulnerabilities of the water system for a long time. All the aqueducts come in from across the San Andreas, so they built dams to create reservoirs on the city side of the fault, such as Pyramid Lake along Interstate 5 and the Los Angeles Reservoir in the San Fernando Valley. But there are concerns about contamination in the event of a quake, sewage lines mixing with water lines.

There are a few things you have to do for your house—make sure it is bolted to the foundation and won't just slide off, and make sure that the gas has an automatic shutoff. But after that, it is just about water. Make sure you have enough water. A gallon a day per person, for a month.

When I bought a big blue water storage barrel from Amazon, my wife thought I was a little kooky. When I bought a second one, she just sighed. But I think she was also quietly pleased.

Look at it like this: are you going to sue the government for negligence after you run out of water and die? The situation in Los Angeles probably wouldn't be quite life or death, but it would suck. You might have to go wait in line for eight hours a day to get water from a National Guard truck. The hot sun beating down on thousands of parched Angelenos? Sounds delightful.

For my friends who live in Los Angeles: this is going to happen during your lifetime, so make your life a little easier. Have a month's worth of food and water in the house. For sanitation, I have five-gallon buckets and a short walk to the ocean. If I lived inland, I might seriously consider a cheap chemical toilet as a backup.

Professor Stewart signed off with the cheery "California is proactive, compared to nationwide. A lot has been done. On the East Coast, they have no clue where the faults are."

The East Coast has been hit by major earthquakes before, just not in a long time. And huge portions of major cities like Boston and New York have been built on landfill. In a quake, landfill is a "liquefaction zone," and it can turn into something like water—buildings can sink.

The final step in my due diligence was to have a structural engineer evaluate the house I was renting. I got in touch with Casey Hemmatyar, a managing director of the Pacific Structural & Forensic Engineers Group.

Casey had been a structural engineer for twenty-seven years, always involved with earthquake-resistant design. Earthquakes, because of their nature, are challenging disasters to plan for.

"The unique nature of earthquakes is that you don't get even one millisecond of warning," he said.

I started to pepper him with questions about liquefaction, about my house, about where to go . . . He held up his hands. There were too many unknowns.

Casey said that when evaluating a structure, there are some twenty variables that he looks at. He uses maps from the U.S. Geological Survey and complex software from FEMA that evaluates distances to active faults. Depending on the distance from the epicenter, Casey takes into account the structure itself, soil conditions, and a whole raft of other inputs.

"Two properties on the same block can have totally different behavior during an earthquake. One might have ten percent damage and the other might have a hundred percent damage," he said. Strong and stiff doesn't mean less vulnerable. Buildings need to be flexible, to be able to move with the earthquake. The real analysis he does is expensive, anywhere from fifty to a hundred thousand dollars, and hospitals are required to get it.

He looked around and grinned at me. "You're okay, here. It's not as bad as I thought. This is a wood frame house, right?"

"I think so," I said, but then my conscience twinged—*is that right?* I'd been living there about three years. I hadn't given it a lot of thought. I tended to view Los Angeles as a place I was visiting.

"Wood is the best for a low-rise building; it flexes a lot," he said.

"Should I try to get outside, during the quake?" I asked. The official word is that no, you shouldn't try to run outside because you'll get injured by flying glass or by falling debris. Stay in your bed. But if the building is coming down? I'll risk it.

Casey shrugged. He didn't love these specifics. Everything is dependent on everything else. He surveyed my yard.

"Here it doesn't hurt you to get outside. But downtown, you have to be careful." Downtown means skyscrapers, and you'd be worried about stuff falling on you.

"In a war, during an aerial attack, there are certain locations that are safe. An earthquake is not like that: everything depends!" He laughed.

So you've got to go with California's recommendation to "stop, drop, and hold on." Get under a sturdy table and hold on to it. That way, when the table bounces across the floor, you bounce with it.

"There are two levels of preparedness: personal and societal," Casey said. The personal one is pretty easy: have that month's worth of food and water. Most of the single-family dwellings in Southern California are going to be fine. Societal preparedness is about local government and regulations, and is harder. Just to protect yourself doesn't solve the problem—your kids still go to school; you still drive on the freeways over bridges; you still want to go to the movies.

Casey told me that most of the essential buildings, such as hospitals, prisons, and airports, will be fine because the government monitors how they're built.

"The problem we have here in LA is the middle, all those unretrofitted buildings on Wilshire—old masonry with no reinforcing, or insufficient reinforcing." He was talking about buildings that were designed and built prior to the 1970s—all those offices and residentials and restaurants.

"They're not going to perform," Casey said.

What a pleasant, dry euphemism. He meant that they will be coming down and crushing everyone inside, blackness, chaos . . . *not perform*.

We walked around looking at my house, and Casey said it would be okay in a moderate earthquake. If a 1 means the building would be totaled and a 5 means that it would be undamaged, he gave me a 3, or maybe a 3.5. *Not bad,* I thought, relaxing.

"Your house is okay from a structural aspect, but there are nonstructural concerns. Make sure all the bookshelves are bolted to the wall . . ." Luckily, I had already done that in my son's room, which earned me some brownie points with Casey. He beamed at me. "What a good father you are!" he exclaimed. I blushed.

Then my wife called out, "Honey, remember that those rooms in back [our bedrooms] were built in the 1920s, and then the rest of the house was added on . . ."

Oh, shit. And the walls were masonry, I remembered now, because I had made several nasty messes hanging curtains and pictures. I'm not what you might call *handy,* but usually I can hang a curtain.

Casey's smile faded. We began tapping on the walls, listening.

"These are usually going to be concrete masonry blocks, they're the cheapest, and if it's from the 1920s . . . It's good that you don't own this house," Casey chuckled. Having a bathtub overhead, that didn't matter much. But the masonry without reinforcing was a problem. This had been a little one-story beach cottage in the 1920s. It was highly unlikely that it had the proper rebar in it.

Casey looked at me and silently shook his head.

So we moved.

—

I decided that one month's worth of food and water was a start. I made my lists: candles and flashlights, tons of spare batteries, line, string, and so forth. I had all my camping gear, but I bought new water filters, tarps, tents, ponchos for the go bag.

For those of you who don't know, the go bag (or the bug-out bag, or the ditch bag) is a small bag filled with essentials that you grab on the way out the door. It's always ready, and so are you. When I worked on boats, we had our passports wrapped in plastic and a water jug in the ditch bag, so if the boat was sinking, you grabbed that on the way to the life raft. This is a survivalist staple. Having a go bag is usually a good idea, something small already in your car, a bigger one in your home. It's easy to get sucked into wanting a bigger and bigger bag (do I add a tent? water filtration?), but try to keep it reasonable.

The more I planned, the less comfortable I felt. My situation was not a good one for a lengthy disaster. I don't mean weeks stretching into months. That's fairly scary. But the real humdinger is when government and society collapse, when a catastrophe of such severity hits that it shatters the man-made world.

Some of the survivalists call it long-term grid-down, or TEOT-WAWKI, a desperate acronym for The End of the World as We Know It, what happens after a widespread nuclear war, a massive comet strike, *The War of the Worlds.* No more sweet US of A. The postapocalypse, the stuff of so many movies and books, a place where we've all spent time: *Mad Max, The Road, Resident Evil.* There's usually a lot of fantasy mixed in with theory.

A great friend of mine told me a piece of family history: "My grandfather was a Jew in Berlin, and he waited and waited to get his family out; he got my father and his siblings out *two weeks* before the Nazis closed the borders." The Nazis officially closed those borders in 1941. If his grandfather hadn't finally gotten off his ass, we probably wouldn't be friends.

Could I give up everything and walk away to follow an instinct, a gut feeling, or even an obvious risk? Could you do it right now, leave everything and go try to look for work and support yourself, maybe in a city where you don't speak the language? Head for the mountains?

Los Angeles is an immense, fragile, vulnerable city. The vulnerabilities are in plain sight. Fifteen million souls, balanced like a dewdrop on a spiderweb. How fragile are these systems? Have we waited too long? The climate change science is right there, whether you believe it or not. The earthquake warnings are out there. Like the song says, just because you're paranoid doesn't mean they're not after you.

So is it time to go? And if so, where?

A lot of "survivalist" thinking means building a retreat somewhere deep in the woods, off the grid. A hidden bunker. Survivalist books contain endless pages on the different guns, the massive freezers, generators, razor wire—all based on an unspoken dose of self-hating fear ("don't let your neighbors see your preparations, they're potential looters").

The more I read, the more I thought, the more hopeless it all seemed. Maybe I was in better shape than when I started—I could lift more weight—but what did it matter? Even if I could afford a proper panic room in LA, or a retreat in Montana, what if it's not what I expected? What if the fallout winds blanket Montana with four inches of fresh radioactive powder? What if we're in New York on a business trip when the bombs start falling? Are you gonna live the rest of your life in the bunker?

When the end does come, it will most likely be from a completely unforeseen cause. A meteor that NASA's forward scattered radar missed (or even one we know about—how would we stop it? Bruce Willis?) slams into the Earth and the ash blocks out the sun for a hundred years. The NORAD computers decide that all humans, not just the Russians, are the real enemy, and launch the nukes. Human beings are notoriously bad at acknowledging the unforeseen, even personally: check the current divorce rate, something like 40 percent. As much as we game scenarios and plan, the "Black Swan" problem will bite us in the ass.

The Black Swan is more or less the intellectual property of Nassim Nicholas Taleb, a stock-market quant who wrote a book with the same name. The concept refers to the societal blindness of pre-seventeenth-century Europeans who, having only seen white swans, would say, "A good man is like a black swan," implying that no truly good men exist. Of course, there *are* black swans, in Australia, and when they were discovered, the term gained a new notoriety: now referring to the existence of the unforeseen. Taleb refers to any extreme unexpected event as a Black Swan, and he makes the excellent point that afterward, everyone can retroactively "see it coming"—this event led to that event—but really, there is no way to predict a Black Swan because of the complexity of the system.

Taleb reiterates a point made famous by Bertrand Russell about the life of a domestic turkey. For the turkey, every day gets better, and it comes to see humans as trustworthy food providers. Then Thanksgiving comes. That day is a Black Swan for the turkey. All of its experience and knowledge actually *hurt* the turkey's survival chances.

We're just a bunch of domestic turkeys. Sorry.

Intuition is set up for understanding small, simple systems—things that primitive man might encounter on the plains of Africa. You're wired for hunting and gathering, for small social interchanges, and to be afraid of predators—not run a nuclear power plant or manage an investment fund. Your intuition, your gut reaction to a single person *might* be accurate, but your gut won't help you identify trends in big systems.

So in the real world we are guaranteed to be surprised by the Black Swan cataclysm. We won't see it coming, at least as a society. But some individuals might do okay—there are always those guys who guessed right, or who were in the right spot to see what was coming down the road.

Maybe, just maybe, I can be that turkey with excellent situational awareness.

I've spent nine years writing about mixed martial arts (MMA), a rapidly evolving combat sport, fought in a cage where fighters can punch, kick, and wrestle. Without a doubt, the more well-rounded fighters, with more options—the fighters who can wrestle well and kickbox well—are the ones who have real success. You've got to be able to do everything in MMA. It makes sense: you want a strategy, but you also want to be like water, flowing with the fight, seeking out cracks and weakness. Never be a slave to the game plan.

As far as the survival-retreat plan goes: the military strategists love to paraphrase an old German strategist, Helmuth von Moltke the Elder, who was probably poaching his instructors when he came up with the nugget, "No plan of operations extends with certainty beyond the first encounter with the enemy's main strength." Or, as Mike Tyson said, "Everyone has a plan until they get punched in the face."

I was surprised by how many people I talked to in LA had the same escape plan: get down to the marina and steal a boat. People in

Malibu and Topanga Canyon, miles away, talked to me about having four-wheelers so they could come down the beach, all the way to Marina Del Rey, and steal a yacht out of the harbor.

Now, I've sailed around the world, more or less. Some of these people had never been on a boat. With the right wind, I could steal a yacht and sail it right out of the marina without a problem. It's definitely something I've thought about. But it's by no means a gimme—there are thousands of people who live overlooking the marina, and many of them have boats. They might stop you. And what if the tsunami trashes the marina entirely? Then what?

We've talked about stress hormones and dissociation, but mostly in the short term. In seconds, minutes. What about days and weeks and months of denial? *This can't be happening.*

Without a doubt, the single biggest long-term problem facing you in a true apocalypse is adjusting your reality. Getting through denial, *this can't be happening* . . . that's the bitch of the bunch.

The horror of Armageddon is of course, unknowable. We don't really know what would happen to people in the event of a zombie apocalypse, or if a superflu kills 99 percent of humanity. But we do have accounts of the worst, most unthinkably horrible thing that ever happened in modern history: the Holocaust. In Terrence Des Pres' wonderful, terrible book *The Survivor,* he analyzed accounts by and interviews with hundreds or even thousands of both Holocaust and Soviet gulag survivors.

He found newcomers to the camps had the highest death rate. Des Pres lists lack of information and grief as primary killers, but most new prisoners died "from prolonged terror and shock; from radical loss, both of identity and of faith in the capacity of goodness to prevail against the evil surrounding them." The adjustment period, before you can come to grips with the new reality, is the most dangerous time. For the newcomer to the camp, mortal danger lay in "the horror and irreparable hurt felt by the prisoner when he or she first encounters the spectacle of atrocity. Moral disgust, if it arises too abruptly or becomes too intense, expresses itself in the desire to die, to have done with such a world." The shock of being thrown into a concentration camp *might* be similar to the shock at seeing your town overrun with zombies or aliens. If you witnessed some unbelievable, mind-bending, world-shattering event, this spectacle of atrocity might kill your spirit, and the body would quickly follow.

If you could survive long enough, Des Pres found, you might recover your will to live. From all his interviews, he set the recovery time at anywhere between a week and several months. Criminals did better, because they were used to breaking the rules. In the camps, if you followed all the rules, you were dead in a month. Criminals recognized the face of this camp social order; they could recognize "us against them"—to the death—earlier than law-abiding citizens. They were in less denial about the changes to their reality.

You have to find a way to survive that adjustment period of shock and help others get through it. You have to find a way to limit denial.

The place to start is with the opposite of denial: acceptance. If you have the imagination to accept that aliens are invading or that the dead are walking, then you'll have the imagination to accept that this earthquake is indeed the Big One. The more you can accept that things have changed, the less time you'll waste on denial and "milling" (disaster-speak for checking in with other people and doing nothing) and the sooner you will take action. If the shit really hits the fan, I'll take a semi-decent plan *right now* over a good plan in ten minutes or a perfect plan later. The faster you can accept that everything has changed, that everything you've worked for all your life is now gone, the better off you'll be during the apocalypse. I'm not talking about actually redefining reality; I'm talking about adopting an attitude— "What's right in front of me?" It's about looking at what you see without preconceptions. If you start limiting your emergency plans to only what you think is likely, then you're screwed.

All my preparations may be for naught, as I will statistically probably be one of the dead rather than one of the living, but that's a fact I can safely ignore, because *it doesn't do me any good.* So let's assume, for the sake of our sanity, that we survive, at least for a little while. And if my family did have the tremendous good fortune to survive, say, a meteor storm that destroys two-thirds of the world, it would be a goddamn shame to die because I don't know how to hunt for food.

Be as ready as possible, be ready for *anything:* climate change, zombies, the undreamed of. Relying on a bunker is a weakness. Worse, it's a mental crutch: the evidence might be saying get the hell out, but you've put so much time into this bunker that you stay when you should have gone. Prepare by readying your mind and body, the things that will always be with you. Sitting in a bunker with a sweaty shotgun in your hand is paranoia, but learning the skills to be self-reliant is common sense. I had learned some basic stuff that I knew would come in handy—stay fit, be strong. But in the unknown world that loomed on my horizon, there was a lot I didn't know.

I could fix that.

We live like gypsies, camping out in our own house. I've rationed us out to one MRE a day for each of us. I have food and water for almost two months at this rate.

Without power, news has been slow to trickle in, and the rumor mill is wild. My neighbor Greg spends a lot of time out walking, and he talks to the National Guardsmen who drive the water trucks in—most people are having to get buckets and wait in line for about six hours to get drinking water. Not us. There's been a riot in East LA, where the trucks took a week to show up.

Greg tells me that the Guardsmen are saying big earthquakes hit all over the place—Washington, DC, Rome, Beijing, and London. Here in Los Angeles everything is pretty calm, as people knew what to do. But in some places there is a lot of fear, a lot of prophecy talk. The End of Days.

At night, we read by candlelight. My son wanders around the house, wearing his own headlamp and shining it into my eyes. The Department of Water and Power is running emergency power lines into various parts of the city, but we don't have electricity here. We cooked and ate everything in the fridge we could.

Although the overall mood has been good, at times almost carnival-like—everybody is on vacation—I know there are some lurking problems out there that are compounding daily. The ocean is starting to stink of sewage, and people are dumping their garbage in there too. It's only been a week, but already the trash is piling high in the alleys. The supermarkets have given away all their food and water, and I've heard that there's a giant crowd of people begging at the intersection of Washington and Lincoln.

The city is starting to feel like a time bomb.

5.

NUMBER ONE WITH A BULLET

In the night, screaming.

That's a bad thing to wake up to. I sit straight up in bed. Screaming again, hoarse, ragged, terrified. My wife's eyes are open.

"What was that?" she hissed. As if in response, another scream, louder. Closer, a different voice. Shouting.

"Shit," I whisper, and slide out of bed.

It's been two weeks since the quake, and things seemed to be normalizing. Some main roads have reopened and power is back on in some parts of the city, though not here yet. The elderly and sick have been evacuated to some of the convention center buildings downtown.

Rumors have started. There was a report on CNN radio for about twenty minutes that China had some uncontrolled flu outbreak, but that report was pulled and never mentioned again. It has all been rumors, wild rumors. The CDC came in and closed the port in Long Beach, followed by a full military invasion of choppers, constant flights. It's creepy, living under the constant whup whup *of rotor blades. We hear different things every day. People wear paper masks, hide inside, and hope.*

I slip through the house, quiet in bare feet, and listen as hard as I can. Up on the roof, I survey the night. The city is dark, although downtown there is the glow of lights. Another shriek, not far away at all. That sounded like a woman. I have a really bad feeling about this.

Inside, I crank up my emergency radio. The local channel has a riot in Koreatown and another downtown. A reporter is talking about a complete news blackout from Washington, DC, then suddenly he's cursing, and then the signal turns to static. I stare at the radio. That can't be good.

Out the window now I can hear gunshots, sporadic, wild. Somebody just blocks away empties the magazine of a handgun: pop, pop, pop-pop-pop.

This isn't a riot, even a citywide riot. This is something else.

I drop downstairs and grab the revolver out of the closet. A Smith & Wesson .357 with a comforting weight and heft, oiled precision. My wife bought it years ago, when she lived alone. I'm careful not to come near the trigger. I deeply regret that we've never fired it. We never even went to the range to test it out. But really, how hard can it be?

I keep watch from the balcony, trying to stare holes into the darkness. The night is strangely hushed, even though sirens and gunshots punctuate and rattle the air. Finally, in the east, a lightening: dawn is on the way. My wife joins me, and we crouch in silence.

"Look," she whispers, pointing below us. There, in the gloom, two figures are shambling up the street. Instinctively, we both crouch down, peering out over the railing. There's a harsh, metallic smell in the air, blood and adrenaline.

I hear a brave voice, my neighbor Tim, down in the street. He challenges, "Hey, what's happening?" and then, "What's wrong with you guys?" I catch a glimpse of Tim's back, and then he raises his flashlight and shines it on the figures.

Their eyes are dull gleams, reflecting back the light like black marbles. Their clothes are torn, and gaping wounds mar their faces. Black blood covers their clothes. Is this some kind of joke? Halloween?

Their mouths sag open, gaping, and a low moan drifts out, an eerie, otherworldly sound. It's not a joke.

Zombies, straight out of a horror movie. As the light plays across them, they surge forward, and I hear Tim's bubbling scream. It's hands down the worst thing I've ever heard. The scream cuts off abruptly. They sound like a pack of wild dogs, snarling and ripping, tearing.

I pound down the stairs and fling open the front door. I burst out of my gate, then stop dead. They're crouched over, and in eerie unison their heads mechanically pivot toward me. They start toward me. I raise the pistol, dully amazed, in the back of my mind, at how hard my hands are trembling. I fire, and I see the shot spark off the pavement. I know I missed by a mile, but I can't seem to control the shake.

. . .

Guns. I knew almost nothing about guns.

What little boy, growing up, isn't obsessed with guns? Squirt guns, laser guns. The nonstop violence of cartoons and comic books gives way to John Woo movies. A few real hippie mothers in my neighborhood hadn't allowed toy guns in the house, but that just meant those poor kids had to find sticks and break them to look like pistols. Poor bastards.

Sure, I'd shot a little with my dad as a kid, with a .22 pistol in the backyard. Even though we used wadded cotton for earplugs, the ringing in my ears would last for three days. I'd gone out with friends in college and blasted off various handguns, but I didn't know anything about guns, really. I knew that what I saw in movies was probably wrong.

Guns scare me a little. There is something about the metal weight and deadliness, the horrific finality of a misdirected bullet, the bang and the kick that frightened me. I've never liked loud noises; that's one reason I prefer sailboats to Jet Skis.

I am not alone in this. That bang and kick are a huge factor on the battlefield. The lightning and thunder are a principal part of the success of firearms. Napoleon used them at a time when the longbow had a better rate of fire, range, and accuracy. However, the longbow's swish didn't carry the moral authority of a musket's bark.

Almost any apocalyptic scenario you can imagine will probably have guns in it, at some point. If you're not fighting marauding bandits, aliens, or robots, you'll be hunting for food. And once you have that, others might want to take it from you. What would I do if something or someone threatened my son, my wife? I'd do what I had to do. And would anybody else act any differently if their kids were starving?

Here in the cozy confines of the first world, we've all grown fat, at least metaphorically; and the lean and hungry may invite themselves to dinner. Better get hold of some guns and learn how to use them.

Interestingly, it is civilians who have led the way in modern combat shooting. The pistol originated as a cavalry weapon, to be used one-handed. While the technology evolved, and individuals learned how to fight with handguns (during the Civil War and in the Wild West), for the military the pistol was something of an accessory, a last-ditch affair. Modern gunfighting can trace its roots to Shanghai in the 1920s and '30s, where British policemen William Fairbairn and Eric Sykes followed the local police into riots and studied what they did there. When they were called back to Britain at the onset of World War II and thrust into military life, they began training commandos with their new methods, such as point shooting—firing without looking down the sights, just pointing the gun at the target, which saved precious fractions of seconds. They also devised the first modern shooting course, which simulated real combat instead of using paper targets. The handgun became an effective close-quarters weapon.

Point shooting has fallen into disfavor now, replaced by modern shooting techniques like the Weaver stance. The Weaver stance is named for Jack Weaver, a famous competition shooter and a member of the LA County Sheriff's shooting team. His stance (trigger arm straight, supporting arm bent, body at a three-quarters angle to the target) first appeared in 1959 in a competition sponsored by Jeff Cooper (the guy who later developed the threat color code). The debate continues as to whether the Weaver or "modified isosceles" stance (arms extended equally, squared up at target) is better or more structurally sound for movement and absorbing recoil. Most professional gunmen (SWAT and Special Forces) will use the Weaver—but they also are paid to train, and they shoot all the time. In stressful situations, individuals are prone to face the perceived threat head on, so the modified isosceles might be more natural.

Jeff Cooper wrote in one of his many essays that this refinement of technique comes not from the military or police departments, which tend not to foster innovation and often discourage it, but by private civilians: "Their pioneering work in shooting was done on their own time, at their own expense, and in some cases contrary to the policies of their superiors."

There are a multitude of schools today offering three- or five-day courses in subjects ranging from Basic Handgun to Advanced Shotgun, but I wanted more than that. Mastery of the gun takes a lifetime of study, and while I knew I couldn't attain mastery quickly, I wanted to leap into the deep end, to find a way to make up for lost time.

Tiger McKee runs his own school in Alabama, a place called Shootrite. Tiger published a training manual called *The Book of Two Guns*, which focuses on using the pistol and the rifle in conjunction—alternating as necessary from one to the other. The title was inspired by the classic *Book of Five Rings*, by Miyamoto Musashi, one of the greatest treatises on individual combat ever written. Musashi was a duelist and sword master of feudal Japan who refined the art of two swords and suggested that mastery of the weapons leads to mastery of oneself. The way of the sword leads to "the Way," in a larger, more profound sense. Tiger is a martial artist, and thinks like one, which I found tremendously appealing. It was a mind-set I was familiar with and would, I hoped, ease my transition into the world of the gun.

Guntersville, Al

—Alabama sweltered under a misty blanket of humidity. Alabama in August, for the hottest summer on record? "You're an idiot," I told myself, driving through rolling green hills and thick southern jungle, around the sweep of Guntersville Lake.

I wound my way into the Alabama backwoods and met Tiger at his local diner, the South Sauty Creek Store.

Tiger McKee is a stocky man with small, strong hands. His hair is cut high and tight like a drill sergeant's, and his blue eyes are unnervingly pale. I had spoken to him over the phone, and his deep, gravelly voice had me picturing a big John Wayne type, pearl-handled six-shooter draped insouciantly over his hip. Tiger was the opposite of that. He was compact, neat, powerful.

He smiled and shook my hand and we made small talk. I wallowed in that mellow Alabama twang, that redneck elocution, part natural and part an intentional disguise. There's a humorous slyness about Tiger's casual conversation, just a hint of playing a hick. He invites you to underestimate him at first, because in the end you won't.

Tiger was happy that I hadn't done much firearms training. "Starting with a clean slate is a really good thing," he said.

We joked about telling people what we do. We both have the same problem. Whenever I tell somebody about the books I write, they want to talk my ear off about the training they've done, or their brother who boxes, or the time they sat ringside for Holyfield–Foreman.

"When we go to parties and somebody finds out what I do," Tiger drawled, "then I have to talk about their grandfather's .38 or whatever . . . so I tell people I run seminars for conflict resolution." He smiled.

"But that's what this is about, really. Someone is trying to do you or your family serious injury, and you have to stop them as quickly and as efficiently as possible. I hate to use the word 'fast' because that takes people in the wrong direction . . ." He shook his head. "We'll get into that, but fast and inefficient is slow. Wyatt Earp even said it: *'Fast is fine, but accuracy is final.'*

"There are two ways to stop a threat," Tiger continued. The Alabama twang was still in evidence, but the laziness was gone from his voice, the relaxed nature. This was the firearms instructor, deadly serious. "The first way is to force them to make the *mental* decision that they don't want to be involved in a fight. This is by far the preferred way. Most people attack because they think they'll get away with it. If, through readiness, or nonverbal cues like our posture, or verbal commands or presenting our firearm, we can get them to change their mind, that works great.

"Now, if none of that works, then we inflict enough damage to their body to stop the threat. So the thing to think about is that *we're not gonna fight unless it's worth our life,*" Tiger said. He warned me about even getting in a verbal confrontation—that can escalate into lethal force without you wanting it to. Better to just avoid the verbal scrap in the first place.

Tiger smiled at me beatifically.

"Think about it this way. If a criminal with a long rap sheet, a murderer, breaks into your home with a gun at night and you shoot him and kill him, you might spend two or three years in and out of court, and several hundred thousand dollars in lawyer fees. That's often the *best-case* scenario, that's with you being righteous and with self-defense and all that. So if a guy breaks into my house and is stealing my TV? I ain't shooting. I'll make him leave, and if I have a real reason to believe that my life, or my wife's life, is in danger, then I'm shooting . . . but not for my TV."

You can't kill someone to protect your property. But, conversely, you can't read the mind of an intruder, either; and if your life is in danger, you must defend yourself.

Tiger went on, "The efficient use of firearms is a martial art where the eighty-pound woman really can, with proper technique, stop the three-hundred-pound man."

"You said efficient," I said. "Why efficient?"

"The threat is trying to injure us, or our family, and the longer the fight lasts, the chance of being injured or killed increases exponentially. Most fights with firearms are two or three seconds."

As I scribbled furiously, Tiger shook his head, changing his mind.

"Those numbers always get thrown around, but they're kinda misleading. Maybe the shooting is only a few seconds, but in my mind, the fight ain't over until everything is locked down and secured. So if I'm at my house and I call the law and then it's twenty minutes before they show up, then the fight's not over. Or, for your Hurricane Katrina–type situation, your end-of-the-world-type deal, that could go on for days.

"But even more than that, *when did the fight start?* Did it start when the threat decided to come to my house and kill me, two days ago?"

He looked at me for an answer, and as I tried to think of something, he continued, "You got to think outside the box a little. When I get up in the morning, I put my pants on and I belt my holster and pistol on, in my mind. I'm saying, *Today might be the day I have to use this weapon.* I pray that I never have to use it, but I recognize the reality of the world we live in. So mentally I am preparing myself, so that if something does happen, I'm ahead of the game because I expected it before I even left the house."

I could see that Tiger was talking about limiting or eliminating the denial stage of a crisis.

As we walked out, Tiger paused.

"Fights are like car wrecks," he said. "It could be anything, anytime, and it will be unexpected. Car wrecks are what they are—you don't leave in the morning and think, *Okay, I'm gonna get hit by a station wagon at the stop sign on that little street.* It'll be a fucking car wreck and you just don't know how or when it's gonna happen."

This is a huge concern of mine, because all the confrontations I've been in have been planned, fights in cages or rings, with months of preparation. The car wreck fight scares me, because you have to react quickly and surely; hesitation can be doom. I'm sure I can be plenty effective if given enough time to prepare, but wake me up from a nap and how would I act?

"When you get in your car, you put your seat belt on, not because you expect the wreck, but because the possibility exists," Tiger said as I followed him out into the blazing heat of the parking lot. Time to buckle up.

Shootrite Firearms Academy is an air-conditioned classroom and a shooting range up a dirt road, hidden away in the woods.

Even after our initial meeting, Tiger and I were both a little guarded. We'd embarked on a three-week training program, just him and me—a crash course in the way of two guns. Two thousand dollars' worth of ammunition was purchased. I had signed myself on to a very serious apprenticeship and wanted to start things off on the right foot.

In the chilled classroom, air conditioner throbbing, Tiger began his instruction, and his first point was a familiar one. My father had always impressed upon me the idea of gun safety with a kind of religious zealousness, an almost magical thinking. He said you should always think of the gun as being loaded. Tiger reiterated that point.

"If sometimes we treat the gun as loaded, and the other times, unloaded, sooner or later we'll get it crossed up." He even treats squirt guns and dummy weapons the same way. It doesn't matter if you just unloaded it, the slide is back, and there's a red safety cord running through the gun: it's *still loaded.*

"When we started Shootrite, in 1995, my wife, Gretchen, came up with the name, and I liked it because it goes along with the martial arts." He meant that shooting and training and practicing is a rite. First, it's a rite of passage, an important step to undertake. But also there are rites or rituals you repeat every time you work with a weapon, when you apply the fundamentals of marksmanship.

"Think about it like this," he said. "Every time you perform a repetition of the action, every time you practice it, you put that repetition in your mental storage box. Now, in a crisis, you have to perform that same skill, and you blindly reach into your mental box and pull out a repetition at random. Hopefully, it's a good repetition, done with the proper form, or you will be in trouble."

Tiger was talking about what Jeff Wise, in *Extreme Fear*, called "overtraining" the poor, weak prefrontal cortex to ensure that the midbrain does it right when the stakes are high. You have to work to ensure that your practice is good.

An eminently practical rule is to never let the muzzle of the gun cover (point at) anything you don't wish to destroy, like your legs, hands, or innocent bystanders.

"You hear 'accidental discharge' a lot; a cop is cleaning his gun and there's an 'accidental discharge.' Well, that's bullshit," growled Tiger. "It's not an accident, it's negligence. It's negligent discharge."

What he meant was, *you are responsible*. And that is one of the deeper lessons behind firearms training. Whenever you touch a gun, own a gun, wear a gun, you have taken on an immense responsibility. Just the act of purchasing a gun has made you absolutely responsible for it. At home, my wife and I had a gun but no safe (before we had a child, not after)—and that's bullshit. If you own a gun, you have to own a safe. Not just for the gun but also for every bullet—you are responsible for *every bullet* that comes out of your gun.

"Every instructor I know—and I'll be the first to raise my hand—has had a negligent discharge. I've had two. If you drive for long enough, you'll have a wreck."

I thought of the old sailing joke: *If you've never run aground, you don't go sailing.*

A critical rule was about the trigger finger, which is your real safety. The finger stays *off* the trigger and out of the trigger guard unless the sights are on the target. If you clench your fist, you'll squeeze all your fingers, particularly under stress, so you have to keep your trigger finger out of the guard until the gun is on target. Conversely, if the sights are on the target and your eyes are on the sights, then your finger *should* be on the trigger.

"That will keep you from *rushing* to get your finger on the trigger and slapping or jerking the trigger," Tiger said. "There's no middle ground here, there's no 'almost pregnant.' That finger is your real safety."

—

We went up to the range to start shooting. Tiger had found this place, half an old gravel pit the county had used for road building, and had turned it into his own private shooting range. Tiger is something of an inventor. He invented his own target system, designed his own rifle and handgrips, and even came up with a lanyard ring for the tactical flashlight. Tiger is always looking to improve everything.

Tiger was neat, all matching drab clothing, everything in place. I was a mess, Carhartt pants and the wrong belt, running shoes, a crushed old sailing hat from La Paz, some free MMA T-shirt. I felt like a clown as I tried to get the earmuffs on over the hat.

Tiger started me with the Glock 19. Tiger carries a 1911 .45, a bigger handgun, a classic of the genre, but at times he also carries the Glock because it is a great weapon: dependable, simple, refined, light, and easy to use.

As soon as you enter the gun world, you enter a world ruled by men and their delight in technicalities, worse than baseball fanatics reeling off statistics. Patrick O'Brian wrote that "sailors are sadly given to jargon," but let me amend that: men, in general, are sadly, hopelessly, given to jargon. Sailing is a whole new language I had learned, and now it was guns: numbers and frames, models and millimeters, grains and feet per second. Is that the two-two-three, or the seven-six-two? Over and under? Breech-loaded muzzle dock? Do I speak gun?

The Glock 19 is a 9 millimeter, meaning it fires a 9-millimeter bullet, a very common round. Gun preferences are faddish, depending on technology and the prevailing wisdom amongst gun enthusiasts, law enforcement, and the military. For a long time, police carried the .38, a revolver, until they switched mostly to "nines." The current trend is toward a larger gun, like the .45 that Tiger carries.

There was a famous FBI shootout in Florida in the eighties, in which two criminals engaged in a gunfight with a dozen or so FBI agents. One of the criminals was fatally wounded in the opening shots, but he didn't die right away, and went on to kill two agents and wound eight more before he eventually succumbed to his injuries. This case is well known and is often referenced for discussions on "stopping power." When the bullet hits something, does it stop the target? The argument goes that the 9 is just too small to get the job done, so the .45 (a much bigger, heavier, but slightly slower bullet) is the bullet of choice. You should carry the biggest gun you can handle. And now we're getting into male ego territory: what can you handle, buddy?

We prepared under an awning, where a thermometer read ninety-nine degrees in the shade. I slipped a holster and two magazine holders onto my belt. "If you own a gun it needs a holster," said Tiger.

First we worked on "presentation"—the correct way to draw the pistol from the holster. Everything has to be done correctly, meaning the safest and most efficient way possible. As the right hand drops onto the gun, the left hand slaps the chest. This is important for two reasons: it prepares you to strike or push if someone is too close for you to get the pistol out, but more important, it gets the left hand out of the way of the muzzle of the pistol as you draw it. Blasting your own hand off is not the best way to start a gunfight.

The gun comes up the side of the chest, angled forward and out so that the ejection port is clear, and then both hands push the gun out into a ready position. The finger stays welded to the gun, out of the trigger guard.

We practiced this dozens of times, for a half hour or more. I was a baby, still crawling, who has signed up to work with an Olympic track coach. The amount of shit I didn't know and couldn't do was absolutely staggering. We'd have to build my knowledge up block by block.

As we rehearsed stance and balance, grip and posture, one thing became clear to me. This was not shooting. This was gunfighting. This was about everything else in the fight as well as the shooting.

"As far as the total picture, you may not shoot at all, and in a real fight shooting is only going to be a small part." Tiger talked about movement, communicating both with your friends and with the threat, and evaluating the environment.

We started in on what Tiger called the fundamentals of marksmanship. Accuracy, for Tiger, is defined by the situation: what do I need to do? At three feet, I don't have to be real accurate to get good hits. As distance increases or the size of the target decreases, the definition changes.

"There are four parts to the act of shooting," he said, almost chanting: "Aim, hold, press, and follow through."

It's all very simple. You have a tube and the projectile comes straight out of it, so you have to align the tube with where you want the bullet to go, and hold it there without moving until the projectile has left. Nothing to it. Except that by initiating the action, by pulling the trigger, you jostle the tube.

Like a golf swing or a tennis stroke, the physical act is subject to endless refinement, and with a mastery of the details you come closer to correct mechanics. For instance, in aiming, bring the gun up, not your head down, for better breathing and for more consistency. As with stroking a pool cue, you want to be consistent in your mechanics so that you can figure out how to adjust your aim.

The "sight picture" means using the sights on the gun barrel to maintain that correct alignment. The three things we are looking at when we shoot are the rear sight, the front sight, and the target. To "hold" the sight picture, you focus on the front sight. The front sight is in the middle, so we focus hard on that and let the rest blur out a little. It's interesting, and counterintuitive, to focus on only a small piece of what you have in your hand while a live attacker is bearing down on you, but that's how you can get good hits.

"The most important part of the process is to *smoothly* press the trigger, because there's a tendency to anticipate when the shot is going to break, so we tense up in anticipation of the recoil," Tiger said. If your sight picture is perfect but your body jostles when you pull the trigger, you won't get good hits.

We trudged out over the scree meadow to the targets. Tiger set me up in front of a cardboard figure (with a stenciled-on gun) at the distance of about ten feet. It seemed insultingly close, but I knew that most gunfights happen at close ranges, inside rooms, so I said nothing. I carefully followed commands and made ready, drawing the gun from the holster slowly and smoothly and coming up to the ready position.

When Tiger said, "Up," or "Gun" (as in, "He's got a gun!"), I would bring the pistol up, try to focus on that front sight, then slowly, slowly, press the trigger. Then came the shock of the bang, a muffled thud, the gun jumping like a live thing, twisting in my hands. I slowly let the trigger out until it clicked—the reset—and again tried to focus on the front sight with sweat pouring down my face, streaking into my glasses.

Within twenty or thirty rounds the sequence had already become familiar, but the results were getting worse—more and more shots to the left, a shotgun spread out from the center to the left edge. My arms ached, and as I was trying to control the trigger reset, I shot another round, downrange, quick as thought. I hadn't meant it: negligent discharge. I didn't have control of the trigger.

I muttered to myself, and Tiger sharply interjected, "Kill that shit. You're in a fight, you don't stop to criticize yourself."

Fighting with a gun demands precision, cool control, and understanding what the gun is doing. Minimize the time not shooting at the target, because fractions of a second count. There's not a lot of time to be looking down at your ammo pouch, or fumbling around trying to get the spent magazine to eject, when somebody is blazing away at you.

At the end of the day, my arms and shoulders were trembling from effort and I'd sweat clean through my pants. We went back to the fundamentals of marksmanship. I was really struggling to get the good hits I had been getting when the day started. I was off by about five inches to the left every time. What was wrong?

"Hold on a second, let me see that," Tiger said, and he took the gun from me. I was relieved. *There was something wrong with the Glock's sights!* He fiddled with it, then handed it back to me. "Now try it."

I made ready, brought the gun up, saw the front sight, and squeezed. The gun clicked, but there was no bang—Tiger had removed the round from the chamber. I jerked the gun visibly, anticipating the recoil, a herky flinch.

After I unloaded and holstered, Tiger and I pulled the earmuffs off.

"Wow," I said, shaking my head. I couldn't believe I was compensating that much for the bang.

Tiger frowned. "You'll be fighting that tendency the rest of your life. Smoothly pressing that trigger is an essential skill, and it takes a long time to master."

I got back to my hotel and simply crashed—from the heat, from the focus, from the effort of holding the gun up. This was gunfighting, not just shooting; the stance, footwork, and intense concentration meant I was utterly wasted, and I barely stirred off the bed as night fell.

The days rolled by, and everything became increasingly complicated as the heat continued to punish me.

Communication, in particular, was a bitch. Tiger had me "communicating" with the threat from the minute he said "Up." So as I attempted to smoothly step to cover and maintain that sight picture and shoot, I was also yelling, "Drop the weapon!" or "Get out of my house!" or "Don't move!"

It was amazing how much my pulse rate went up simply from yelling. I could often hear it thundering in my ears against my earmuffs, and could plainly hear it thump faster as I rushed reloads or manipulations to clear malfunctions. For complex motor skills, like shooting, the optimal heart rate has been found to be between 115 and 145 beats per minute. I wasn't getting into bad territory, Condition Black or anything like that—but I could feel my heart rate climbing just from the stress of yelling at a cardboard target and having Tiger's unremitting gaze on my every move. How much greater would the stress be with an actual armed opponent who might be shooting back? It was nearly unimaginable.

It became very, very clear to me, very quickly, that unless you train for this stuff all the time, there is absolutely no way you are going to be able to do it during the car accident of a real fight. Even here, just in training, I got flustered, made mistakes, and started rushing, which only made things worse. *Slow is smooth and smooth is fast.*

Tiger taught me to fight with one arm, as if I had been injured.

I learned to do the reloads and fix the jams, and it wasn't too hard, as long as I rehearsed it and stayed slow and smooth. But if I hadn't ever practiced it? If I were trying to do it in a real gunfight? Forget it. "A fight is not a place to develop new skills," Clint Smith, a famous gun instructor, has said.

Afterward, gazing at the target, I was dismayed to see how my shots spread out. Tiger said, "You can expect, in a live situation, to have your shots spread out to three hundred percent or more." So although I'm getting hits, from a distance of five to maybe thirty feet, I'm not getting good hits all the time.

Particularly troublesome was the head shot. It's such a small target that I can see why it's often abandoned. The head itself is not the target, as the thick skull protects it, but a triangle between the eyes and mouth, the "ocular cavity." That shot proved impossible for me to make while moving.

Tiger and I spent a lot of time together, and we'd often get to chatting underneath the awning as I reloaded the magazines. He made me reload without looking at the bullets or magazines, with my head up and scanning around, making sure I didn't get "head-down" complacency.

Tiger's father had been a colonel in the Special Forces, in command of the Twentieth Group, based in Huntsville, and Tiger had grown up shooting. "I can't remember not shooting," he said. "Also, my dad would take me with him when the unit was training, running ambushes, riding in C-130s and some of that fun stuff."

"So why didn't you do the military route?" I asked him.

Tiger smiled wryly. "When you grow up with a dad that's a colonel, that's a little like being in the military. By the time you're leaving home you get pretty tired of being told what to do."

Tiger had been a little wild in high school. "I was basically a professional street racer, with a manager who booked opponents for me. But I was always shooting. It wasn't until I started taking classes that I realized how little I knew about it. So I started approaching it as a martial art: here's something I can do with the rest of my life, study and improve."

He started Shootrite because he was ready to teach things his way. "I wanted to bring in things from other martial arts—boxing, karate, muay thai, jujitsu, a little bit of aikido, tai chi chuan."

Tiger had found the most crossover with tai chi. He found the movements, the footwork, and the ability to "root" to the ground for stability all very applicable to shooting.. Tai chi is considered a *soft*, or internal martial art, and Tiger thought of firearms in the same way. "Hard" arts are about meeting force with force, like a punch; and the "soft" arts focus on redirection and using an opponent's force against him.

Tiger frowned, knowing how the soft arts are seen by MMA fighters, "I fully believe that if you apply your internal energy you could apply it through a firearm or a sword or an open hand. I know people will laugh, but I think you can channel energy into that weapon and into that bullet." The Zen master archers would describe the true archer as being both the archer and the target at the same time.

The mistake that people make is they confuse Zen sayings with mastery. They think of *The Karate Kid* and assume that if you learn "Wax on, wax off" and your heart is pure, you can beat up a black belt. The myth is seductive, but mastery has to come first. Once you've shot every day and taught firearms for twenty years, then *maybe* you too can start to channel energy into your weapon and place the bullets where you want them. But mastery doesn't fall into your lap when you read the Zen wisdom or begin studying tai chi. After ten thousand hours of diligent, intelligent practice, you can start thinking about the internal energies and finding ways to be the shooter, the bullet and the target.

—

"If you knew you were going into a fight, you'd want a rifle," Tiger said. The sun ticked off the metal awning, and a tiny breeze eddied the lush Alabama jungle around the range. Cumulus clouds towered to the east, and heat lightning flickered.

"The pistol is a defensive weapon, but it's a tool, like a hammer. A rifle is something you'd take into bed with you at night." He's named all his rifles; his sniper rifle is named after a coldhearted ex-girlfriend.

"The pistol is easier to learn on than a rifle, and the same principles apply. But something like eighty percent of people survive being shot with a pistol, and maybe ten percent survive being shot with a rifle."

"Why is that?" I asked. The bullet weights or the grain are similar.

"Velocity," Tiger said. "The AR, which is the civilian version of the M16, fires the .223 round, which isn't all that big, but with the much longer cartridge case and more powder it has much more power and velocity."

Tiger lent me *Terminal Ballistics: A Text and Atlas of Gunshot Wounds*, a forensics guide. It is a truly horrible book, but in its photographs you can see plainly the difference: the handgun wounds are small dark holes, but the rifle wounds are massive eruptions, with heads split open like burst melons.

Tiger has designed his own version of the AR, and he calls it the Katana, after the long sword of the samurai. The AR is an immensely popular rifle and has become a platform for accessories—special sights, grips, and tactical flashlights, everything but the kitchen sink. Tiger stripped it back down to its essentials.

"In my opinion, the samurai took personal combat to a much higher level than any other culture has. In feudal Japan, even a big battle was a massive series of individual combats. So I named this rifle after their sword."

It may sound odd to think of a rifle as a sword, but when you start to look at the history of firearms, basic designs have not substantially changed in a hundred years. John Moses Browning, an American inventor who died in the 1920s, made the last real changes to modern firearms, introducing the slide action and autoloading. Since then, plenty of bells and whistles have been added, but the structures are essentially the same. Modern gunfighters—SWAT and Special Forces guys, for instance—should think about what they do in terms of martial arts, in light of a hundred years of study. A rifle can be pure like a *katana*.

Tiger pulled his two prototype rifles out. They are not beautiful things, these Katana ARs. They are strict black utility, alien, all hard angles and notches. Maybe an elegant simplicity could be ascribed to them, but that would stretching the aesthetic issue. My first impression of vicious, lethal metal was compounded when I brought one of the rifles to my shoulder. The gun had a hard edge and was uncomfortable. But it was light.

Tiger was even more cautious about the rifle than the pistol. "Don't even touch it without respect," he said, when I picked it up off the rack by the barrel. "Don't pick it up like it's a rake. Imagine that's a giant laser beam that is always on, and it will cut in half anything the muzzle sweeps." Every time you touch it, you should bring it up properly and check that it's "clear" (that is, unloaded). Just in case the gremlins had reloaded it.

The semireligious clinging to the ritual is the mainstay in the battle against complacency. The weather was hot and I was shooting when I was tired, for days on end. If little mistakes started to creep in, they would cascade into a big one at some point. And any real mistake with a rifle was going to be supremely dangerous.

Out on the range, just holding the rifle was hard work, and I learned to seat the butt not in my shoulder, but high on my chest, in the pocket of the collarbone, just the very bottom inch or so of the stock. There, my eyes aligned perfectly with the iron sights, and my "cheek weld," where the gun hits the cheek, was correct and tight. It just felt right.

Shooting the rifle was far easier than shooting the pistol, partly because I had no interest in rushing this scary black laser beam at all. It was a whole new world, a new level of power and emphasis. The AR was emphatic compared to the Glock 19. I shot with the plain metal sights on the rifle first, and accuracy was much easier. I made headshots at ten or fifteen yards. I couldn't see the bullet holes, but I could hear Tiger telling me where the shots were going. If he was silent my heart fell, and I knew that I'd missed—so I would take a breath, slow it down, find the front sight, and prreessssss. At the end of two thirty-round magazines, my forearms were blazing with the effort of wielding the rifle.

With the AR your ability to fight is extended to three or four hundred yards, but we did much of our work within twenty that first day. "Most rifle shootings happen at pistol range, ten yards and less," Tiger said. "Even police snipers are usually shooting across the street, which is well under a hundred yards." Tiger teaches sniping to SWAT and FBI officers.

I practiced properly reloading, correcting malfunctions, even slinging the rifle over my shoulder and unslinging it. Every move should be made with maximum safety and efficiency, minimum effort. Learning to handle a gun reminded me a little of learning chess. When I started I thought that the chessboard was wide open and there were a billion ways to win. But in chess, as in a gunfight, there are correct moves to make and there is a best move.

As we walked off the range that day, soaked through with sweat, I asked Tiger, "Why do you think shooting is so much fun?"

He looked a little startled, as if maybe no one had ever asked him that.

"It's just cool, man," he said at last, in his laid-back regular voice. "As a kid, you think explosions are cool, and learning to hit and break stuff, and then hunting . . . it's fun."

Shooting is fun, and not because we have power over life and death: that's too cerebral. It's a far simpler pleasure, more like skiing. The power and thrill are primitive, rooted in our fear and love of thunder. The first time you fired a gun it scared you, even if you can't remember. When you learn to master the elements, now the thunder and lightning come under our control. It's exhilarating, the ability to put a bullet *right there.*

The next day we started with the red dot, a kind of scope that is attached on the top of the rifle. With the red dot, you keep both eyes open, and wherever you put the dot you put the bullet. It's the magic of technology, basically a small lens that reflects a laser dot back toward your eye.

The red dot is kind of a miracle. It basically idiot-proofs shooting the gun. With the red dot, I'm Deadeye Dick. I'm Annie Oakley. I'll shoot the wings off a fly. It inspires a confidence that can get out of hand.

Tiger has built what he calls the Wall, a strange conglomeration of structures about sixty yards from the targets. It's a straight wall composed of varying types of cover: a roofline, a chain-link fence, and cement blocks, with various styles of windows and low holes.

We did a dry run first, moving down the line, heads swiveling, and from each of the ten or so positions I was supposed to get two good hits. Some were kneeling, some prone; one was angled up on a piece of roof.

One position in particular was tough. Called roll-over prone, this position was for firing the rifle through a hole maybe six inches off the ground, simulating firing under a car, as had been done in the shoot-out following the famous 1997 North Hollywood, California, bank robbery. In that incident, two felons wearing body armor and carrying automatic weapons had waged World War III on the local police, until finally nearby off-duty police officers went into a gun shop, commandeered weapons, and shot one of the guys from underneath a car. Interestingly, the felons had taken the muscle relaxant phenobarbital, and when you watch the security camera footage, they are slow and calm, which made them vastly more dangerous.

Finally, I stood at one side of the wall, smoothly pulled the rifle out of the slung position, put in a magazine, then ran the correct readying procedures. My eyes and the weapon pointed downrange at the target. My intention was to get the record-setting slowest time on this course.

"On you," Tiger said behind me.

I stepped quickly behind cover and climbed up the "roof," and as I came over the top, I awkwardly braced myself, found the sight picture, and touched the safety off. I had absolutely no idea how hard anything would be to hit at this range. I fired, and the steel target gave a *ping*. I controlled my breathing, let the sight settle, and pressed again. *Ping.*

Turns out, with that red dot, everything was pretty easy. I took my time and moved under control, scanning, weapon ready, trying for smooth as I went down the line. I climbed up and down, I crawled in prone and backed out. I didn't rush it, and I only missed once, from roll-over prone. The roll-over prone was particularly hard because the rocks were boiling hot from the sun. But I let everything drop out of my mind—the discomfort, the searing hot rocks, the odd body position—concentrated on that front sight, and press, got my *dings*.

I had finally internalized the principles of shooting. You can move at varying speeds, but when you actually have to shoot, everything has to slow down. You *can* hurry—but not during the shooting part. So what if I was a little slow? I was getting good hits. I felt deadly.

When I finished the Wall, I could really understand how the rifle was much more effective than the pistol. There's an old military maxim that "the rifleman controls everything he can see," and now I knew how true that could be. Where the red dot goes, so goes a big, scary bullet at supersonic speeds, straight as a laser, pounding down. I could control the landscape, I shaped it, I owned it.

That night in my hotel room, I glanced over *Terminal Ballistics* again, and it made me deeply sad: all those dreams gone up in smoke, all that life cut short into dead meat. I was also reading a book about the siege of Stalingrad, one of the more horrific chapters of human history, and that was weighing on my mind too—the utter breakdown of society into warfare, then into total warfare, and finally into mindless killing, deprivation, cannibalism.

My one thought as I turned out the light, the thought that kept me twisting and turning, was: It must never come to this. We can *never* have this, any of this, for my son. The whimsical, comical aspect of training for the apocalypse felt very far away.

—

Toward the end of my stay we began to work on transitions from the rifle to the pistol and back again. Tiger had a special timer that reset at each loud bang, and he timed me in all my motions—shooting the pistol from ready, from the holster, reloading, and then shooting again with the rifle. It turned out that reloading the rifle took me almost five seconds, while switching from rifle to pistol took only two and a half seconds. So instead of reloading the rifle, you might switch to the pistol until you can move to cover or the threat is down.

Think about it like this: if you were standing in front of a guy who was shooting at you, five seconds would feel really, really long.

And it was here, in practicing these transitions, that I really began to feel the martial arts element of shooting strongly—because it was so physical, smoothly flowing between one action and another, safely, efficiently, with no wasted motion. Tiger would bark at me anytime I didn't have an active weapon up on target—and if the threat was down, better get back to that rifle and get it cleared and reloaded, because another old maxim is "The pistol is what you fight your way back to the rifle with." The actions acquired a smoothness that felt like boxing, like ballet, a beautiful, smooth, economical action that is also fast and deadly, as it should be. I danced the way of two guns.

Up on my roof, I smoothly bring the AR to my shoulder, light as thought. The red dot flares on.

The zombie is standing at the gate to our yard, sniffing, hunting for the living inside. He bangs against the gate, then starts to climb it. Another zombie slouches up behind him. The first climbs slowly, moving as if he's underwater, and the red dot settles on his forehead. I breathe; watch the dot rise, fall, and settle; hold my breath; and gently press. The rifle cracks, and the zombie crumples and falls.

I breathe and adjust. The red dot finds the other zombie, clambering over the first. Breathe, hold, and the dot settles . . . crack, the zombie splays out. I am mechanical, detached, a smooth-functioning machine. I lower the rifle and scan.

For now, the street is empty. I know there will be more, a lot more. But I have a lot more bullets, too.

6.

I'M NOT A DOCTOR (BUT I PLAY ONE DURING THE APOCALYPSE)

I sit and watch in silence, most days. Sometimes Greg sits with me, and we stare out over the city.

The view hasn't changed in a week. There are a few piles of bodies, zombies shot to pieces. There's been no radio, no communications, just rumors. We no longer fear the worst. The worst is with us.

For about a day, we were surrounded. Hemmed in by a sea of the undead, we were counting bullets and saving enough for ourselves.

Then the carnage really took off inland. There were massive columns of smoke pushing up out of Hollywood, and more in the Valley—black smoke pumping into the air in muscular, shimmery pillars. A thick haze like a fog settled in. For several days, the city inland from us burned and raged.

It was a relief. The noise drew the zombies off my house, off our block. We still potshot the lone zombie, now and then, lurching up our street—but the masses had gone. I could only imagine what was happening in there. One day there were massive explosions from downtown, near the National Guard Armory, and then, almost abruptly, the quiet came.

We holed up and went into hiding for a week. No lights, no sound, dumping our waste into the storm drain. The stench of rotting bodies, the flies, the sun baking things hard—the desert was reasserting itself, even now. The ash and smoke made the air hazy and glittery.

The zombie virus seems to have run its course. Whatever demonic plague animated them for a few weeks has run out of steam. We have found a few that could still crawl, but mostly, they have returned to being truly dead. Still, we don't celebrate or let up our guard. The new wariness that we've adopted is implacable. Our fears own us.

The city noises are gone, and it's impossible to remember them. The silence feels like it has existed forever, the quiet of the earth showing its hand. Man had assumed he ruled the world, and the world had pulled back the veil to show him the truth: you are here for a brief moment, with your noise; before you was silence, and after you there will be silence. Apocalypse *means "unveiling" in ancient Greek.*

This morning is different. I hear something—a whistle, the scrape of feet. Greg signals me. Then, over on Washington, I see them.

It's a band of men, not zombies. Their quick steps and sure movements are almost a relief after the lurch and shuffle of the undead.

They're dressed in black and carrying military weapons, and a lot of their gear looks like army, but they've hidden their faces behind black masks or bandannas. They've got machetes in their belts. I study them carefully with binoculars. The sun is behind me and shouldn't shine off the glass.

They move swiftly and surely, and communicate by hand signals. Not a gang, but some remnant of the police, maybe the National Guard.

Greg looks over at me. "They've got to be zombie hunters, cleaning up the city," he whispered. "I'm going down to talk to them and see what news I can get."

I'm not so sure. Something about the masks, the machetes . . . doesn't feel right. I tell him to be careful.

Moments later I see Greg on the street. He's got his own handgun in the holster, and both his hands are up, and he's talking.

The men in black flank him quickly, rifles leveled right at him. They surround him. I think about going for my rifle, but they're far past my effective range. I can only watch.

One of them nonchalantly draws his pistol and blasts Greg in the chest at point-blank range. Three times. The shots pop, and in the echo Greg crumples.

Armageddon is a contact sport, and somebody's going to get hurt.

The thing about medicine is that it's a young science. Medicine has made more progress in the last 150 years than in all the previous centuries combined, and the achievement of the modern practice is perhaps the single greatest monument to man's ingenuity, dedication, and (dare I say it) divinity. For all that, the days of witch doctors, bile, and black humors ain't that far behind us. Medicine is still a rough science, and more low-tech than doctors would have you believe; the practice of bleeding, which dates back *at least* to Hippocrates, is out, but in a hundred years we may very well look back on chemotherapy and radiation the same way that we look at leeches and lancets now. So don't pat yourself on the back too hard.

Emergency medicine as a specialty can trace its official roots in the United States to the 1960s and the Alexandria Hospital in Virginia, where doctors created the first 24/7 emergency room and started training the first emergency medical technicians (EMTs). EMT training was created to help physicians deal with the large numbers of patients in emergency rooms, to spread the reach of each doctor by making doctors more efficient.

The emergency system is about time. The system sprung up, partly by design and partly by evolution, to get a hurt person into the emergency room or the operating room of a hospital (where they can perform miracles) before they croak. The training of first responders, EMTs, and paramedics is based on the premise of the golden hour: if you can keep a patient alive and stable for an hour (the time it usually takes to get someone to the hospital), you can save a life.

There is a decent argument that the decline in murder rates in the United States since the 1970s has simply been a product of advances in the emergency medical system: the combination of the 911 system, ambulances, and paramedics has suppressed the death rate enormously, and without them the murder rate would be astronomical. What that says about our society as a whole I have no idea. Similar advances for combat medics on the battlefield have arguably reduced battlefield casualties.

Back in 2003, when I was a wildland firefighter, I wanted to become a hotshot (a member of a Type 1 federal crew, the elite of the ground crews) and eventually maybe a smoke jumper (the elite initial-attack firefighters who parachute into remote fires). However, being from the East Coast, I had started in firefighting late—I was twenty-seven years old when I took my first job. Most of those guys begin much younger, right out of high school, and fight fire through college. They receive a lot of federal training. There are hundreds of courses, such as Helicopter Crewman and Extreme Fire Behavior. The more courses you complete, the easier it is to get hired, and I had the bare minimum. But hotshot crews also need EMTs, so I decided to become one.

The most famous wilderness medicine school in the country is in New Hampshire. Called SOLO, for Stonehearth Open Learning Opportunities, the school is well known on the outdoor adventure circuit. I had read some review in a backpacking magazine that said, "*If you want to be the essential, 'go-to' guy for any extreme expedition, SOLO is the place to start.*"

In 1975, a boy was hiking in New Hampshire and broke his arm. The EMT training at the time dictated that you splint the arm "as is," in place, and then transport the patient to the hospital. But the boy was so far in the backcountry that he missed his golden hour by eight hours and lost the limb. Transfixing the limb in an unnatural position had probably restricted blood flow, causing all sorts of terrible problems. The idea of straightening the fracture first, pulling traction in line (which I'll get to) and then splinting it, is fairly straightforward. It would allow for normal circulation. But at the time, that was outside the scope of care that EMTs could legally provide, and it wasn't taught or practiced. That simple action would have saved the limb. One EMT who was on the scene, Frank Hubbell, realized it.

SOLO was born from the quandary facing emergency technicians in an area with a lot of hiking and camping, and evolved with the efforts of Hubbell and his wife, Lee Frizzell, both of whom are EMTs. The question was simple: how does emergency care differ when the golden hour is out of reach?

The Wilderness EMT (WEMT) program arose from a common-sense approach to thorny issues like this. If the person can't be in an operating room in the next sixty minutes, and the EMT knows how to pull traction in line and splint the arm safely, then he or she should do that. A wilderness EMT is still focused on stabilizing, packaging, transporting, and not harming the patient, just like a regular EMT, but with a more improvisational side.

Frank Hubbell would eventually go on to become a full-fledged doctor with renowned expertise in wilderness medicine, and SOLO emerged as one of the first wilderness emergency medicine programs in the country.

I tramped up to New Hampshire in January 2003 for the Wilderness EMT course, a full month of intense class and fieldwork. I remember deep, thick snow like a blanket, freezing cold, and the rime of ice on the roads.

The SOLO school is tucked away in the forests of New Hampshire like the Ewok village, a product of the earlier hippie generation that went to Vermont and New Hampshire to get into nature. The school is dominated by a large, beautiful wooden building, designed by Frank and his brother Kent, who was the chair of the architecture program at the University of Michigan, as a "barn for people." It was something between a barn and a church: cozy, spacious, comfortable, utilitarian, and lofty, all at the same time.

New Hampshire in winter was thick with snow and under a dense blanket of arctic air. Every day we'd have class for hours and hours (yawning in the indoor heat), then suit up and tramp out into the woods to do fieldwork. We'd improvise litters for moving people who couldn't walk and then carry them, a painstaking, careful process.

(Carrying someone on a litter requires teamwork and good communication, and the speed averages out to one mile an hour; however, zombies might be an excellent motivator). We splinted arms and legs, examined each other for mysterious ailments, and acted out complicated injuries. There was an amusing amount of role-playing and ham acting.

The other students were mostly young outdoor professionals, such as ski patrollers and river guides, although there was also an ex–Navy SEAL who was going into personal protection with some international security firm. He was always good for a laugh.

One of my instructors was Bill Kane, an eloquent, slightly larger-than-life figure who talked a blue streak, with a professorial command of the material. He'd been a lifelong climber, an EMT, and an Ironman triathlete, as well as a businessman. He had started as a physical educator and worked for the YMCA before becoming an outdoorsman and adventure racer. Bill barraged us with jokes, stories, and knowledge with an energy that could spike into manic. He was something of an unstoppable storyteller, but a charismatic and enjoyable teacher.

Bill was an adventurous guy. He'd traveled, and guided, all over the world (South America, Alaska, Nepal) and pushed his limits; and when he talked about being an EMT, he imparted a slight thrill to the tales of gore, like a kid describing a horror movie.

I can't revisit here all the material you need to become a wilderness EMT. The course requires a full 180 hours of study. The practice of medicine is all about knowledge, which is why doctors make the big bucks and have to go to school for eight years (for comparison, first responder training is forty to sixty hours, and paramedic training is twelve hundred or more hours). Even to be a lowly EMT you have to do a tremendous amount of memorization, learn dozens of acronyms, and then drill. Everyone should do it; it's great knowledge to have and

SAM SHERIDAN

wonderful for your understanding of the world. Reading this chapter won't cut it, believe me.

But can a little information make a difference? When I called Bill up and asked him about medicine in a postapocalyptic world, he said, "If it's a trauma-based problem, like large soft tissue injury or a fracture, there is quite a lot you can do. You can take care of wounds, clean wounds, close wounds, splint and cast fractures. You straighten limbs as best you can, pull traction in line, make it look like it's supposed to look, and splint them. It may heal with a bone spur or a slight deformity, but it can heal."

What Bill was saying is that you can only help people heal themselves, especially in a long-term grid-down situation. "Modern medicine looks to save and preserve and also prevent loss of function. A lot of things will heal, given time, but you may be severely impaired.

"But if they have *medical* problems, they're in trouble. . . cancer, diabetes, heart attack. You might get them through the heart attack, but now they have a damaged heart. Without surgery? It's pretty bleak."

Surgery has become a standard part of our lives. Almost everybody I know will get at least one surgery during their lifetime. For TEOT-WAWKI, forget all that. We're going back in time.

I'm going to focus on a few simple things, and what might change during the apocalypse. Forget the golden hour, it means nothing. You're not stabilizing somebody in hopes that the chopper can make it here or that a three-day rafting trip will get you out to a road and an ambulance. There is no more hospital.

This is not just a fantasy; wilderness medicine deals with this type of situation now. SOLO has practitioners and runs schools and programs in Africa and all over the world, and there are plenty of places where there is no ER and no OR and there isn't going to be one. With wilderness medicine, improvisation is the rule.

So, the world ends, aliens invade and reduce our cities to smoking rubble. Your ten-year-old daughter is out scavenging for food, and she's late coming home. You go out looking for her and find her unconscious, in a partially collapsed building.

Perhaps the most important lesson of WEMT, and the biggest one for the postapocalypse, is that you really, really need to assess the scene. Don't rush in and create another victim. Don't be in a hurry as you approach a hurt person. Stop, look, listen, survey; figure out, as best you can, what's going on. Situational awareness, or SA, is a catchall term used to refer to the trait and skill of being aware of your surroundings and how they are changing. SA is absolutely critical here. Are you and the hurt person in immediate danger? The SOLO newsletter says, "When something has gone wrong, it seems so obvious and simple that you should stop and take time to look around . . . yet, it is probably the most commonly skipped step in emergency response . . . you need to make sure that whatever just happened is not going to happen to you or the others with you." So, make sure the building isn't coming down on you. Make sure you and your daughter don't have any immediate threats. This is easier said than done with a loved one, but try.

Once you're sure that the scene is safe, you can move on to helping somebody. Can you determine what happened, or ask the patient? Can you establish the mechanism of injury (MOI)? Patient A tripped and bumped his head on a low doorjamb, and Patient B was in a car that was going ninety and blew a turn and flipped over eighteen times before he was thrown clear. Patient A and Patient B appear to have the exact same bruise on their head; but if you establish MOI you can start thinking about other, more serious problems that might be hidden.

But don't forget rule number one: don't make more victims.

If a person is unconscious, the first things to check are the ABCs: airway, breathing, and circulation, in that order. When you come up to your unconscious daughter after carefully surveying the scene to make sure that the roof isn't coming down, check her airway first: Is her mouth open? Is there obstruction? Checking breathing goes hand in hand with this. It's why EMTs love a screaming baby—the airway is good! And then you check circulation: Is she bleeding? Is there a pulse?

Everyone should know CPR, which stands for cardiopulmonary resuscitation. It's easy to learn, easy to get certified in, and not all that hard to remember. CPR is protocol for dealing with basic problems in the ABCs. It only takes a day to learn, and the practical test is on a dummy.

If a person isn't breathing, if the oxygen supply system is down, CPR allows you to work the system from the outside, mechanically. You blow into the lungs and then pump the heart, and although it does a shitty job of moving oxygen through the body, it's better than nothing.

By the sixth or seventh time I was CPR certified, I felt like I could actually do it in an emergency. I'd reached the point of overtraining. There are slight changes from year to year, so it's always good to get recertified. As with shooting a gun, so with performing CPR: overtraining is crucial to using any skills in what will almost certainly be a high-stress environment.

CPR is great for treating drowning victims, particularly the younger ones. To a lesser extent, it also prepares you to deal with electrocution, a shock (from lightning or a downed wire) that merely disrupts the electrical signals to the heart but doesn't do a lot of damage. For almost everything else, you're shit out of luck. Without the ambulance and the OR and the golden hour, CPR won't help much if a person lacks a pulse, whether this is caused by stab wounds or cardiovascular disease. The American Heart Association "concedes that resuscitation without advanced life support (such as defibrillation and intravenous medications) is extremely unlikely to be successful." But still, a 7 percent chance is better than nothing.

So you check the ABCs on your unconscious daughter, and she's breathing with a pulse. Just then, you see an alien slime creature crawling toward you out of the darkness, and you need to take care of it. Another simple, useful tool is the recovery position. This is how you protect an unconscious patient by keeping their tongue, vomit, blood, and saliva draining out of their airway. It's also known as the three-quarter-prone position: lay the person on their side, down arm out, top arm bent around the head, top leg in front. Go on YouTube to see how it's done. It's very simple but somewhat complicated to describe. A lot of unconscious patients suffocate because they can't maintain their airway. Bill would repeat in class, like a mantra, "The tongue is the most common thing to block an airway."

After you deal with the alien, you return to your unconscious daughter, and now you see a sharp, unnatural twist to her arm and a massive gash that's spilling blood. For this situation, there's another basic skill that's useful to know: traction in line (TIL). Anyone can perform TIL, even without training. I did it myself before I was an EMT.

I was a thousand miles off shore in the Indian Ocean, sailing with a friend of mine and his girlfriend on a thirty-eight-foot Hans Christian. We were passage-making, meaning we were headed a long way, from Australia to South Africa. I was on night watch, alone, and needed to see if there was any chafe on the jib. I stepped forward in the blackness, and I thought I was stepping onto the small bowsprit, but my foot dropped right off the boat and I slammed into the deck. I wasn't in any real danger, but I jammed my right forefinger. When I stood up, the finger was bent ninety degrees at the big knuckle. It hurt like a bitch. *Hmm, that doesn't look right,* I thought. We were a week's sailing out of the nearest town. That's a long way to an ER. I didn't give myself time to think. I instinctively grabbed the finger and pulled it out and away from the hand, then back over to where it should be, "in line," and let it snap back into place. It swelled up like a sausage, but eventually recovered fully. I had pulled traction in line.

TIL is simply pulling the hurt or dislocated limb out and away from the joint (or the body), and then "in line" with the rest of the limb, which usually allows the tendons and tissue to reset so you can slide the limb back the way it's supposed to be. With a broken limb, it can also really help alleviate pain and reestablish circulation. Then you need to splint it in place, which is where your improvisational skills can come in.

What about wounds and bleeding? You pull traction on the arm, but now you've got the gash seeping blood to worry about. Actually, this is where you can really help. To stop bleeding, the move is simple: pressure. Apply firm pressure for twenty minutes and the body should start clotting. If that's not working, you can sometimes find the artery that's pumping out blood and apply pressure with a finger. If that's not working, tourniquets are now back in fashion and have seen considerable use on the modern battlefield. The tourniquet is meant to be an emergency stopgap solution, cutting off circulation to the whole limb. The danger here is that in a few hours, the limb will be lost, but it's better to lose a limb than a life. You can buy premade tourniquets for your medical gear, or improvise with a belt, as gunslingers in the Wild West used to do. Tie a rope around the limb, "upstream" of the wound, and tighten the crap out of it, cutting off all circulation: that's a tourniquet. But maybe the bleeding still doesn't stop.

Which is where cauterization comes in. Sure, it sounds a little Hollywood, but surgeons cauterize all the time; they just do it with special electrical or chemical equipment, under tight control. So if someone's lost an arm and it's pumping blood and you can't stop it, don't just stick the stump in the fire. Instead, see if you can heat up a piece of metal and cleanly cauterize the wound. Damage and burn as little tissue as possible to get the desired effect. Bill pondered that one, but in the end said, "It's a little dramatic and sacrificial, but if I was handling a traumatic amputation in the woods, with no hope of a hospital? It might be the way. Wound cleaning would be difficult, because you have to be careful not to start the bleeding again." People used to think that cauterization fights infection, but this is not the case. In fact, all that dead tissue can be a breeding ground for infection. Dead tissue is a petri dish, all the more dangerous when you can't clean aggressively. Cauterization is a last-ditch, desperate ploy, but hey, it beats dying.

Cleaning a wound, fighting infection—those are probably the most important things you can do. Even in a hospital setting, all the antibiotics in the world won't stave off infection if the wound is dirty. Now comes a critical step for you and your daughter in the postapocalyptic city. Once you get her home, you'd better clean out that gash in her arm thoroughly.

"Cleaning the wound is the most important thing you can do. Wound cleaning is *so freaking huge,*" Bill said. "There is no medication that replaces the physical removal of dirt and bacteria." We're so used to antibiotics and creams that we've lost our fear of infection. But it's absolutely deadly. You have to get in and scrub the wound, deeply, painfully clean it, or else the person is doomed.

Infection, historically, is what gets you. In pretty much every war, infection and subsequent disease kill more soldiers than the enemy's bullets. Even in the modern hospital, infection is what kills most people: it wears them out, beats down the immune system over time, then lays them defenseless at the doorstep of pneumonia, rings the doorbell, and runs away. So clean the living crap out of the wound, rinse it with a 2 percent iodine solution if possible, and sew it up. Pouring alcohol over the wound like a gut-shot cowboy will help, but alcohol does traumatize tissue. Honey is actually an excellent short-term solution, because sugar will not support bacterial growth. If the wound has been open for twelve hours, you're too late: don't sew it up, because infection will already be in there. Clean the hell out of it, but the wound needs to stay open to drain. Pack gauze in; the gauze acts like a wick.

Let me reiterate this point: if you don't thoroughly, painfully clean the wound, the patient will die.

Infection starts out with redness, swelling, and pain, and eventually manifests as red streaks running up and down the limb. When this happens, you're just about toast, as the infection is spreading to your whole lymph system. You are in dire need of antibiotics. Your blood is becoming toxic.

Bill had told me a story in class, and I made him retell it.

"There was a woman from Arizona on a rafting trip on a river in Asia (this event was actually officially reviewed by the SOLO founder, Frank, but the names remain confidential). She was in her mid-twenties, healthy, no problems. She's wearing a pair of Tevas for the hike in, and she raises a blister. No big deal. There's the usual pressures of the first day, off they go, and paddle all day. Like most rivers in Asia, this river serves a lot of different purposes. It's for drinking and cooking and waste disposal and a toilet for the people who live on it. So now, the blister is popped open and starts to hurt a little. It's a little red. She tells the guide at the end of the day. They clean it out and put a *waterproof* bandage on it."

Bill's voice drops to indicate that this is a questionable move.

"They get back in the boats and finish the day. Next morning she wakes up and it's really swollen." Here's a real red flag: if a wound is getting redder and more swollen, your body is losing. Whatever you're doing is not working, so do something different.

"So they clean it again and put another watertight dressing on, and they'll check it at lunch. At lunch, they think it's starting to *streak*."

We've all had a million little infections. You get a cut, it gets red and painful for a day or two, and either you put Neosporin on it or you don't—but it goes away. What happens when it doesn't go away? The redness gets darker and more painful, and then red streaks start appearing near the wound. This is a huge warning sign. This means the infection is becoming systemic.

"So now, at the end of day two, they realize she's in trouble, and they're in a bad part of the river to get her out. So they call for the chopper, the chopper picks her up, I think it was the next morning, into day three, and she comes off the river. They take her to the nearest hospital, where they realize that this is beyond them, and they get her to Singapore either late on day three or early on day four.

"Early on day four they remove her leg, and she dies the next day."

Even though I knew the punch line, it was still a shock. Just a little blister, and the leg comes off and then she's dead, within five days.

"Frank reviewed what had happened. The waterproof bandage was a mistake. You can't really make something waterproof in the water, and bacteria love dark, hot, and wet. If they could have kept it open to the sun, and gotten it to dry . . . but the biggie is they had antibiotics in their kit and either weren't prepared to use them or thought they needed to save them for something more serious."

These bacteria are everywhere. They're probably on you right now. But your body is fighting them off, your wonderful skin is intact, and your immune system is winning.

That story always scared me, because I could see myself having the antibiotics and not knowing when and how to use them.

"If you see streaking, you need to start a course of oral antibiotics right away. An injection is even better, because now speed is essential—you have to try to get out in front of this thing."

Talking to Bill convinced me of one thing—I needed to talk to a specialist. I got in touch with Dr. Robert Winters, a doctor in Los

Angeles who is board certified in infectious diseases and internal medicine. He runs a clinic on travel medicine, preparing travelers to go all around the world.

"Common bacterial infections would include staph, strep, and several Gram-negative bacteria, including *E. coli*, *Pseudomonas*, and *Klebsiella* species," he told me. Some bacteria have developed resistance to antibiotics.

In India and Mexico, all kinds of powerful antibiotics are available over the counter. "It's created a huge problem; that's why there's so much drug resistance there. Anytime you get a cold, you take Cipro or Augmentin, and more exposure inevitably leads to more resistance.

"I see these extremely virulent forms of staph all the time. They've become quite common, these forms of staph and strep that have a *virulent gene*. I was taking care of a guy who came on a bike ride from San Francisco to LA. He got a little cut on his leg and within twelve hours he was in the ER and they had to cut off his leg. Necrotizing fasciitis," said Dr. Winters—far, far too breezily for my taste. I was horrified. That was just another day in the office?

"What could he have done?"

"Nothing. Every time you get a little scratch, you can't go running to the doctor." That dude didn't get hit by a car on his bike ride, but a nasty, ultravirulent form of staph was lurking just the same.

There are some very common bacteria that can kill you, too. "I see this all the time," Dr. Winters said. "Cat bites, or a deep scratch, because the claws have cat saliva on them." There's a dangerous bacteria in cat saliva, and within twelve hours the bitten hand would be red, painful, and swelling to twice normal size. Something like that could kill in seven days. The cat's needle-sharp teeth can bury the bacteria too deep under your skin to properly clean.

"If the world was ending, I would have Leviquin or Cipro, Augmentin, and Bactrim or Septra. Those last two are drugs from the sulfa family, and they are antibiotics that will handle resistant strains. All of these can be had in pill form." Easier for us laymen than dealing with syringes. Dr. Winters thought for a moment, and then added Doxycycline because it treats atypical bacteria such as *Rickettsia*, which causes Rocky Mountain spotted fever and typhus. "Typhus," he said, "which is flea- and tick-borne, was incredibly deadly for refugee camps." Certainly, typhus is one of the great killers in history, like the plague and dysentery, and typhus epidemics changed history. In a refugee camp, or in a city with no electricity or plumbing, it could strike again.

These drugs deteriorate over time—most of them have expiration dates of about a year. Dr. Winters said that you would, of course, still try them if you had nothing else, but you couldn't expect much. Within five years, most of the stores might be inert. In a long-term grid-down, we're headed for a time of no antibiotics.

Dr. Winters had hit on the true terror of the postapocalypse: it's a return to the Middle Ages. If you stay alive long enough, you're going to miss the hell out of your dentist.

Medical reference books are great—doctors use them all the time. *Where There Is No Doctor,* a "Village Health Care Handbook" intended for aid workers in remote areas, is a wonderful resource. The Physician's Desk Reference (PDR) is also good. Medicine is a little like cooking: read the recipes and follow directions. Of course, it's not that simple, but it's worth trying if that's your only option.

Here comes the boring survival advice that has to be said: the most common cause of infectious diseases is drinking water that has human or animal fecal matter in it. These diseases are usually diarrheal; our system recognizes the problem and tries to flush the invasive bacteria out of the intestines. Fighting these bacteria is the norm in most places on earth.

Heat kills, so bring any water you intend to consume to a rolling boil. If you're above eighteen thousand feet, you have to boil it for a few minutes, because at high elevation water boils at a lower temperature. Or use chemicals—chlorine or iodine are the common ones. Or filters. There are a lot of neat little filtration devices out there. Water is a big deal. You can last a month or more without food, but without water you're dead in three days, maybe a little longer.

—

So, in any sort of postapocalyptic scenario, medical care is deadly serious. The golden hour is out the window. There are no paramedics coming. No ambulance. No operating room. No highly qualified surgeons with a lifetime of study and an army of sterile technology behind them. Those days are over, my friend. If you get seriously hurt, you're probably dead. Prevention is the name of the game. DO NOT, under any circumstances, GET HURT.

I was flipping through the channels and I saw a survival expert jump into a whitewater river and float down it. He floated downriver correctly, on his back, feet first, and as horizontal and close to the surface as possible. I'm sure it was probably part of some scenario the producers had cooked up. But it was terrible survival mentality. *What are you doing in the river, my friend?* Another survival instructor with a TV show once told me, "Real survival is bad TV. It's people sitting around under a tree, conserving calories." A classic survival mantra is "Don't stand when you can sit; don't sit when you can lie down." But TV producers know that nobody will tune in to watch that, so they need contests, goals, action.

This is part of what I call the little stream problem. Anybody who hikes a lot has run into the situation: not a big raging whitewater, but a little stream with boulders. You don't want to get your feet wet, so you hop from boulder to rock and get across.

Frank Hubbell wrote in the SOLO newsletter about a pair of hikers who were halfway through a day hike when they came to a little stream. One of them went leaping from stone to stone, slipped, fell in, and dinged his knee. It wasn't too hard, just a ding; nothing catastrophic. When he got out of the water, more embarrassed about getting wet than hurt, he was surprised to find he couldn't straighten out his leg. There wasn't much pain or any bleeding. Turns out he had come down on a sharp rock that cut his patella tendon, which holds the quadriceps in place. Right through his skin. Now, as Frank wrote, "This is not a serious life-threatening injury, but it does make it very difficult to walk. It will require surgical repair."

See where you're totally, utterly screwed here? Surgical repair is out, my friend. You're dead. You can't walk—you can't gather food, you can't get out of the woods unaided, and you can't outrun the aliens. You just died because you hopped from rock to rock instead of getting your boots wet, or taking them off and wading across, which seemed like a pain in the ass.

The solution is to stop, switch your boots for a pair of Tevas, and cross the stream slowly, wading, with the help of a staff. Then, on the far side, you put your dry socks and boots back on. So now crossing a little stream takes twenty minutes instead of twenty seconds of hopping rock to rock. But you can still walk when you get to the other side.

In a grid-down, badass, TEOTWAWKI scenario where the ambulances aren't coming, running around pretending to be Rambo won't end well. You'll need to be deliberate, careful, cautious. Watchful. Prevention is your only option for a lot of serious injuries. You have to rethink your risk analysis.

It's not sexy, it's not good TV, but brushing your teeth and flossing—with something—is going to matter. Dental health is critically important to long-term overall health. Think long and hard about all your medications. Can you survive without the prescriptions? Can you fix the problem with diet?

I was diagnosed with a thyroid disorder, early-onset Hashimoto's, about four years ago. I was prescribed Synthroid, which I had to buy every month. Remember, in the grid-down scenario, the local pharmacies are going to run out of everything in a few weeks. Instead of the medications, I removed wheat and gluten from my diet for about a year and my most recent blood tests showed my thyroid was functioning perfectly. I'm not convinced that it will hold up, but the preliminary results are promising. Food is medicine.

I read a fairly paranoid TEOTWAWKI writer who made a great point: Better to get all your elective surgery right now. Get your vision fixed. Following that advice, I had a badly deviated septum (from having my nose broken three times) surgically corrected.

Take off your boots, put on your Tevas, and wade slowly across the stream with a walking stick. And by stream I mean the *stream of life*, friend.

When I finally reach Greg, it's almost too late. I had to wait until I was certain the men had moved on. Luckily for Greg, they moved quickly, looting the small corner deli and retreating back the way they came. Finally, half expecting the ambush, I go out with my kit and scuttle across the street.

He's awash in blood, but I find a pulse. He's barely conscious. I see his eyelids flutter weakly at my presence. He doesn't speak, but he knows I'm there. That's a great sign.

The first thing I have to do is plug the holes. I have to stop bleeding and any air movement into the chest, if possible. I prop Greg up and look for the exit wounds, because they may be bigger and bloodier. On the back of his blood-soaked shirt, I find three, dark with pooling blood.

I know I need to seal them and keep him in a position where he can breathe. Shock is going to be big issue, but right now I need to control bleeding. It looks like the gunshots all went right through. I jam four-by-four-inch gauze pads in the wounds. I'll clean them later, after the bleeding stops.

I'm pretty sure he's hit in at least one lung, so I'm worried about tension pneumothorax. His lungs may be leaking air into his chest, into the pleural cavity. The pleural cavity needs to maintain a vacuum or the lungs can collapse, so I have to make sure that if his lungs are leaking air into his body, I let it vent through the bandages. They need to operate like a one-way valve. It looks easy in the books, but Greg is a bloody, sweaty, hairy mess—I'm not sure I can do it.

Another neighbor, Clark, helps me apply pressure, and we stare at each other as Greg breathes wetly, coughing slightly. His skin is cold and clammy, diaphoretic (sweaty). Shock is setting in. Still, I've got QuikClot in all the wounds now, and the bleeding is vastly reduced. My wife brings a blanket and we cover him, and I start to think about a litter to get him inside—Greg is six foot four and 220 pounds, not an easy load.

The bleeding is stopping. Greg is a big, tough guy, and he's healthy. If he regains consciousness, I'll start him on antibiotics.

7

GET THE HELL OUT OF DODGE

Right before dawn is the best time for scavenging, the safest. The city streets are quiet, every window pitch black. Abandoned cars line the street, some overturned and burned out. Everywhere is fading evidence of the fight against the undead, drying bones and bodies. For a time, scavenging was good, but now it's harder and harder to find water.

The city is an entirely new landscape; somehow we've been transported to this desolate, empty space. Not quite empty. There are people out there, and you have to be careful.

On the first morning I come home with my water bottles all empty, I know that we're in real trouble. I have some left in reserve, but not much.

We talk it over with our remaining neighbors. Clark wants to bunker in and hide. Greg's touch and go, and there's no question of moving him. They have water for a month, if they adhere to strict rations.

We consider the marina—a boat would be the easiest way out of the city. But the earthquake has wreaked havoc in there. A small tsunami sank enough boats to block the entrance, a barricade of wrecked yachts.

I don't like my options, but we're going to run out of drinking water in a week, maybe two. There's no helping it: either we go, or we die.

We reluctantly start to pack, to plan. It's incredibly hard to pick gear, to boil things down to the essentials. We'll have to carry a two-year-old in a backpack. There's something irrevocable about leaving; somehow everything becomes real. We'll never be back here. Life will never be what it was.

The morning comes for our departure, and we set off, boots crunching on glass in the dim light, an hour before dawn.

I take "point" and my wife takes "slack." I'm focused on the ground close ahead, the immediate; while she's got her eyes up, looking downrange. Armed and nervous, we scuttle from cover to cover, senses all cast wide, listening and looking and smelling.

There are people out here, rough gangs, families. We see some signs, even writing like graffiti, marking territory. The sun rises, and the heat of the day begins to pick up.

A few times we're spotted, but we manage to keep moving without a confrontation. A couple of kids shadow us for a block or two, but we drift on. Most people want to be left alone. The sun climbs in the sky, and we're not far from the freeway. I wonder if we can hike out of town on it.

My wife hisses, and I freeze. She's seen something.

We pause in the silence, crouching. Then she's moving.

I don't even see what she saw, but I hustle after her into an abandoned building with doors smashed, windows broken and gaping. The place still stinks of fire. My son is quiet and watchful on her back.

We hunker down on the second floor. I take a spot where I can see some of the street, set back from the window.

"What was it?" I whisper. She puts her finger to her lips.

Minutes later, I hear them, coming down the street from the opposite direction. I carefully peer out the window. I'm back far enough to be invisible in the darkness.

It's a gang. I count five, armed to the teeth. A raiding party? A war party? I can feel the danger vibrating in the air. They wear dark glasses and dust masks or bandannas, all of them faceless. Ripe with menace.

I look too long; one of them peers up at the window. I shrink back. No way he could have seen me. I risk another look. He's still staring, but he hasn't raised the alarm. His companions move around him, down the street. He's thinking about it.

I give my wife the thumbs-down and quietly check the AR. One in the chamber, ready to go. I'm a little low on ammo, but I've got enough. My wife carefully checks the Glock. Truth be told, she's a better shot than I am.

I risk another peek. He's crossing toward the entrance to my building, and now some of his buddies are taking notice. He's got a pump shotgun and he racks it, noisily.

I move to cover the stairs. My wife moves the backpack with my son into the shadows and crouches in front of it, gun at low-ready.

Silence, and in the silence, there's another noise. A distant thudding. Bam bam bam bam, pause, bam bam bam bam.

What the fu—heck is that?

Whatever it is, it's coming this way fast. It sounds almost like a pile driver, but much faster, staccato. The sound is starting to ring off the street and echo off the buildings.

I dart over to the window and catch a glimpse of the armed men, fleeing. I hear a few gunshots, and shouting. They're sprinting flat-out and I see one ditch his gun and pack. The thundering pounding increases, and I shrink back into the shadows.

Something flashes by the window. Something huge. Black metal, like a gun. Higher than us here on the second story. The pavement is splitting, a deafening din. Stupefying. This can't be . . . real.

I peek out after it. I just catch a glimpse as it rounds the corner, following the men. My impression is of a giant black spider, at least forty feet tall, some kind of robot nightmare, moving with a terrible speed. A dozen legs like needles spearing the ground.

"What the hell was that?" my wife hisses. I can't answer.

The sound is fading. But there's no denying what we saw, the malevolent intent behind that terrible speed.

A shadow blocks the sun. I squint at it, then stare. Not a cloud—a black shape, as big as a cloud, sharp-edged, like a fistful of knives. Nothing like that has ever been in my sky; nothing has ever been so big and strange.

My wife joins me at the window, and we stare at the thing. It drifts on, and the sun emerges brilliantly.

"That's . . . not from around here," my wife says, finally. As we watch, tiny black dots drop from the ship. I watch one fall. It slows before it hits the ground, and legs splay out. Another giant spider machine.

"We gotta get out of here," I say.

The urban environment is a neglected one in current survival thinking, which is odd, since the abandoned city is a hallmark of most doomsday fictions. We've all seen the movies and read the books. The city is nothing without man, an empty nautilus shell, strange, ordered, but nonsensical. An abandoned city is terrifying for what it signifies— something is horribly wrong. Millions of people aren't where they should be. When I imagined any grid-down situation, visions of an empty Los Angeles always played a part. What was it about the concept that held so much fascination?

I reached out to Matthew Beaumont, a senior lecturer at University College, London. He specializes in nineteenth- and twentieth-century literature on cities and wrote a book called *The Spectre of Utopia* that contains a chapter called "The City of the Absent."

"I was watching *28 Days Later*," he told me over the phone in his soft, cultured accent, "and I wondered, why do I take such pleasure in this empty city?" The movie is about a character who wakes up in an empty London and gradually realizes it's filled with zombies. The most poignant moments come from the incredible views of major city landmarks—famous bridges, Piccadilly Circus—all empty and littered with trash.

Dr. Beaumont coined the term *socially empty space.* He writes, "Socially empty space is a species of space in which, because one expects it to be filled, densely populated, like the emblematic spaces of metropolitan modernity, the absence of people is perceived almost as a presence. It is urban space that vibrates with a sense of absence."

Over the phone, he said, "In movies like *28 Days Later,* there is an eerieness; the palpable empty atmosphere becomes *uncanny,* in the German sense: *Das Unheimliche.* Empty of human life, the buildings acquire a life of their own. They watch you."

He was referring to the classical Freudian idea of cognitive dissonance best illustrated by a doll. A doll with some humanoid characteristics is cute, but if it becomes too lifelike, it's creepy. Horror movies with things like zombies or killer dolls constantly play with this: something is familiar, yet foreign.

But what, then, of the undeniable thrill, the pleasure from seeing these empty cities?

"The destruction of the city is associated with a new beginning," he says. "The sense is, the city is the problem, and if it can be cleansed, we can start again."

Certainly, TEOTWAWKI means that nothing you know in the world—your job, your car, your shitty apartment—matters anymore. The world is over. The boss you hate and your suffocating mortgage payments—none of that is important. You can start over and build a new society. The dystopian is actually utopian.

But there is something simple, *childish,* about the joy of the empty city. It's like being a little kid in the mall when everyone goes home. When I was in fifth grade, I found a way to break into my grammar school and did so on numerous occasions, without vandalizing anything. Why would anyone break *into* school?

"Being alone in a city, I can go anywhere," said Dr. Beaumont. "We live in these cities with such strict rules, existence is utterly routine and defined by regulations. In a postapocalypse, the city becomes a game, a playful space. We can go into any forbidden area. It's thrilling."

In his book, he writes, "In a metropolitan society dominated by the routine experience of a mass of people, in all its positive and negative aspects, and of a spatial regime that is at once anarchic and elaborately regimented, the city of the absent is simultaneously a dream of being freed from the constraints of capitalist modernity and a nightmare of being cut loose from its consolations."

I could all too easily imagine the nightmare for Los Angeles. A big city like LA is a wonderful, complicated machine with some tolerance for error, but overwhelm those tolerances and the machine grinds itself to pieces. If the disaster was nationwide and help wasn't coming? Then there would be a power vacuum in Los Angeles, and as they say, nature *hates* a vacuum. Gangs would be the natural outcome. Tribes, family groups, and neighbors banding together for survival might wage war for the precious remaining resources.

—

Los Angeles, Ca

—It was a pure SoCal day, the sky unbroken blue, the air hot and still, the sunlight a liquid presence lying down on top of the streets and cars. May, the temperature already in the high eighties, summer on the way. I was cruising way inland, in the neighborhood of Boyle Heights, on the Flats, at what used to be Aliso Village. Who do you go to in Los Angeles to talk about survival in the city?

"Rule number one down here is, you know who plagues where," Spade murmured, as we cruised down the side streets. "You got to understand the invisible boundary lines, especially if you're in the game. If you're an outsider, you still need to understand your surroundings." He told me that if you could read the signs, the territory was all clearly marked. If a gang member gets out of prison after ten years, he needs to start reading the graffiti, the "writing," in his old hood to see what has changed, where he can go.

Spade's an ex–gang member from Boyle Flats, a thin Latino man in his late thirties. With his long black hair slicked back in a braid, arms covered in tattoos, and heavily lidded eyes, Spade looked the part. He survived "the game," barely, and had been a lot of things—a tagger, a tattoo artist, a gangster, a meth dealer and addict. Through a combination of good fortune and hard work, he's managed to put all that damage behind him. Spade is a full-time painter, a muralist, and a councilor to ex–gang members.

We pulled through a stop sign, and Spade's eyes carefully scanned the car mirrors.

"They are definitely watching you, even now when it looks empty," he said. His voice was quiet, sibilant with the Chicano accent, just a murmur. "There's a gang on every block here, every street has a clique."

We crossed the quiet avenues, Spade pointing to alleys and routes, "holes" where you could see into enemy terrain.

"Here's where the heart starts to beat faster," he said with a smile as he turned into hostile territory.

"How come we can come through here now?" I asked.

"It's mellowed out—the generations are different, the law has changed things a lot."

In the early 1980s in Boyle Flats there had been black gangs, East Coast Crips. They had been pushed out—now all the black gangs were in South Central. Before that, it had been other immigrant groups. "In historical times it was the Russian Flats, even the Jews back in the day," Spade said. But always, the poor.

"This is the park where I used to play as a kid. My father used to sell drugs out of this park," he said. We paused in the cool, air-conditioned car, and I watched Spade's face as he told me the story. If your father is a drug dealer, how much of your fate is decided?

"My father was a construction foreman in Mexico, but because of his immigration status he couldn't get that job here. He had some family connections to Juarez, to the cartels, so he started transporting heroin—tennis balls of heroin." Spade uses the careful diction of the ex-con with a GED; for instance, he never says "meth," always "meth-amphetamine."

"He had to stay out of jail, so the best way for him was to use his son. So I was holding for him. We were going for quality time, to play ball, but I was possessing the heroin. He'd whistle and I'd come, I carried it in my pockets wrapped up like candy. I must do what I must do to get the love of my father."

I could imagine this early training in awareness, how different his time at the park was from that of the other kids. Playing ball while all the time aware of the men, the buyers, the police.

His father had started using, which sent him in out of prison. "I wanted to be an artist, or a break-dancer," he said as we pulled away. "So I became a tagger."

Tagging (usually done by kids) is just putting your name out there in spray paint, marking territory, letting the world know "I am here." Taggers only want to write; they sign their name and the name of their tagging crew. For them, prestige is about getting your name seen, especially in hard-to-reach places—on freeway signs, atop tall buildings.

Anything artistic, with a lot of flourish, the stuff that's hard to read, is tagging. Gang writing is different, it means "We control this," and gang writing is simple, in block letters, readable.

Spade told me about his tagging crew and how he got home every day. "I used to sprint, I used to just run straight home. I wouldn't look left or right, I was on a mission—no looking, no eyes, no *whatssup fool?* I just focused on running, on my footsteps." Spade was ten, twelve years old, trying to avoid the yawning chasm all around him. To interact, on any level, would begin the process, start the snowball rolling, and the gangs would end up controlling him. So he ran home, pretending to be invisible.

He smiled. "But eventually, you get caught up and you join the gang."

Spade drove me for hours through the neighborhoods, showing me examples of gang writing versus tagging, and places where territories clashed. These were danger zones, and one way you could tell was if there was "crossing out."

"If there's crossing out, there's beef." He meant if gang writing was getting crossed out, there would be problems. I wrote the name of my gang and you crossed it out—that means you disputed my claim. Fighting, shooting, conflict: all equals "beef."

There was an interesting moment, driving with Spade, when he said, "Yeah, there's definitely a lot of activity in this neighborhood, they're active in here . . ." I looked around and then asked, "How can you tell?"

Spade was silent for a moment, then he laughed, shaking his head. "I can just tell, they're everywhere here." Spade smiled. He could feel their presence. He was relying on his intuition, his subconscious, to pick up subtle clues that he couldn't consciously register.

Gavin de Becker wrote *The Gift of Fear* about intuition, fear, and trusting your own instincts. The take-home lesson is that your subconscious is much more in tune with the surroundings than your conscious, so if something feels off or funny, or you get a bad vibe, *pay attention*. You're picking up subtle cues that your conscious isn't quite aware of. Your intuition, which may be terrible for making stock market picks, is excellent for detecting hostile people.

Don't let politeness lead you into danger. If a stranger feels odd, stay away. De Becker uses the story of a woman who is about to get onto an elevator when she sees a man in there who makes her uncomfortable, even scared. But she goes in anyway, because she doesn't want to be rude, or think *that* about a stranger, or appear racist. What animal in nature would enter a tiny steel box with something they were afraid of?

To paraphrase de Becker, acts of violence are never truly random and senseless. Somebody's got a reason, and your instincts are honed to detect it: you just have to listen to them. The bottom line is that if someone makes you uncomfortable, no matter how polite they are, you are being warned—the animal in you is picking up their intentions.

Intuition alone is not enough, though. Paramount to survival is the learned ability I mentioned earlier called situational awareness, or SA, which can be defined as being aware of the environment and changes to it. Or, as a captain I used to work for would sweetly remind me, "Don't have your head in your ass."

Spade and I cruised into a new area and paused at a four-way intersection. It was a poor neighborhood but fairly clean, a million miles from the *favelas* of Rio or the shantytowns of Johannesburg.

"Look, look here, see it?"

I didn't.

"Look at the pavement, you see all those doughnuts? You can tell there's activity."

Then I saw it, skid marks on the street, dozens of overlying circles.

Guys had been out spinning doughnuts at night in their cars, laying down rubber. This was their spoor, like the paw print of a bear.

"One time, I was driving through here, creeping, maybe ten at night, and I stopped at a stop sign, and thank God I looked in the rearview mirror because I saw three guys holding their big-ass pants, and when I checked back they were right behind me, so I hit the gas and they shot up my car, hit the door and the edge of the window. They knew I was passing through a lot, so they thought, *Let's just wait for this fucker, he's gonna come, dog.*"

God had nothing to do with it. Spade was always checking his mirrors; his restless eyes danced up and down the streets. His head swiveled ceaselessly, taking everything in, looking for signs. A habit from childhood he would never break.

SA is a skill that is linked to intuition but not purely of it, an ancient talent. Firefighters, pilots, and the military have all taken on the term for training purposes. When we studied SA for firefighting, it was to avoid getting so focused on a task—say digging, or cutting down a tree—that you miss the subtle event, like a wind shift, that can bring danger your way.

For a rookie firefighter, my instructors told me I had good SA, probably because I had been a professional sailor. Out on a sailboat, you become naturally in tune with SA, because that's what sailing is: using the environment. You're always looking ahead, into the future, to see what's coming.

I had the good fortune to talk to Jeff Wise, the author of *Extreme Fear,* about situational awareness. He told me, "I just took a road trip with my brother, and he was watching the GPS the whole time. I'm the kind of guy who drives around with a map open in my lap, trying to figure things out. I became very aware of the differences between the two approaches. For instance, he wanted to go to McDonald's, and he plugged that in and the GPS gave him a complex set of instructions.

But if he looked out the window, he could see that if he just drove over the sidewalk he was going to be in the McDonald's parking lot."

For Jeff, that lesson was even more important when flying a plane. "Look out the window when you're flying, don't stay buried in the gauges and instruments and miss the obvious."

The modern study of SA actually comes from flight training, most notably a military strategist named John Boyd, who in the 1970s developed the idea of a decision loop. The way for a fighter pilot to beat another was to get inside his decision loop. Whoever had a better grasp of the situation, whoever made critical decisions not only sooner but *righter*—decisions that more accurately reflected the entire environment and predicted the future—would win the dogfight.

Jeff continued, "Reading and orienting a map is harder than using the GPS. So you had to invest yourself, and what was it that you invested? Attention. Attention is a hard thing to invest right now, that's what's in the shortest supply—people can't spare it."

The frenetic pace of modern technology means that attention is in critical demand. You can't have dinner without checking the score on the game; you can't watch the game with texting friends. Our attention is spread thinner and thinner.

"The GPS means that you don't have to think or plan beforehand," said Jeff, "and so you have no *context*."

There are famous cases of people following the GPS right off a proverbial cliff. A Canadian couple drove to Vegas, and on the way back, following the GPS, they somehow ended up driving down a long dirt road in the Humboldt forest and got stuck in the mud. The husband set off with the GPS (like a devil perched on his shoulder) and was never seen again. The wife was eventually rescued *seven weeks* later. They had no context—somehow the dirt road made sense.

Jeff writes: "Information technology is a two-edged sword. It both empowers and cripples. It convinces us that we don't need to worry about background, about context, about details. It seduces us into overlooking the difference between knowing and understanding, between information and knowledge."

Tiger McKee and I spoke often of situational awareness on the shooting range. Some undercover policemen talk about practicing SA by observing little details about people on the street in order to figure out their backstory. For Tiger, it is a skill, like all others, that requires practice: "You always play the 'what-if' game. When I pull into a gas station food mart, before I get out of the car, I do a quick scan of the parking lot. Are there people just hanging around? I look at the windows. Are they covered in posters? Can I see what's going on inside? If I can't, maybe I'll go down the street. In a restaurant, I sit where I can watch the room. I know where the normal entrance and exit is, but I also know that the kitchen will always have an exit, too—so where's the kitchen? How can I get there?"

When he made me reload the magazines by feel, always looking up, scanning the horizon, he wasn't just being a hard-ass. He was teaching me a skill, trying to make it a habit.

"You definitely have to develop this skill," said Tiger. "Not too many years ago, you'd have it because you'd be using it all the time, for hunting and survival. But nowadays, the majority of people can make it through their whole life and never have to worry about it. The best way to defeat your enemy is to deny them the opportunity." He meant that by being aware of the situation, by seeing further down the road into the future, you can avoid the enemy, avoid the fight. Good situational awareness, more than any other trait, is critical to survival. See the problem before it manifests. By the time it arrives, you can be somewhere else.

Being aware of your surroundings, urban or otherwise, is crucial, but at some point you're going to have to get the hell out of Dodge.

Being mobile is an excellent survival strategy because of the flexibility it grants.

What's the ubiquitous mode of transportation, across the whole country? You never know when you might need to "borrow" a car. In all the *Terminator* movies, they're stealing cars left and right. I should know how to do that. What if my car was trashed? What if I were chased into a parking lot by mutants? I asked Spade about it. Did he ever steal cars? Could he teach me? He laughed. He knew just the guy.

"This is it, this is the tool," Luis said. "This is the moneymaker, like a calculator for an accountant." He showed me a slim flatheaded screwdriver, maybe six inches long: a Craftsman 41584, the perfect weapon, and all Luis needed to steal a car. He slouched in my passenger seat on the way to a junkyard, where he was going to teach me.

Luis was a good-looking older Mexican man, maybe mid-forties, with short salt-and-pepper hair, a neat thick mustache, and watchful eyes. His face was hard, his hands wiry and strong. Luis (pronounced *Louie*) was an old-school gangster from Cuatro Flats (Fourth Street). He was *veterano*, he's survived—when a gang member turns thirty-five, he is allowed to begin to get out of the life (but not at thirty-four).

"I have no tattoos, none. It's a dead giveaway. I never use a nickname. The cops ask me, 'What do they call you?' 'Nothing, just my name, Luis.'" His face was impassive, innocent, the same way he would speak to the police. Aggressively cold.

When Spade had mentioned Luis, he spoke of him almost reverentially. "He's the *mano peludo*—the hairy hand. There was an old Mexican TV show that had a hairy hand on it that would come out at night and steal shit. That was the perfect name for Luis, he could get whatever you needed, he was his own black market. The hairy hand that always takes." Spade laughed. "Watch your shit! Luis was the kind of guy who could steal anything."

Luis had been clean for quite a while, though, and said he would only talk to me because he was sure the statute of limitations was up for him. He says the statute won't run out on capital crimes, but we weren't going to talk about those.

While his clothes and his skin were innocent, Luis couldn't quite hide the edge of the street and the ex-con, etched in the lines on his face. I've seen it before, those long years of living in constant hostility, fear, anger, burned into your features. Just as sailors get crow's-feet wrinkles around their eyes, prison produces a look of habitual anger and guardedness. It stamps a person's face as surely as the sea and sun.

"I grew up in Boyle Heights, and it's hard to grow up in a housing project and not get into trouble. You get caught up in the mix, Juvenile Hall, then camp, then placement, to county jail, and finally prison— whoa! It hits you in the face. Thirteen years for me, in and out. I've been in twelve of California's prisons."

Luis didn't say this with pride, however—he said it with mild regret and deep embarrassment. "I look at people my age and they have a home, a family, and I think, *Damn, I could have had all that. I traded it for a high, for the thrill of taking shit that didn't belong to me. I can do this, I can hit this place, and I'm going to get 'em good,* and I did." He laughed softly. His brown eyes watched me carefully, cautiously. Spade had vouched for me, but he's still not so sure.

He was still hustling. When we ate lunch together, I heard him tell the cute waitress in Spanish that I was writing his life story, revealing all the bad things he did so that young kids will learn from his mistakes.

Luis had agreed to show me how to steal a car. It's considered so easy that it's almost not worth doing; he could just tell me how to do it, but I insisted.

. . .

The junkyard was dense, a working place, with grease-soaked pavement and shattered glass, maybe an acre of derelict cars lying in neat, tight rows. They seemed thoroughly picked over—could anybody really have missed anything valuable? But if you needed a part for your car, this was a cheap place to hunt for it. We wandered between the rows, crunching glass under our sneakers, angling sideways to avoid metal.

I asked Luis what the easiest and fastest thing to steal would be.

"If you want it fast, you pick something typical, a Honda or a Toyota—but usually somebody is asking for something. The front end, the motor, seats . . . The older it is, the easier, but it doesn't matter all that much."

He slid into the shell of a '92 Honda Civic and sat behind the wheel. As I slipped into the passenger side and pulled out my camera, he shoved the screwdriver into the keyhole and began prying—and the shell came away almost like tinfoil. "This is all just shit, it's die-cast metal, it comes right off," he said. The old Civic is a classically easy car to steal.

"This is kind of a waste of time. What you would really do is dent-pull this, but we can do it." (We'll get to dent pulling a little later.) He pried out the stuff in the ignition—the tinny metal cap, the lock itself—and cracked and peeled back the metal around it. In about three minutes, he popped all the crap out of the ignition and turned the switch with his screwdriver, just like a key. It was that simple. Basically, the only thing keeping the car from starting is the ignition lock, which is right there on the surface of the steering column. Pull that off and you're good to go.

Luis couldn't help himself, he was a little tense. I asked him about it, and he laughed. "It's bringing back memories, I haven't done this in a long time. But yeah, my heart is beating fast." His energy was rushing, nervous, a little furtive. I could imagine the memories this must dredge up; Luis claimed to have stolen about a hundred cars in his career.

I asked him about the wiring, like in the movies. "Yeah, that stuff is idiotic. It takes time, sometimes you don't have light . . . you're in a parking garage, no power . . . don't have time to be looking, and you can't use a flashlight because that attracts attention. Get in there, sit up straight, and *boom,* get out. Messing with the wires is old school, it's not necessary, nobody does that anymore."

He reached right up under the dashboard and fished out the wires. "You still got it here. Always the white wire with a red stripe is hot. Tie it to the blue, then tap it to the yellow." He bridged with the screwdriver. "But you don't need to do that. What I did is flare the ignition switch"—it looked exploded, almost like a bullet spread out—"but with a little three-pound dent puller, it would be effortless."

We left the car and prowled the rows. What we were doing was somewhat illegal, although not really *badly* so. Luis showed me how he gets in—right through the door handle. He slams the little screwdriver through the metal edge of the door and door handle, prying in under the latch. "You slide in here, right at the handle, and you can hook the latch from the bottom. Honda is up, Camry is down. You just get the hang of it." He demonstrated on a car door without an inside, so I could see the small latch that the handle maneuvers. If you really developed the feel, it could be so fast that from a distance it would almost look like you had keys.

"You go in through the passenger side. A lot of times the alarm from the factory is on the driver's side only. But a lot of stupid idiots break in to the driver's side because they don't want to hop over."

It's all about knowledge. You have to understand, to some degree, the make and model of the car you're stealing. Luis is a mechanic, and he was called on to fix cars as much as steal them. Also, the more modern the car, the harder to steal—new cars have computer chips in the keys. Luis said in passing, "Oh, they still steal 'em, but now they get a set of dummies from somebody at the dealership."

"On some cars, the steering wheel locks into place. You know what I mean, you need the key to unlock the steering. But that's easy to handle, too."

Luis showed me how: on the top of the steering column, right underneath the steering wheel, the pin mechanism for locking clicks up into place, holding the wheel. "You can break it with the screw-driver, but that shit can still lock on you—and you don't want that to happen when you're driving," he said. "But you just use your body weight and crack it . . ." He wrenched the wheel over; it resisted, then, with some effort, cracked and moved. "But the pin is still catching, you have to break it all the way off."

"Side switching" is what you do to GM cars, Cadillacs and such—you don't even go near the key. Luis showed me how he pries into the steering column and finds the mechanism—a kind of rod connector—that you break apart and that starts the car. American cars you side-switch, Japanese cars you dent-pull.

Unsurprisingly, many of these cars had already been side-switched or dent-pulled—they'd been stolen already and had somehow made their way here, through the insurance companies and tow trucks, or perhaps illegally. Row after row of cars with the ignitions pulled out or the columns cracked open.

We were sitting in another car and Luis was demonstrating some-thing when suddenly he pushed back, almost angry. "You're not gonna do all this," he snorted. "You can't be messing around in the car like this." His voice was full of tension, because his internal clock was ticking, and he was spending too much time fiddling in the car. If he were really stealing it, he'd be caught by now. Situational awareness on high alert.

In the end, we got caught. My large camera, slung around my neck, turned out to be a problem, and the guy who was running the yard made me put it away. No cameras in the junkyard. I'm not sure why; business secrets? *What makes your junkyard so awesome?* Probably he could just sniff that we were up to no good.

—

Another hot day, another junkyard, somewhere in the middle of East LA, a dense maze of derelict cars stacked two deep, a warren of glass and metal. We sat inside a shattered '98 Camry, with another stripped Camry parked on top of it.

I prepared to dent-pull this little Camry. The owner of the yard hadn't loved the idea, but I'd pulled out a book to show that I really was a writer, and gave him fifty bucks. I told him I was writing a survival book, and this was what to do if you lost your keys. He smiled politely, not buying that for a minute.

"You guys need a few hours back here?" he asked.

We laughed. "No, half an hour, tops." *Ah, hubris.*

I had my new dent puller, something I had never even seen before. The dent puller is a tool for bending the metal of a car, for pulling the dents out. It's a long rod with a handle at one end, a screw at the other, and a weight that slides along it. Dent pullers are various sizes according to the size of the sliding weight.

I went to work, with Luis watching. I put the dent puller against the ignition and, *bam,* drove the weight down the rod. This was supposed to seat the screw at the tip, so that I could screw it in. *Bam. Bam.* I couldn't get the screw to start.

Luis looked at the screw tip and decided it was the wrong one, so we searched the junkyard for the right one—brass, more like a drywall screw, sharp. Luis said you could often find them in a car, holding down the trim.

When I finally got the new dent puller screwed in, I couldn't yank out the ignition, and neither could Luis. The sun was beating down on the yard now, and we were sweating and cursing freely inside the dirty metal hulk. There was grease and broken glass everywhere. I kept slamming the small two-pound weight back and trying to yank at the same time, and I was getting nowhere.

Luis eventually borrowed a much bigger, five-pound dent puller, and with that screwed in tight, I slammed the weight back and pulled, *wham,* and the ignition switch started to bulge. It was awkward. I had to pull around the wheel and across my body, and it took me several tries to yank it all the way out. Suddenly, the whole thing cascaded out in a column of shattered plastic and metal.

But I hadn't gone quite deep enough, so for another ten minutes I beat on the hole where the switch used to be, prying out shards of plastic. We borrowed a bigger screwdriver.

Luis was grimly resigned and amused. "It's been fifteen years since I used to do this," he said. "You kind of forget what you need."

Finally, with a snap and pop, the last chunk of the ignition switch came out of the hole, and reaching in with my Leatherman pliers, I turned the nub. Bingo, you could feel that the action was the same as starting a car. It had taken me about an hour.

"You'd get much faster with practice. You have to practice," Luis said. "You get a feel for it." Crossing the United States, after Armageddon, I was going to get a lot of practice.

"Why not just carry a big dent puller, like a ten pounder?" I asked.

"You can't be walking around with a massive dent puller in your pocket," he said.

But I could put a big dent puller in my go bag, I thought.

All bets are off. This is an alien invasion. No more sneaking around. We hustle through the streets back up to the freeway. Speed is of the essence now.

We see two more of those spider alien robots land, and we can hear them tearing up the city. We trot up the on-ramp, breathing hard, with glass crunching under our boots.

The freeway is littered with cars, most of them pushed or driven to the side and abandoned. Somebody, maybe the National Guard, bulldozed their way through—there's more or less a road down the middle.

Right there, on the edge of the ramp, is a good prospect, a Japanese-made truck, old but in good shape.

We pause by the side of the truck, huddling for cover, as a screaming roar like thunder splits the sky and two F-18s streak overhead, rattling our bones. The last remnants of the air force? We turn to watch them, and as we do, one of them fireballs, incinerated, with a boom I feel in my teeth. The other fires missiles, and I can't see where they hit, and then something hits the plane, and it starts to stream smoke and nosedives for the hills.

So much for our resistance.

"Let's go, honey!" my wife snaps. Right.

I break the glass and yank open the truck, and we pile in. I've brought an eight-pound dent puller and a few screwdrivers, and the sense of urgency flooding my system makes short work of the ignition switch. Fuel gauge is at half a tank. A lot of these cars have been siphoned, so we're lucky to have found this one.

How long will that battery last? This car wasn't abandoned during the big quake, it was afterward. Probably during the zombie attacks. Maybe three weeks ago. The battery could still be alive.

The city is burning again, and the fires are everywhere now. Those massive black metal spiders stride through the smoke and flames with the poise and assurance of conquerors. I get the feeling that in a few hours, Los Angeles is going to be a wasteland.

I bend to my work, trying for fast. It's hot, stifling, cramped, and frustrating.

"Uh, honey?" murmurs my wife.

"I'm close," I say, not unkindly. I smash the big screwdriver in and pop out the remnants of the ignition. Inside, gleaming, is a little metal nub, the hidden nipple of the car.

"Honey!" There's some urgency in her voice.

I look up. One of the tarantula-robots is on the freeway. I can hear the pounding of its legs, I can feel the vibrations. Time to go.

I fish my Leatherman out, carefully reach into the ignition, and turn. Just like a key. The battery is almost dead, but the starter goes, goes, goes . . . and the engine catches. I look up at the robot, almost on top of us, and throw the shift into reverse.

"Seat belts," I say, and stomp on the gas.

8

MAD SAM

The noise is deafening, the thunder of alien metal on asphalt. I look up to see the spider machine flashing down on us, legs spearing into the road, tearing through the rubble. It's unimaginable that something so big and heavy can move so fast, its legs in constant shuddering motion.

There's some kind of awful mouth underneath, surrounded by a forest of whipping tentacles. Yikes.

The tires on the truck squeal as I stamp on the gas. We surge backward, but with the monstrosity maybe a hundred yards away and closing, I need to turn this car around and drive it the right way, forward—thirty miles an hour in reverse is going to get us killed.

Rosamund, Ca

—The tires squealed in a long, shuddering scream, and the smell of melting rubber filled the car. I slammed against the harness, first one way, then the other, the world outside whipping around in a mad cartwheel. I ignored it, staring at the stuntman's hands and feet as he fluidly slammed the wheel around and popped the car into drive. We blasted forward. Piece of cake.

"That's the reverse one-eighty," the stuntman said lightly. His name was Chris and he looked like the young Unabomber: massive wool watch cap pulled down tight over his head, the anonymity of wraparound dark glasses, wispy beard. But his voice was friendly.

My turn. We switched places, and I felt the now-familiar rumble and power of the V8 as I goosed her up to the mark. The car was a Chevrolet Caprice, built in 1978, massive and boxy, probably an extra from the original *Starsky and Hutch*. Yellow Car was her name, and my name when I was in her. I lived to hear *"Good job, Yellow!"* over the radio—but mostly it was *"Come on, Yellow, you know what to do, try that again."*

I gripped the wheel, my left hand at about three o'clock and my thumb wrapped. This was the one stunt that required what they called the death grip. Usually, you keep your thumbs outside the wheel in case you hit a curb, a parked car, or a manhole. The sudden jolt could jerk the wheel so violently it might shatter the bone. My right hand shifted her into reverse, and I craned around backward to look at the cone mark, directly behind us, some seventy feet away.

"Ready, and *action*," Chris muttered.

I touched the gas, got her lined up as we started to roll backward, then stamped deep on the gas pedal. Yellow leapt backward, engine roaring, tires clawing up the road as she pulled us toward the mark.

Small inputs, I thought. Another stuntman, Danny, had lectured us about driving backward. "The car isn't designed to go backward fast," he said. "It's supposed to go three miles an hour as you back out of your garage. When you start putting some speed on in reverse, it's going to get squirrely really quickly. So keep the inputs small." He meant steering maneuvers had to be tight, incremental.

We came up on the mark, where the pavement had been wet down by a sprinkler truck to make the trick easier.

One-two, I thought. *One,* I lifted my foot off the gas, and in time, *two,* I ripped the wheel counterclockwise, over the top and all the way to six o'clock.

A fraction of a split-second pause, and then the world spun, madness, out of control, just noise and sound and surging forces slamming me against the seat belt. Somehow I knew what to do, the car knew what to do, and as the nose came around I pounded the shift into drive, stomped back on the gas, and we finished through 180 degrees and surged forward, rocketing out of the "gag."

Holy shit, I thought.

"Pretty good," muttered Chris. He didn't even have his harness on and slouched across the seat like he was watching TV. "But you were slow on the shift to drive. Try and get that happening when we're at ninety degrees. Remember, at ninety, the back wheels have momentarily stopped rotating, and the car thinks it's standing still—that's the perfect time to shift."

"Right, right," I muttered, stupefied at what had happened.

On the next one, things happened a little more slowly for me. I could actually feel where the car wanted to go. I threw the shift from reverse into drive at ninety degrees, and it went in slick as goose shit. Chris was right; at ninety degrees, skidding along, the back tires are momentarily frozen, transitioning from rolling backward to rolling forward. For a brief moment, the car thought it was in park.

In the small town where I grew up, I walked to school. I didn't get my driver's license until I was seventeen because I didn't need it—there really wasn't anywhere to go. My dad taught me to drive on two different standard-shift cars—a 1985 Chevy truck and a truly massive GMC Suburban (we could seat eleven kids in there). He said, "If you can drive these, you can drive anything." And they were both horribly difficult to maneuver, made more so by my father's particular teaching technique.

He'd make me drive to a steep hill, turn the car off halfway up, then try to start it again as it was rolling backward. I'd sweat bullets during the half-hour driving lesson, stalling and grinding. My dad was a former Navy SEAL, EOD (Explosive Ordinance Disposal), and his nickname at my high school was Iron Mike. When he wanted things to be stressful, they were.

I'm not a car guy. I just want a car that starts when I turn the key. I don't care about performance and I could never afford the speeding tickets. I had a motorcycle in college that I rarely drove, and I bought my first car for a grand, a 1988 Chevrolet Corsica. My mechanical skills ended with checking the oil on that thing, even though I drove it across the country four or five times. Then I bought a Geo Prizm, a tiny car that got forty-five miles to the gallon. Obviously I was never out to get girls with my automobile choices.

Surviving the apocalypse could come down to a single car chase, or a long war with *Mad Max* mutant bikers. Now I knew how to steal cars, but I'd better learn a little more about driving them.

—

I got up well before dawn and drove out of the darkened city, heading north. I was on my way to the Rick Seaman Stunt Driving School, also known as the Motion Picture Driving Clinic, at the Willow Springs Raceway in Rosamund.

I climbed out of the city on the 5 North as the day began to lighten, sunlight streaming through the green hills under a low, heavy bank of clouds. The winter in Southern California had been the rainiest in years. I felt like I was climbing into the *altiplano* in Peru, the high desert. As soon as you leave Los Angeles, California gets rustic in a hurry.

I found the school, nestled into some hills on top of a giant mesa, the ground covered in scrub and sand. I drove through to the back toward a small track. A variety of vehicles littered the lawn, so I knew I was in the right place; they looked like smash-up derby contestants, with dented, colossal hoods, built in the late 1970s or early 1980s when American cars were solid.

Rick Seaman greeted us warmly, a barrel-chested man with gray hair and a ball cap. He was what a stunt driver should be: Vietnam vet, rough growling voice, deep war chest of stories, thick bristle mustache. His school was a pretty serious operation. He not only had cars for us, he had a crew of stuntmen and -women, more than one for each of the students. The crew worked quietly getting the cars ready, checking radios.

We milled around in the bitter cold and watched the sun try to filter through the dark clouds, sipping coffee from travel mugs and waiting for things to get started. The class size was limited to five, designed for professional stuntmen who wanted to get into car stunts or just work on their skills. Being a stuntman is all about getting jobs, and the more skills you have, the more work you can get.

I took stock of the other students. One of them was just having fun, a lawyer's assistant from Chicago on vacation, and the other three were stuntmen. One of them, in fashionable jeans and fine leather driving shoes, had been a Belgian race-car driver and looked it. Dashing, with model black hair, all he was missing was a long, white silk scarf.

I had never been a kid who pulled doughnuts in the parking lot. What the hell did I know about driving fast? I was nervous because I knew that I was quickly going to be found out as a nerd, the kid with absolutely *no clue* as to what he was doing. I secretly hoped the lawyer's assistant was as green as I was. We all gathered around Rick, sitting down at a folding table set up on the blacktop, shivering.

"I've been in this business for forty years," Rick said, almost regretfully, "and we know what works and what doesn't. This is about what the car can do—it's not rocket science. You partner with the car, you dance with the car like you're dancing with a woman. You have to lead; and some cars are easy to dance with and some are hard, just like women." I wondered if Rick had a different version of this speech for coed classes. Probably not.

Rick admonished us to drive aggressively, to not be timid. But we also had to learn the speed limit "bracket"—what we could and couldn't do in a particular car.

We all took radios and climbed into our cars. I got Yellow, the battered and dinged old workhorse. There was no ignition key, just buttons to push. She was set up like a race car, with thick steel tubes inside for safety and a three-point harness.

We went out to "shake down" the cars, which means familiarizing yourself with your car's unique qualities. We drove tight slaloms and played with "understeer." If you try to take a corner too sharply for the speed of the car, the front tires "push" and slide out from underneath you—they can't give you what you want. The turn is too fast, or the road is wet or gritty, or your tire pressure is too low or too high. The application for me was obvious: when you're driving a slalom course through a zombie-infested city, you need to maintain speed so the zombies don't catch you, but maintain control because if you lose it and crash, now you're zombie food.

Then we each took on a stuntman driver, and they guided us through the course, talking about ways to correct for understeer: how to take a better line, how to use a technique called "pitch and pull," taking little bites with the wheel, steering in and then out of the turn, demanding less and then taking more.

I rode with a nice guy named Harry, and he drove with both feet—one on the brake and one on the gas. For me, because I had learned to drive on a standard, with one foot for the clutch, I did everything on an automatic with my right foot, leaving my left free for a now non-existent clutch. It made sense to learn to drive the automatic with both feet, for quicker or simultaneous inputs.

"Remember," Rick's gravelly voice crackled over the radio, *"a skidding tire has no directional control."*

That pitch-and-pull technique really worked. You could head into the turn too hot, and the tires would start to push, but with pitch-and-pull you could miraculously clamber back into a tighter turn. You could pull your ass out of the fire and narrowly avoid the cones that marked a parked car, a hundred-thousand-dollar movie camera, or a postapocalyptic biker gang.

"A lot of it is about wheel time," Harry said. "You just got to get a lot of wheel time, and that's why this course is good—you get it!" Practice, that old chestnut, once again.

We met back in the classroom and began to get into the nitty-gritty of what stunt driving is all about.

A huge part of what they do relies on "lock-up," on getting the rear wheels to lock up with the emergency brake. This allows the back end of the car to "come loose," which is where almost all the moves come from: the skid turns, the 180s, the 90s. The skid turn is just what it sounds like: you send the car skidding around a sharp corner, in control but with tires screeching. The 180 is when you come flying up and skid to a stop, turning through 180 degrees, to finish with your rear end right against the mark. The 90 is half of that; you come driving up hard and the skid into a ninety-degree stop, ending up broadside to the mark. All of these moves are made possible by getting the rear wheels to lock, through use of the emergency brake.

"This is not something the car is designed to do—the main brakes are hydraulic, and they have a lot of power. The e-brake is mechanical, it's just a cable, and it can be iffy. The engineers that design cars, they don't have stuntmen in mind." He chuckled. "They make it harder every year." The e-brake is designed as a backup to the hydraulic braking system.

One of the critical things to do was to make sure the e-brake catch was disabled. In every car, the e-brake is designed with a catch of some kind, so that it stays locked down when you use it, either with the foot pedal or with the handle. Rick told us the various ways to disable the catch so that you can pull and release the e-brake smoothly, as if you were applying hydraulic brakes.

We all rushed to our cars like kids, hot to try the 180s. Rick split us up in two lines around the track, and we listened to the radio and waited for our "action" call.

I was pretty nervous coming into that first turn into the straightaway that led to the 180. Rick sat against the wall, deep behind two sets of cones that were the mark, the spot our rear end was supposed to end up in. I had seen one of his stuntmen demonstrate it, and I knew I had to be aggressive with the speed, so I got on the gas and the car roared. I had no idea where to start the move, the "point of initiation," as Rick called it, so I just went—I got lockup with the e-brake, I could feel and hear the skidding, and then a sharp quarter turn of the wheel to the left, and the car spun and shuddered to a stop.

I ended up about two-thirds of the way around, and maybe twenty feet from the mark. Rick's dry voice crackled over the radio, *"Okay, Yellow, that's the first one, you got that out of your system. More speed, and better line of approach."*

I quickly drove out and back around the track to get back into line, switching sides so that the next 180 would be in the opposite direction. My heart was pounding.

So it went through the day. Gradually, the process became clearer, the timing of when to brake, the tightness of the quarter turn, and countersteering out of it. Once the car went past ninety degrees, the front wheels could be turned the opposite way—countersteered— which would help bring the nose straight behind the rear end.

I got a little better at it, but my nervousness rarely subsided. It was exhausting. I felt almost out of control the entire time. The need for sharp judgment and fast hands to countersteer was demandingly physical, and even though it was bitterly cold outside, inside the car it got blisteringly hot.

Getting the lockup was critical, and then I usually made too big a move. The speed got to me, and I often jerked the wheel violently and ended up unable to counter, making a mess. You had to do a lot of different things, in the right order; some of them were powerful and fast, and some of them were small and controlled. Making it all come together in a truly stressful situation would be a nightmare.

The 90, coming into the mark and skidding to a stop broadside, was actually much harder than the 180—the quarter turn was smaller, more delicate. You had to "ride the slide," get lockup and then gently turn and guide the car into the 90. I really struggled going from the big, stamping-on-the-gas-pedal move to a small move.

I've never been a finesse guy. At my best, I'm a two-by-four carpenter, not a cabinetmaker. I'm good at smashing things, digging holes, and grunt work, and bad at delicate finish jobs.

Rick sent a young stuntman, Danny, into the car to hold my hand and try and get me through the moves, to nail the 90. I was the only one of the students who was struggling so hard with it. Even the lawyer's assistant did better.

Danny could see where I was going wrong, and he instantly

helped. He had me rehearse the physical actions. While I was waiting for my turn, he made me put the car in park and run through the motions. Repetition was the key. Just like when I was running the gun drills with Tiger, I got a little better over time.

The Belgian race-car driver was flawless, of course.

We broke for the day, and I stumbled back to my car for the hour-and-a-half drive home. I was utterly drained from the stress, but also elated for having survived and excited for what the next days might bring.

The next morning was clearer, the sky a perfect blue wall. Without the clouds and the moisture, it was noticeably colder, too.

We started the day taking the wheels off a car and looking at the brakes, studying the differences between the disc brake and the drum brake.

"What makes a good driver is not your natural ability, but being able to connect with the machine," Rick growled at us. "Some people don't understand and they don't connect. When the car starts doing weird stuff, they don't know how to compensate or make repairs. A little bit of gearhead in you really helps."

You'll certainly need to embrace a little bit of your inner gearhead if the grid goes down forever. The more you know about getting technology to work, the better off you'll be. In fact, maybe the best thing you could put in your bug-out bag would be a certified mechanic. Barring that, in a postapocalypse we'll all become part-time mechanics. You might as well start learning something now.

We got back to work, back in our cars, flying around the track. I spun out on the first few skid turns we did; instead of making the ninety-degree turn, I came in too fast, made too big a quarter turn with the wheel, and blew it, sending poor Yellow spinning through the cones that represented a city street—smashing into parked cars, pedestrians, the hundred-thousand-dollar camera. I wasn't alone, either; it seemed everyone was struggling to get back into the groove.

Then, slowly, things started to click, just a little bit. I started getting good results with a little less speed.

When I was in line, waiting for my turn, I would watch the other students go and think about them as they spun out or nailed it. When it was my turn, my mind filled with nonsense as I bore down on the mark. There was the stress of performance, of getting it right in front of Rick, all the stuntmen, and the other students watching. Then there was the stress of the car, the roar of the engine, the shriek of the tires, the out-of-control feeling.

But as long as I got it together and focused in the final seconds of the first move, just *the exact motions required for the first move*—I was okay. Time started to slow down to where I could step-by-step my way through the entire gag.

It was a paradigm shift. We were learning to drive in new ways. I felt out of control, but I wasn't. I was steering with the e-brake and momentum, using the front wheels as pivot points. I was getting a feel for the weight of the car, something I hadn't thought much about. When you give it gas, the weight shifts to the back wheels; when you get on the brake the weight shifts to the front; turning forces the weight onto the outside wheels. We were learning to drive in ways the car was not designed for, in directions it wasn't meant to go.

When we next gathered at the table in the bitter cold, I asked Rick a question that was nagging me.

"What's the real-world application for all this? Are we just learning how to make it *look like* we're driving fast, or are we really learning how to drive fast?" This, of course, was hugely important to my reasons for being here.

"There's a ton of real-world application," said Rick. "If I was the driver for a bank robber, the first thing I'd want to do would be to fix the e-brake. Think about it: when you take a turn too fast and merely try to steer through it, you get that understeer problem, you'll *push*. But if you can hit nice skid turns, you can keep up a lot of speed and zip right through a sharp turn. If you can blast a 180 out and your pursuers have to stop and do a three-point-turn, you'll gain a half mile on them."

So if you were going to have to drive through a zombie slalom, you'd want to fix the e-brake. If you knew that a mutant biker gang was pursuing you for cannibalistic reasons, you'd better be able to hit that 180 clean.

We talked about "getting pitted," a maneuver the police will sometimes use in high-speed chases if they're worried the suspect is a danger to himself or others. They use their car to tap the one they're pursuing on the rear quarter, so it spins out of control. "PIT" stands for precision intervention tactic—tactical ramming, really. You've seen it in countless movies.

"Well," said Rick, "if you saw somebody coming up behind you and setting up to pit you, you can time it, then touch the brakes—at fifty or sixty miles an hour you'll be behind him in a split-second, and then you get on him and *you* pit *him,* and drive him into the wall or the ditch. 'Course, the timing on it would be tight." Indeed.

—

In the afternoon we went back out on the skid pad, and now Rick really started to hammer home "the package."

We were all getting the physical acts of the gag; we could do skid turns and 180s. But now we had to learn control, how to land them in the right spot for the camera, or, in a real-world situation, how to avoid an accident, make a turn, or fit through a tight spot. Refinements, adjustments—the devil in the details.

What Rick meant by *the package* was speed, depth, timing, point of initiation, and line of approach. All these things had to come together, under your control. I particularly struggled with the last one, the line of approach. I often finished my 180s or 90s far outside of where I wanted to be, way off the mark. The gag was good, but the line of approach was off.

Rick's voice crackled over the radio. *"You've got to look yourself into the mark. If you look at what you're trying to avoid, you'll hit it."* He had talked about this before, and it was something I had learned driving motorcycles—if you stare at a pothole, trying to avoid it, you end up steering the bike right into it. You have to look up, especially through sharper turns, and look at where you want the bike to go. Sliding into stunts is the same: you have to avoid staring at the cones you're trying to miss, and instead look at where you want to be. That could be tricky if you were trying to hit a skid turn through a fiery maze of burning cars, pursued by an alien spaceship, but just remember—look at the daylight.

Rick wrote in his class handbook, "Bringing a perfect 180 to the perfect depth and end mark is mainly a result of you having the 'feel' to put it there . . . it becomes you and the car and the mark working in perfect harmony and union. It's like Zen. . . ."

The concept of Zen mind is definitely applicable to stunt driving, because you need to *not* be thinking. Whenever I was thinking, I screwed it up; whenever I came into the turn focused on steering smaller, or worried about the next line of approach, I blew a part of it. When I almost blanked, and let my mind flit like a butterfly from one step to the next, I came closer to getting it right. I had to empty out.

There is a Zen saying that goes, "Falling into Zen mind is an accident, but you can have more accidents." Stunt driving is like that, too. Rick said, "I get an experienced stunt driver in here and he takes a skid turn ten times, every time it's a little bit different. But if he's experienced, he can play in there and make every one a good one." He can have them all be happy Zen accidents.

The key to all this is time behind the wheel. In *Extreme Fear*, Jeff Wise writes about stunt pilots who have performed incredible feats to save themselves and their planes, because they had so much experience that they didn't fly a plane so much as *wear the plane*. They strapped the plane on like a suit. When they discuss how they fly, they can sound mystical. They feel what the plane wants—but it's just about mastery. Ten thousand hours, whatever you want to call it. Rick and his experienced veteran stunt drivers were like that. They knew their cars so well they were essentially wearing them.

"Okay, gentlemen, time for your test," came Rick's gravelly voice over the radio. This was the moment I had been dreading, the final exam. We had to do a medley of gags: first, coming out of the corner, the skid turn, then the 180 at the mark, then the skid turn into the 90. You had to get both gags right, back to back, before you could move on to the next pair. Nightmare.

We were halfway through the third day, and according to Rick, this should be no problem. To add to the pressure, he had given us a half-hour to complete the test—as a whole team! If all five of us didn't do it, we all failed.

Of course, we all knew that failing meant nothing, really, but it sure felt like pressure, which was what Rick was after. On a movie set, having three hundred people watching, a half-million bucks' worth of cameras set up, with the film spooling through at thousands of dollars a foot—that was a pressure situation, too. Like Rick said, you *might* get two takes to get a gag right, but then they were going to call somebody else, and there went your paycheck.

What about real survival pressure? What happens if you and your loved ones will be dead if you spin out in the turn and blow this gag? If you miss the skid turn, that means that the mutant biker gang is going to cook you and your family in a pot. That's pressure on a whole different level.

Sitting in line, Yellow thrumming underneath me, the sun beating down and the din of cars all around, I had the sinking feeling that I was probably going to be the one who blew the whole thing.

Rick started with the action calls, and I inched along until I was next up. I watched the Belgian race-car driver, in Black, perform his first turn and 180, slamming it home, perfect.

"That's a money shot, Black," came Rick's voice. A money shot is a keeper, the shot the director wants. Black only had three more to do. Why did I always have to follow that guy?

"Action, Yellow," crackled the radio, and I pounded on the gas and felt the car roar to life. My mind was cluttered with a hundred different concerns, but as I bore down on the first mark, I just thought of the first step: *get lock-up.* And I did. I skidded through the turn, past ninety, but with a lot of gas I saved it, and I roared down at the next mark, swerving wildly to get the right line of approach, and suddenly I was *boom,* in my 180, and finally somehow I got everything to stop.

As the dust settled around me and the smoke from the tires whirled away, I heard Rick's voice: *"That's a money, Yellow."*

I absolutely flew through the course, perfect, right behind Black and not missing a beat, until it came to my last gag, a skid turn and then the 90 going right. I missed the first one. Then the second. Dread filled my heart: *Watch, I'll have done everything before this right the first time and now I'll be on this one trick until time runs out.*

Black hit his last gag, and Rick's voice crowed over the radio, *"That's a money, Black, you have graduated!"* and then I heard the same for Red and Silver, as I went around and around, trying to land this 90. I skidded in with a bad line of approach. But I was getting closer and closer. I knew it couldn't avoid me forever. Again, ripping through the skid turn and into the 90, *riding the slide,* a little countersteer and a shuddering stop. Was I too far away from the mark? Then, finally, the words I was dying to hear:

"That's a money, Yellow—YOU ARE NOW A STUNT COM-MANDO!"

The truck engine screams shrilly. I have the pedal all the way down, in reverse and doing forty miles an hour already. The giant metal spider is closing, legs flashing like knives. In a split-second glance, I feel something: an evil intelligence, an angry god. Maybe fifty yards out.

I stay cranked around, looking out over the backseat. I catch a glimpse of my son, staring wide-eyed.

And then I see it, an opening, a piece of the freeway with no cars, big enough for me to hit the 180. Within a heartbeat we're in it. With no time to think, I grab three o'clock with the left and whip it into my hip, right around. The tires wobble and roast, the world slews wildly around; I wait patiently for 90, then slam the shift into drive. I plant my foot on the gas.

The truck bucks forward, that spider is nearly on us, something slams into the truck bed and the truck jounces three feet to the right, but the speedometer is climbing and

*pushing, past sixty . . . suddenly, a nightmare of cars, jumbled
in front of me. I hit a nifty skid turn, then another, pumping
the e-brake as best I can. We slam through. I spare a glance
for the rearview mirror and see the spider falling behind.
No doubt about it.*

We're through.

9.

NAKED INTO THE WILDERNESS

"What are we going to do?" my wife asks in a whisper, crouched in the deepening gloom, the forest thick around us. The twilight has reduced all color to shades of bluish gray.

We'd driven for a few days, siphoning some fuel, seeing almost no one. Nervous strangers had run off the road in front of us. We were heading into the great West, away from the cities, away from the dangers of the alien spiders. But our luck had run out on a country highway that ran alongside a broad river.

There was no warning. We were driving along, the hum of travel and the quiet of the road lulling us almost into complacency, when I caught a flash in the rearview mirror, something massive—then our truck was being lifted off the road. A brief impression: mechanical tentacles crushing effortlessly into the car frame, yanking us up in a heartbeat. A different kind of alien monster, something we hadn't seen. The truck went up like an amusement park ride, and we shrieked in unison. I looked down and saw we were over the water, and without stopping to consider, I grabbed my wife and son and went out the door.

During that sickening moment of free fall, time slowed down, and we watched the truck rise without us, locked in the metallic grip. Then came the utter shock of cold water, the silence, plunging deep. I surfaced gasping, my son bawling and my wife coughing next to us. We bobbed in the river, took one final look at the vanishing truck being crushed to pieces, and then we were swept downstream.

It felt like a long time, but we were probably in the icy water for less than five minutes before we crawled ashore, gasping, trembling. I knew we had to get moving, to get away from the road, so we plunged into woods. A tall, dark forest, with the smell of Ponderosa pine. After an hour, we dragged to a stop, almost too tired to continue, feeling the cold. The adrenaline finally wore off, and my hands were trembling. I'd never been this tired.

Now, in the silence, the mundane hum of mosquitoes. The whisper of the wind in the pines and aspen. My wife and I look at each other. We've lost everything but the clothes on our backs. Now what?

Kansas in July is a serious proposition. The temperature was over a hundred, the humidity levels such that the briefest activity, such as slowly answering a cell phone, resulted in shirt-drenching sweat. The sky was a hard, parboiled blue, with low clouds scudding by, the breeze a small mercy. The flat, gently rolling grassy landscape was notched with rivulets of cedar. Farmland, cows, silos, big trucks, and the oily heat all reminded me of western Massachusetts, where I grew up and picked corn.

John McPherson climbed out of his massive red diesel pickup to meet me at the local gas station in Randolph, a town of a few hundred. He appears an archetype of the Vietnam vet: long white hair and beard, sweaty bandanna around his temples, gold earring peeking out, and massive glasses with tint control and some kind of thick surfer frames. He's like Dennis Hopper in the *Easy Rider* era—a small, strong man, grinning and chatting, aging but irresistibly vital and sure. He wore a T-shirt, cargo shorts, and hiking boots with thick socks. Gypsy the German shepherd is his sidekick. Nearly every day he makes it down to the Quick-Stop to get a small dish of ice cream for Gypsy.

John and his wife, Geri, are experts on "primitive living" who run a company called Prairie Wolf. John has written and self-published half a dozen instructional books that have sold hundreds of thousands of copies. They used to teach classes to the public, but now only teach the military—Fort Bragg sends the SERE instructors to John and Geri to learn the essentials of primitive living. *Primitive*, in this world, has a strict meaning: no steel tools allowed.

John's books all have the subtitle "Naked into the Wilderness," and he teaches the skills necessary to survive with nothing in the deep woods, skills that would have been second nature to primitive man: breaking stone to make sharp edges, starting a fire without matches, building shelters, trapping animals, preserving and cooking meat, tanning hides, weaving plants into string or rope, and making containers for carrying water. John is an original. He's been doing it for forty years, and many of the modern names in survival, including Cody Lundin of *Dual Survival* and Les Stroud of *Survivorman,* took classes with John and Geri at a nascent point.

John McPherson looks a little like a hippie, but he isn't one.

"Survival is a dictatorship of whoever knows what he's doing.

While you're here, you do things my way." He looked at me inquisitively, and I nodded. I had absolutely no problem with that.

John also carries a Glock on his hip. "First rule of a gunfight is to have the gun on you," he said, smiling. "It ain't gonna do you any good in the glove box or in the bedside table." He is very serious about his gun rights. "What good is any right if you can't defend your own life?" he asked me rhetorically. Good question.

I followed John up onto his land, through a couple of cattle fence gates. He owns about fifty acres of woods overlooking a lake, bordered by a state park and ranchland. We drove over a high (for Kansas) plain through a thick stand of cedar trees into John's compound. He lives in a log cabin he and Geri built themselves, off the grid. I'm not sure what I was expecting, but it wasn't the spacious, beautiful house I saw, filled with warm wood tones, lovingly decorated with primitive western artifacts—buffalo robes and skulls, stone axes, saddles. He shows me his solar panels and banks of batteries, a well-appointed three-hole outhouse, and his own shooting range.

Geri is a bit younger than John, handsome, at ease. This is her lifestyle as much as his. She loves the house they built, and she loves her life. "You'll have to kill me to get me out of here," she murmured to me once. She was going to teach me some supplementary skills, like making jerky and pemmican, and rendering fat for lamps and candles.

I had come to John McPherson to learn the same skills he teaches the SERE instructors. He offered me lodging in a tent on his property, with dire warnings of summer in Kansas. I wasn't scared of a little heat and humidity. I should have been.

We started with fire, not because it's necessarily the place to start, but because it's awesome. "It's magic," John said matter-of-factly. "I made my first bow drill fire in '74 or '75, and it never gets old, because it's just magic. Of course," he added with an instantaneous afterthought, "the magic don't always work." John was full of those qualifiers. "That's how you can tell if the survival shit you watch on TV is real," he said. "If it don't always work, it's probably more real." I thought of the hour it took Luis and me to steal a car.

The bow drill is dependable, the standby, the way to make and get fire on a damp day with damp wood. There are several pieces to it— the bow, the drill, the bearing-block, the hearth, and the cord—that all have to be made by hand. The first time around, we made them with steel (our pocketknives) but all of it can be done with stone. "It just takes longer," John said. And indeed, over the next few weeks I fashioned another one, making each piece using stone flakes I had chipped myself, and it did take longer. A whole lot longer.

The bow drill is an example of simple mechanics: you spin a wood drill, hard and fast, into a wooden hearth until you get a smoldering coal. The bearing block is used to apply pressure to the drill. The bowstring is wrapped tight around the drill. The drill mates with the hearth on the bottom and is capped by the bearing block on top.

Before crafting my own, I worked with pieces John made. The cord on the bow was 550 parachute cord, another ubiquitous survival item (a lot of survivalists replace their shoelaces with 550 paracord, just in case). It all was good stuff that worked, and had already produced fire. Later I would spin my own cord from hemp fibers, and it was agonizingly hard. My homemade hemp string would stretch, weep moisture, and break repeatedly. It's hard to really appreciate just how good our tools are until you try to go without them.

"What I want is for you to really understand how this works in the right situation," John explained. There was always a definite method to his madness. He is perhaps the most hands-on, "what works" guy I've ever met.

"I want you to get your mechanics of doing this perfect. That way, when it's not working in the field, you know that *you're* not the problem. You can rejigger the hearth or the drill, tighten the bowstring, try other things—but your mechanics are sound. That's important. We don't want you putting a lot of time into something that won't work."

I understood that quickly. As I started trying to get the drill to spin, I got frustrated, because it wasn't working the way it should. It's not easy applying just enough downward pressure while sawing with the bow to spin the drill.

If you weren't 100 percent sure of your technique, you might worry at it all day, doing something wrong when all the pieces are right. Get the mechanics right, and then you know there are five or six other variables to adjust, instead of thousands. I could imagine sawing away on a rainy day, huddled in the wreckage of a small plane in northern Canada, the frustration building.

Making fire is an athletic event. Learning the balance—how to maintain pressure on the bearing block and the drill while spinning the drill by razing the bow back and forth—took hours. The drill wanted to skip out of the hearth and flip over, or bind, or slip on the bowstring. I perched on one knee, braced and crouched over the hearth and drill, and sawed away. It was stressful, hard work in the muggy heat. Sweat poured off of me, which I tried to keep from falling onto the drill.

But then, the sudden exhilaration of fire! Not real fire, not at first—but smoke, first a trickle and then a gusher from the bottom of the drill, where it met the hearth. The smoke filled my eyes and nose, but it didn't matter because I knew I was winning. Now the quest was balanced on a knifepoint. Now was the realm of potential heartbreak, because my muscles were sore and hot, sweat dripped into my eyes— and yet somehow I had to muster up *more* control, speed, and precision. "Don't lose your poop," counseled John.

I was well on my way to losing my poop, but things were happening. Wood dust coagulated around the base of the drill, blackened, tacky, shredded from the drill and hearth by the heat and pressure. Smoke twirled in stringy coils from the drill.

If I had done it correctly, there was supposed be a deep, almost cone-shaped notch in the round hole in the hearth where the drill fit. Eventually, I got it right, so that the smoldering dust could drop out and collect below the hearth. Cutting the notch in the hole where the drill went was a painstaking process of cutting the hard wood and cleaning it, but there were no shortcuts, because that's where the glowing ember would eventually fall. I learned this by doing it wrong, of course, several times.

Any mistake (and that first day there were plenty) just meant the process had to be repeated, and more precisely! There was no backing out, throwing it in. This was survival. If you make a mistake, you have to repeat the task until you get it right. Methodical precision pays dividends—*slow is smooth and smooth is fast* is the firearms mantra that Tiger had burned into my brain. It really applies to all things in life, particularly in the survival endeavor. "You can't be in a rush and make fire," John told me.

I took that to heart, but later John had to prod me—because there is a moment when you have to "get after it" and saw as fast as possible, breath heaving. Don't lose hope, don't panic, do just a little *more* of what you are doing, with a little more pressure and speed, muscles seizing with lactic acid—and finally, there it is!

In the brown dust underneath the notch, on a leaf, was the smoldering coal, just a thin, tiny trail of smoke in the unremarkable dust. Just a promise, but that was what all this work had been for. Still no fire, but the promise of fire, and only tender loving care would see it through.

Filled with adrenaline, I was in danger of fumbling, of moving too fast, and John cautioned me. "You've got a lot of dust, a good ember there. You've got a few minutes, maybe even three or four minutes. Go slow, be careful, don't lose it."

The key now was in the preparation. With John's help I had prepared a bird's nest of shavings, shredded bark, anything else airily flammable, the lightest fuel we could find or make. Ever so gently I tipped the leaf and the smoldering coal into the nest, a brave trace of smoke pearling up.

Now I held the bundle high and "blew it up,": I used my breath and a kiss of wind to fan the embers into flame. Confident, hard, steady breaths infused life into the coals. The ember glowed cherry red and spread throughout the nest. Suddenly, the flame leapt up and seared my hands, the promise flaring—but still so tenuous, for in a brief second the fuel would burn out.

I turned quickly to our preparations. I placed the bundle, too hot to hold, down in the spot where we planned to put the fire, and I added twigs and tiny kindling. There was the crackle and real heat, then I added bigger kindling, and suddenly the promise delivered. I had fire, I was gonna live! Our fire became durable, beyond the whims of wind and error.

John and I stared down at our creation, flushed with adrenaline and success. "It never really gets old," he said.

It is magical, drawing fire from cold wood. Mastering man's oldest skill, the skill that truly separates the tool builder from the rest of the animal kingdom, a skill that has essentially vanished. I reached back across the millennia into the dark prehistory of the cave and worked shoulder to shoulder with ancestors.

John and I had spent a whole day just starting a fire. Over the next two weeks this pattern was repeated. We were up at 5:00 a.m., working by 6:30, and done at 5:00 p.m., but usually we only got one or at most two things done. Because these skills required a different mind-set, and the mastery John wanted to impart took time.

Ever since I was a kid, I've been in a hurry. I got decent grades in school, but every report card was the same: "Sam rushes through his work." Every teacher from kindergarten on wanted me to slow down. The modern world has conspired to exacerbate this problem. Here, in the woods in Kansas, I had to slow down. I had to absorb some of the slow patience that John exuded, because these skills just take time.

—

The fallout from being forced to learn patience is that John and I talked almost continuously for the next two weeks. We talked as we separated plant fibers to weave into string (it sounds complicated, but it's almost embarrassingly easy); we talked as we cleaned clay we dug from the ground; we talked as we broke flint. All these activities were marked by hours and hours of painstaking work. I got to hear John's story, starting from childhood.

"I knew what the early explorers and Indians did—they could live without modern gadgets—but I didn't really have any way to pursue it at that point. But the big thing was that a real outdoorsman could make a one-match fire. So I spent a lot of time doing that," John told me.

"I did some hunting in my mid-teens, but not a lot. I had an old .303 jungle carbine I'd carry on hikes, which was cool, made you feel like an explorer. But me and my friends, we didn't know much."

Eventually John ended up as a paratrooper in the 173rd in Vietnam, where he was wounded and received the Purple Heart. After some twists and turns of fate, he found himself stateside, twenty-seven years old, with no possessions but the clothes on his back.

"I had this opportunity to really go after whatever I wanted. I spent a good deal of time trying to figure out how to take advantage of this. I've only done a few smart things in my life, and this was one of them."

John went after his dream, which was the log cabin in the woods and total self-reliance. Not some job to support the log cabin, but the log cabin and frontier living, period.

"I thought if I could start fire, I'd be god of the wilderness," he says lightly. "But then I realized I didn't know shit."

He became a kind of self-taught anthropologist, rediscovering skills that had essentially disappeared. Some other isolated hobbyists pursued this survival lore, but there was little published literature on the subject. John taught himself tanning by studying Otis Tufton Mason's anthropology reports written for the Smithsonian in the 1890s. And Mason had never done it himself, he was just recording what he saw. John had to rediscover the methods through laborious trial and error.

In the 1980s, John "came out of the closet," as he put it, and started to attend meetings of groups called Rendezvous and Rabbit Stick, informal gatherings of people who were hobbyists or enthusiasts of primitive skills, drawn to the imagined romance of the Old West. In terms of technical skill, John was surprised to find that he was way ahead of most of the folks there. He was dismayed by these "mountain men" who claimed they could re-create the buckskin lifestyle of the early American West. "My first Rabbit Stick, I had on buckskin everything, and there were only a couple of guys there in buckskin and they had chemically tanned leather moccasins," John recalled with disgust. "I thought, Well, this is bullshit." John went from being the new guy to a graybeard in a few days, because he was so advanced his own exacting self-study. He'd brought twenty or thirty skins he'd tanned, and sold them all. He was soon teaching individuals and then classes, and started self-publishing his manuals.

—

Flint knapping is the art and science of breaking rock to get flakes of stone, breaking rock "predictably." Anybody can take some flint, smash it down, and maybe get a piece or two with a sharp edge. But primitive man could pick up a chunk of flint and strike a dozen knives off it in a few minutes, in the course of fashioning an axhead from the main block.

John has evolved his own peculiar physics on how this works. I watch him pick up a big piece of flint and start knocking flakes off with a "hammer stone," just as easily as tying your shoes.

When I try it, I find that it is considerably harder than it looks. You have to direct the force into the flint at the right angle and you have to strike accurately, which takes time to learn. The blow produces a cone of force, and you have to angle that cone correctly into the flint in order to produce flakes without breaking too much or too little. Accuracy is important. You must make grazing strikes, forceful and clean.

And, again, patience—if you miss, don't swing again, trying to hit that tiny spot. You've changed the rock with your striking, and need to slow down and reassess.

After a few days, I've got enough facility to strike flakes, even some long flakes, from a good-quality rock. But the "bifacial," the axhead or arrowhead, is out of my league, at least for now. Still, in a pile at my feet lie a dozen knives of various sharpnesses, shapes, and lengths, and I use them sporadically for various tasks, which is more satisfying (but slower) than using my pocketknife.

"Well, you don't have to be an artist," John said to me. "Survival isn't about making beautiful arrowheads, it's about being well rounded—you get a sharp edge, you can use that to get fire, shelter, and make traps." He stressed the need to be flexible, adaptable, because each situation is different.

"A lot of 'survival' people do short-term bullshit. They don't realize the amount of work required. If you and I had between now and October in the wilderness we'd have a hell of hard time making enough clothing, with tanning deer hide or whatnot, and putting up meat stores for winter. The effort is *huge*. Most of these guys go out for a few months at most. Who cares?"

I knew what he meant. I could go out for a month and essentially live off my fat stores. Even if you ate nothing, you could probably last for three to five weeks (although you'd be pretty badly off toward the end). John was talking about being real, true, alone into the wilderness, for the duration. Not in the tropics, but somewhere with snow.

"To be honest, one person alone probably couldn't do it. You just wouldn't have the time. Now, the primitive people and the Indians, they were naked their entire lives and they were acclimated from youth to the cold and exposure. Going naked into the wilderness can be done, but time and resources to make winter clothing, that's a killer."

He paused, thoughtful. "Of course, everyone always talks about edible plants, and I know I haven't really studied those as I should. But there's twenty years of study or more right there, just for one little ecosystem. You got plants that are edible that look exactly like plants that are poisonous, and it takes a botanist to tell them apart. You got plants that are no good in summer, but in winter, when you can't find them, that's when their roots have the nutrients. So to do a lot with plants you also need time to plan and make storage. Acorns are wonderful, a miracle food, they got everything—but they're only good for three weeks a year. In a survival situation, you need meat. You need to be trapping, opportunity hunting, fishing. And then you eat the whole animal."

John and I talked about "rabbit starvation," which is a famous term describing the plight of early European explorers who had all the rabbit they could eat and still starved to death—the meat had no fat and not enough nutrients; it was all lean protein. They didn't eat the organs. Living alongside the Inuit, they starved to death, while the Inuit consumed almost everything of the animals they caught, and survived. You have to eat brains and certain other organs, everything but the intestines and bladder.

"Geri once said, 'A deer is Kmart.' If you need to, you can use just about everything." Later, he showed me how to cut a deer's backstrap of sinew, a terrific source for cordage and lashing. There's meat, which can be dried. You can make glue, water containers and clothing from the hide, arrowheads and tools from the bones.

I had read *Into the Wild* years ago, and I remembered that Chris McCandless had killed a moose, but the meat had spoiled on him. "What should he have done?" I asked John. "Should he have smoked it?"

"You got to cut the meat into strips less than a quarter-inch thick and dry it. That's all, really."

"What about flies, maggots?" I asked.

"If it's thin enough, they don't lay eggs in it. I don't know why, but it works."

Later, I tried it with some raw venison and it dried in about two sunny days. The flies buzzed around some but didn't really bother it much. It made for some tough, bland jerky, but I'd be more than happy to eat it in a pinch. The Indians and explorers would also make pemmican—jerky pounded up and mixed with fat and dried berries. Geri and I made some in her kitchen and I ate it later, out on the road. It was greasy but certainly delicious.

We walked out into the sweltering Kansas heat to do a little scavenging. John had always thought he might move farther west, to Montana or Wyoming, but he realized that this part of Kansas has everything he needs. He's got flint, clay, and all the flora and fauna he requires on his own land, within walking distance from his house. "In Montana, flint might be three hundred miles away, in a certain part of the state, and good cordage fiber might be in the opposite direction. Here I got everything."

He continued, "As I walked, I'd be looking for flint, for places to put traps, for wood I could make a fire from. You got to be economical, efficient—you might see some good flint and then end up three miles away making camp, and it's not efficient to come back for it." That's one of the reasons he stresses the need to make containers, to efficiently hold the things you find as you gather.

Marijuana, or hemp, grows wild in Kansas. (My wife, who went to high school in Lawrence, Kansas, remembers being surprised to learn that anyone would ever pay for weed.) John and I harvested the stalks, not for the THC but for its other great use—the fibers. Hemp was the source of almost all rope in the Western world until the invention of nylon.

We had to be careful to strip the leaves. John had a basic understanding with local law enforcement, but he didn't want to push it by bringing leaves home, even by accident. He showed me how to check other types of plants as we strolled, which is what you would do in a survival situation.

"You can tell if a plant will make decent cordage by breaking a small branch and tearing it—if you get long strips, you can weave those to make string or rope. I don't teach the various names of plants, because those will change from location to location. I try to teach characteristics, to make it more universal." Cordage, meaning rope or string, is a highly valuable survival item. You can use it to lash your structure together, to make traps, to make the bow part of the bow drill, or to construct a bow and arrow.

He tore off a tiny limb of hemp and watched to see how the bark held together. Hemp bark itself is basically a ready-made lashing, amazingly strong. Compared to the other plants and trees we stripped, the marijuana was miraculous. Small wonder everyone made rope from hemp. A marijuana field would be a gold mine in a survival situation.

"A lot of places, you won't find fibers this good. But you can still make a decent string from a lot of different things, including animal hair or even your own hair."

Once I learn the basic pattern for twisting cordage, I do make a short piece of rope from Gypsy the dog's hair; and although it's a pain in the ass, it's doable. Compared to hemp, making rope from anything is a pain in the ass.

About shelter building, John feels that it is so basic, obvious, and time consuming that aside from a few basic principles, it almost doesn't need to be taught. When I asked about waterproofing the roof, he replied, almost angrily, "There's really no such thing as waterproof in a primitive situation, just degrees of water resistance. That's just the way it is."

Water drips on to your shelter, runs down along the roof material a certain distance, then drips again. You need multiple layers, and the tighter they can be laid the better, so that rain drops down, runs along, hits the next layer, runs along, and so on until the rain drips down outside of your shelter. The smaller and closer together the material, the more effective this is, so grass is superior to small round sticks, for instance, which intuitively makes perfect sense. You'd need several feet of sticks, and maybe just a foot of tightly bound grass bundles. But it all depends, of course.

John mentioned a student he'd had who frustrated him, a student who always wanted too many specifics: how many inches high should the lean-to walls be, how many feet of grass for the roof? John snorted angrily.

I realized that John was teaching me that survival is improvisational. It's like jazz. You make it up as you go along, provided you understand the principles of what works and what doesn't. No lean-to situation is exactly like another. No wilderness is a mirror of another. The weather, the flora, and the fauna all play into your choices. You might build a lean-to in a forest with easily accessible materials and the need to get out of the rain, while the desert has totally different requirements and limitations. The igloo is a perfect example of improv. You've got no wood, no trees, and yet you can make a shelter.

"Is it E and E?" John asked, and I knew he meant "escape and evade," the stuff the Special Forces guys are working on. In that case, you better make sure your shelter is well hidden, which takes precedence over comfort.

"You learn the rules, the basics, tools, things you *know* work," John said as we stood in the blessed breeze on a high hill, watching his two horses graze, "but then you continually improvise." That improvisation is the skill I was honing, through instruction and then trial and error, just like primitive man.

⌒

Another day, another vital lesson.

"Small traps, that's your bread and butter," John said. "You put enough of those out for pack rats and mice, you can do okay. I like deadfalls because they fall on the animal, kill it, and protect it from coyotes and whatever else is out there.

"Traps are economical. They're working for you while you're

building the shelter or looking for a water supply. If you get good at making them and placing them, you can get to a success rate of fifty percent or better—if the animals are there. And then you have strings of traps, fifteen or twenty this way, fifteen or twenty that way. You can dry the meat and start storing food."

John and I were now near the house, practicing setting up traps. Looking at the pieces of the trap, a pile of sticks, a piece of cordage, and a large, flat rock, I could tell there was some kind of unique logic to them, but I could never have figured it out on my own. Once John showed me the simple, elegant way the pieces fit together, I practically slapped my head with how obvious it was. It makes perfect sense, a trigger underneath a rock. The rat "busies" the trigger, and the rock comes down.

After a full day of practicing setting deadfalls, often referred to as Paiute deadfalls, we headed out to see what I could do.

John and I walked over the low-slung grass hills under a stinging-hot sky, moving through cow pies and scrub brush, dusty and hot, until we found a pack rat house, one of the infamous middens I had read about. I was looking for some small hole in the ground, but the pack rat midden was more like a beaver lodge, a high pile of sticks.

"Well," John said, "I would have been collecting the pieces I need to make the trap on the walk here, but you better go do it now." I felt foolish as I scrambled around to find the ingredients.

There was something childish about setting the trap, down in the grass and bushes, fiddling with twigs. It took me back to my youth, when I would make forts for my toy soldiers. I crouched down next to the midden, shaping the sticks, cutting wedges, balancing the stone. I could imagine doing this in a survival situation, gnawed by hunger and fear, and there would be nothing childish about it then.

The work was hot and scratchy and I killed about six ticks that were climbing on me—but, as usual, to rush was only to lengthen the job. If I screwed it up, and things didn't balance smoothly, I would have to start over. The sun beat down on my hat, and the blurring buzz of cicadas and grasshoppers rose in a deafening hum around me.

Setting traps was hard work, but it got easier. The first day it took me about an hour to set two. On the second day, I set four in that time.

"Always set each trap like it's your only one," I heard John call from somewhere above me on the hill. The clink of breaking rock told me that he'd found some flint to work on while he patiently waited for me. "Make each trap a ten, each part of each trap a ten. This trap could be the only one that produces for you." John always said, "Make it a ten," meaning make something perfect—because you might be limited in what you find. If most of the pieces that you can make are tens, and then you only find a six for another piece, then you have enough quality built in to still make a trap that works well.

I sat cross-legged in the dirt, surveyed my delicately balanced deadfalls, crushed the seventh tick I'd found on my leg, and thought, *You better produce for me, you son of a bitch.*

Over the next few days John and I would walk out early in the morning, long before the day got hot, to check the traps and reset them. I had mastered the basics, so I could make the trap, set the rock, and place the bait (a dab of peanut butter, but it could be a bug or anything that might draw attention) usually within ten or fifteen minutes—but my luck was bad, or my traps weren't tens, and I caught nothing.

John explained that the problem probably lay in the trapping sur-face: rats could squeeze out of the gaps and escape. I needed to fill in any holes in the ground the rock was falling onto. The rock and the ground had to mesh like puzzle pieces.

I figured that I was just unlucky. I have bad luck fishing, too;

friends who catch lots of fish mysteriously go dry with me. My vibes are wrong, or I lack patience. I felt a familiar disappointment with these traps, and I could only imagine the heartache I'd feel if I was actually starving to death.

I've been hungry before. I've gone on monthlong camping trips, run out of food, and lost thirty pounds, and I was never a fat guy to begin with. In the Amazon I probably lost thirty-five pounds because we ran low on food and my guides had only two bullets for the ancient shotgun, one of which turned out to be a dud. Hunger permeates your soul and takes over your mind. You start having four-hour conversations about food, about what you're going to eat when you get out of whatever shitty situation you're in. I used to get olfactory hallucinations—suddenly, deep in the jungle, I'd smell glazed ham. If I had been truly starving, my disappointment at finding empty traps might be overwhelming.

John wasn't buying my "unlucky" line, either. "That's just bullshit," he said. "Every man who fishes goes through his dry spells. You just don't fish enough, so you had a few dry spells and think that's it."

I was reminded of the famous race to the South Pole between the Englishman Robert Scott and the Norwegian Roald Amundsen in 1910–12. Amundsen used sled dogs and ate some of them, while Scott felt that this was "unsporting" and pushed his sleds with his men. Amundsen was first to the Pole, and all his men lived; Scott perished along with his entire party.

The journals of both men are part of the public record, and Scott is always talking about "God's Will" and "fate" and saying "we've been unlucky with the weather," while Amundsen's journal is filled with numbers—calories carried, kilometers covered, and so forth. Amundsen even wrote later, "Victory awaits him who has everything in order—luck, people call it."

Another lesson: luck is a critical element of survival, but you have no influence over it, so make it as irrelevant as possible. Don't let bad luck beat you, and take advantage of good luck by being prepared.

—

"I always say that you should be an *opportunistic* hunter," John said as we walked out one morning, the dew soaking our legs.

"Hunting by itself is inefficient. You'll spend a lot of time and energy with usually very little payback. But walking in the woods you come upon animals—rabbits, deer, anything. And if you have a bow and arrow in your hands when you check your traps, you can take advantage."

John showed me how to make a primitive bow, and we spent days shaping the bow stave according to the physics of the curving wood. As the bow curves, one side stretches and the other side compresses, and compression is where failure happens first. So when we shaped the bow, we spent hours removing wood equally from the top and bottom on the compression side. Adding sinew to the elastic side and horn to the compression side would have increased the bow's power, since those two materials are better for their respective roles than plain wood, but that was too advanced—John wanted me just to see that a simple bow was possible.

John spent another day teaching me to make an arrow, which is widely regarded as more important than the bow. We heated a wood shaft and straightened it, chose a piece of bone for the arrowhead, and attached the arrowhead to the shaft using sinew and hide glue.

"With this little bow," John said, "if you had a chance encounter with a rabbit or deer you could at least make an attempt. And if you were serious and had time, you could easily make a bigger bow that had a fifty- or sixty-pound pull. And then you'd have a chance of wounding a deer at twenty yards or so."

My first two traps of the morning were down but empty. There is some suspense when you approach a down trap, a slight thrill: It's tripped! Something happened! Multiply that emotion a hundred times if you're starving to death.

John and I ambled over to the other set, and I slogged through the wet brush to see that both of them had also tripped. Up came the rock on the third trap and there was nothing underneath. Sigh.

My fourth trap boasted the biggest and heaviest rock I'd used, maybe sixty pounds. I yanked it up, not expecting anything at this point, and there it was! The gray fur of a pack rat! I hooted with triumph, startled John with a high-five, and shouted, "We're gonna live!" at the top of my lungs.

The pack rat was healthy looking, with thick fur, big as a pet gerbil. We were concerned about hantavirus, a fatal disease found in the dried urine of rats and mice, so we carefully picked up the rat with a plastic bag, as if scooping up dog poop. When we got home we threw it in a bowl with water and bleach, then thoroughly washed and rinsed it. John showed me how to clean it. Pulling off the furry skin felt like like pulling a tight sweater off a doll.

We cleaned the rat and we threw out most of its organs, which in a survival situation you'd probably eat. Another reason to make containers is that boiling the rat in water would be the most efficient way to eat it—no protein or nutrients would drip off into the fire and be wasted. If you had one rat to dole out between three or four people, with a stew you could be fair.

I fried the rat on a hot "griddle" rock with some deer fat and salt and ate it. It was gamy and delicious.

As I finished and licked my fingers, John gave me a funny look and said, "I believe that's the first time anyone's eaten a rat and not offered me some." I was instantly contrite. My wife was completely unsurprised when I related this story to her. I'm not sure what that means about my eating habits, but it doesn't feel complimentary.

I certainly wasn't going hungry. Geri was cooking three meals a day and at night we were eating desserts like pecan pie with fresh-picked blackberries. After dinner, John would usually throw on one of his own instructional DVDs (powered by his solar array and battery bank), a warm-up to the next day's lesson, or a survival-themed movie. We watched Werner Herzog's documentary *Little Dieter Wants to Fly*, a tremendous story of an American pilot shot down in Vietnam. In the documentary, the pilot escapes from his captors with nothing, not even shoes, and he destroys his feet running through the jungle. John talked to me about constructing footwear and showed me some sandals he'd made from cordage.

"We didn't learn survival skills in the military, not like what we teach here," John said. "It was all about using flares, getting rescued."

John has decorated a large corner of his house with Vietnam memorabilia: pictures, clippings, letters, and citations. Faded photographs of a much younger, skinnier John grinning ear to ear, with a long M16 in his arms. John was involved in a firefight and was wounded. We talked about the particulars for a long time, the tunnel vision he'd experienced when being shot at. Tunnel vision is often described as a narrowing of perceptual focus; as your eyes fill with the image of the threat, you can't see anything else.

"I ain't no hero," John said. "Hero is risking your life to save another, *and succeeding*. If you don't succeed, well, you're maybe a little heroic. I've been involved in some heroic things, but I ain't no hero. Now, shit, if somebody calls 911 they're a hero."

He laughed. There was no rancor in his words, just amusement at our changing world.

In 1975, John had been talking a lot to his friends at a bar about how he thought he could start tanning skins. One day when he came home from work, he found a dead calf on his doorstep. He knew who had dropped it off and why. They were calling his bluff.

"So I dressed it out, and tanned it with the brains as I had read in that Otis Manning book, and most of it was like cardboard—but there was one little piece, about as big as my hand, that was perfect. Soft and supple. I knew I had to get the whole skin like that."

John assaulted the problem, experimenting on a succession of hides, reading what paltry literature there was, sometimes having a conversation here or there with somebody who knew a little. And eventually, he figured out a system that worked for him.

Clothing is an essential survival tool. By wearing the skins of animals, our ancestors survived and flourished. John showed me how it could be done.

Basically, the animal skin has to be cleaned of tissue and membranes on the inside and hair on the outside. I asked about that. Wouldn't leaving the hair on make it much warmer? Yes, but it would also make it ten times harder to tan.

The raw skin of the animal is supple and soaked with moisture—it is recently living tissue, after all. So you could kill a deer, skin it, and throw the skin over your shoulders—a nasty, sopping, clammy cloak—but when it dried, it would be as hard as wood. This is *rawhide*. You couldn't wear a rawhide cloak unless you kept wetting it.

To tan a hide, you coat it with oils, which allows it to dry but stay supple. The way John does it is with "brain oils," which are just what they sound like—the oils from the brain of the animal.

I spoke to John Shea, an anthropology professor at the State University of New York at Stony Brook, about the origins of tanning. He told me that it's hard to be sure but that the first real hard evidence is eight hundred thousand years old, and that some researchers suspect tanning might have been invented even earlier.

Early humans would have experimented with many processes—saltwater helps the tanning process, and tanning can also be done with uric acid, from urine. "At some point, somebody probably noticed the detergent effects of stale urine; it could be used to drive the fats out," the professor told me.

John and I scraped the meat, membranes, and hair off a deer hide. Then we soaked it in brain oils (John bought pig brains from the supermarket). You have to really work the oils in, soaking and wringing the hide out dozens of times. Wringing the heavy hide dry like a chamois is laborious work, but the hide needs to soak up the oils completely. Leaving the hair on makes the job harder because then the oils can only penetrate from one side.

After you've really imbued the hide with brain oils, you need to work it as it dries to keep it from becoming a piece of rigid cardboard. John showed me how to push and pull, stretch and grip the hide as it dried. Slowly, imperceptibly, the hide begins to turn into *buckskin,* that soft, supple, wonderful stuff that feels like a velvet blanket.

It's a ton of work. John claimed, "If you know what you're doing, you can kill a deer in the morning and be wearing him by that evening." I thought, *You better shoot that sucker early.* You can't leave the skin alone for ten minutes during the drying phase, or you'll be screwed and have to go back to the brains. I worked the skin for almost four straight hours. Professor Shea told me that for early humans this would be a familiar, routine skill—like driving a car is for us.

Finally, you take the lovely soft piece of skin and smoke it, locking in the oils, so that afterward, even if it gets wet, it will dry soft. Geri sewed the skin into a cone and attached a piece of fabric to the bottom (to extend the cone). John and I gathered cedar branches with a lot of leaves, and we smoked the skin over a long thin smokestack from a tubby iron woodstove. "The Indians would either use the tepee, and smoke a lot of skins at once, or build a fire pit in the ground with a low entrance and a natural chimney," John told me. The skin slowly turned a lovely, rosy dark brown, and within another hour it was done— smooth and soft and wonderfully supple. The whole process had taken an epic seven hours of straight work.

Holding up the skin, I again felt that connection to our ancestors: *this is how we all used to do it.*

"The thing to remember about so-called 'cavemen' is that they were smarter than us, probably," Professor Shea said. He meant that because of constant survival tension, they would be more "on point" than we are. The common fallacy is to think of cavemen as grunting savages, but physiologically, they were exactly the same as us. They were pure *Homo sapiens,* with the same brain, same bones. From birth they were under incredible stress from the world around them, which would have made them phenomenally strong and motivated. You see what we're capable of: Mozart, the space shuttle, the atom bomb. They had all that same brainpower, but they used it on their small patch of ground, their immediate environment.

"There were no dumb cavemen," said Professor Shea. "The lions and wolves made sure of that. These were a profoundly intelligent and spiritual people."

To survive in the wilderness, I would have to rediscover that strength and spirituality. We all would.

The fire pops. Shadows flicker off the walls of the lean-to, creating depths in darkness. Outside, the night is black and pricked with stars.

My son picks at his rat, gnawing at the end of a bone. His face is greasy with fat.

"Can I have some more?" He grins. My wife grimaces. "I never thought I'd say this," she mutters, "but I wish there was more rat, too."

It hasn't been easy. We're gaunt with hunger, on the edge of starvation. Those first few nights—before we got a fire going, before we really figured out the trick of building the lean-to and burying ourselves under pine needles—those nights had been hell. But we are still alive.

The wind gusts and sparks shower out of the fire, some spiraling up and out into the night. Somewhere a coyote calls, but the sound is far away and feels reassuring—the coyote is telling us we're alone.

10.

THE DIE IS CAST

The silence has become monstrous. My wife hasn't spoken for almost a week. At first, I wanted to give her the space she needed, but now I'm worried. And of course, I'm slowly going insane myself in the quiet. She still works, gathering what she can, and she lovingly cares for our son, but she won't talk to him or me. He's become deadly quiet, too. It's taken months, but we're through the "I just wanna go home!" whining and screaming. He finally understands that we can't—ever—go home. In the moment he understood, his eyes went from four to fifty years old.

I rarely sleep. Instead I fall into a daze at night, only to be startled by some noise—an owl, a shift of the wind, a log settling in the fire—that makes me leap to my feet, heart thudding wild in my chest, my handmade club thrusting into the dark. I can't trust myself in those moments, when shadows harbor monsters. For long moments I'm convinced that we're under attack, and only after minutes of silence, seeing my wife and son fast asleep, can I catch my breath. Sometimes

I see her eyes gleaming in the dark, but she doesn't speak to me. Those eyes judge me. I should have avoided this; I should have prevented it.

I can feel an overwhelming numbness in my heart, a distance setting in. At times I don't have any idea who we are, scuttling along like roaches at the lip of this great forest. What is this world?

At other times, moments of fury strike me, and I rage in the woods, alone, like some mad gorilla, thrashing and hooting, breaking branches, tearing the skin on my hands.

I have traps to check, long lines of traps, and that's what I do from morning until dusk. My world has shrunk to a tiny misery of little deadfalls, stone and string. Sometimes I bring in five or six rats, sometimes nothing. But at least I have something to do.

One day I come in after hours of setting traps and see my family in a frozen tableau. Their eyes are open, and I think they see me, but they barely respond. As I watch them, I realize I don't think they've moved for the entire day. They're a little sunburned and dusty . . . they've been sitting for five or six hours straight.

It's the scariest thing I've seen so far. We may be eating, but we are not surviving.

Bill Kane, the EMT instructor who gave me the lowdown on medical preparation for the big grid-down, had muttered in passing, "Of course, mental health matters in the care scheme. For EMTs and patients in traumatic situations, PTSD [post-traumatic stress disorder] is not abnormal, and doesn't require diagnosis to treat."

What he meant was that after severe trauma, your patient might be mentally "messed up." You might be, too. You don't need a doctor to tell you that.

I hadn't even thought about mental health until that moment— but of course, it was obvious. Survival is so mental. We know how stress hormones and fear can mess with our heads in the moment, but what about after the moment, when we have to get busy living or get busy dying?

In a *War of the Worlds* situation, the psychic damage is going to be pretty ubiquitous. If you see a family member turn into a zombie, or a town melted by aliens, you're going to be traumatized.

How can you help people who aren't coping, or help yourself if you realize you're not functioning well mentally?

The second casualty of the zombie apocalypse is going to be your sanity, to some extent. Any apocalyptic event is going to be mentally traumatic—turns out, the *definition* of mental trauma is basically a feeling of personal apocalypse. Your world becomes strange, unrecognizable, and terrifying. Just like TEOTWAWKI.

Through the help of friends, I made contact with Dr. Ghislaine Boulanger, a clinical psychologist and psychoanalyst in New York City who has worked extensively with adult-onset trauma and taught at NYU and Columbia. Her book *Wounded by Reality* is fascinating. She's been deeply involved in the field since the 1970s, beginning her work with Vietnam veterans.

This is a vast and possibly foolish oversimplification on my part, but here goes: the basic difference between massive mental or psychic trauma in childhood versus in adulthood rests partly on the fact that children's perceptions of trauma differ from adults'. When children are very small, how they react to terrifying events depends very much on how the adults around them are reacting. Hopefully the adults are protecting them from terror. But when children are unprotected, frightening events are *incorporated* into their personality as it forms— so an imprint, a shadow of the earlier trauma remains in their adult selves.

Adults can't do that, because their personalities are already formed. Instead, some adults appear to break apart. Their self collapses.

When I finally reach the good doctor by phone, her voice sounds perfect for a psychoanalyst: warm, smooth, with a lovely, slightly posh English accent. It's an intelligent, reassuring voice you could tell anything to.

Dr. Boulanger was pretty wary, at first. *What's this about zombies?* She is a serious academic and respected psychoanalyst, and not to be trifled with. But as I quickly and urgently pleaded my case, she reluctantly saw where I was coming from. In the end, her natural passion for the subject won out, so I asked her about the denial stage during a hypothetical apocalypse.

"What you're referring to as denial, during a traumatic event, I call *catastrophic dissociation*. People go on autopilot, not to be completely overwhelmed with terror. 'I did what had to be done,' they often say. 'I didn't feel a thing.' It's an important safety measure."

I thought of Charles Morgan, the Yale researcher testing Special Forces guys in SERE school, and his description of dissociation from stress: experiencing perceptual distortion. Dr. Boulanger was referring to another facet of the same experience, almost a by-product.

I asked her to define *dissociation*. "When an experience is dissociated, it is unacceptable to the conscious mind, or parts of it are. Those parts that are not acceptable are put in a little package and shunted away. They are not understood. They are sensations, sounds, visions, thoughts, and feelings that are unmanageable, so they are shoved aside. Catastrophic dissociation is a term I use for the most extreme form of dissociation. It happens when you think you are about to die violently, to be extinguished. Not a slow coming to terms with death, but the thought that it is happening *right now*."

We've already discussed the things happening in the brain under extreme stress—the flood of natural drugs that can overwhelm the system, Condition Black. We know that the frontal cortex, the decision-making box that separates us from animals, can be essentially turned off by stress chemicals.

But there's more. Dr. Boulanger writes, "In extreme stress, the increased secretion of norepinephrine disrupts hippocampal functioning necessary for the consolidation of memory." She goes on to state that cortisol (another stress hormone) can actually damage the hippocampus, that "adrenaline ultimately devastates the explicit memory."

She told me, "When I was in New Orleans after Hurricane Katrina, a number of people talked to me about Cormac McCarthy's *The Road*. They could relate to it. A crisis changes the world, and, in a way, so does massive psychic trauma. The familiar is gone, and the failure to return to a familiar state is very disorienting to some people. People will sometimes wonder, 'Did I die back there? I think I'm alive, but I don't feel as if I've survived.' That's a very disorienting feeling, you're among the walking dead."

She laughed at the unintentional zombie reference.

"You can't rely on things, you don't have faith in your own ability to make changes, to *have agency*, to protect yourself." She theorized that perhaps the marauding bands of killers that seem to populate many postapocalyptic scenes from pop culture are people trying to persuade themselves, through acts of violence, that they do have agency, that they have some control.

Anybody who is trying to raise a two-year-old understands his struggles to establish *agency,* his need to gain control of his life in some way. My son and I battle like Godzilla and Rodan. "I wanna wear that *dirty* shirt!" makes sense when you start thinking about how little agency a two-year-old has. You wake me up and put me to sleep, make all my food, schedule my day . . . give me *something*.

"But perhaps the most alienating thing for people is to find themselves really quite numb. Not scared, but numb. Soldiers in the military very often find this. If you can't find your familiar feelings, you don't know yourself, which is disorienting.

"What you thought you should have feelings about, instead there is indifference. Not depression, not sadness—just indifference, detachment, numbness. It's very hard to have a relationship with other people, you don't have the depth of feelings that make that possible. Where feelings have carried you in the past, they don't carry you anymore, and this leads to further estrangement from others, and from yourself."

Dr. Boulanger dislikes the term PTSD because it has been politicized and monetized. Insurance companies have gotten involved in the diagnosis of PTSD, and where money goes then corruption and distortion follows. Still, it bears mentioning, because PTSD is what we were talking about, more or less.

PTSD is just the most recent name for a long-standing human condition. It was called shell shock in World War I and battle fatigue in World War II. It's a collection of psychic problems caused by experiencing some terrible things.

The diagnostic manual that health professionals use describe it as the result of exposure to a traumatic event, such as death or serious injury. The event is reexperienced through recurring, unwanted recollections, during which the person often feels that the actual event is recurring. The person will try to avoid anything that reminds them of the traumatic event or stimulates their recollections of it. Symptoms include diminished interest in activities, detachment from others, insomnia, hypervigilance, and exaggerated startle reactions, among others.

Imagine a healthy young man with a good job, a loving wife, and a tight group of college buddies. He experiences an extremely traumatic event during which he thinks he's going to die, but he doesn't. Two years later, we see that same young man. He has lost his job, his wife has left him, and none of his buddies will talk to him. PTSD may explain what happened to him.

Because money is involved, there is controversy about who gets diagnosed with PTSD and who gets treated for it. There are also ancient social inhibitions and ideas that distort our thinking on the subject. You should be able to *just get on with your life.* Suck it up, be a man, rub some dirt on the wound and get back in there! If you can't, then something is wrong with you: you must be a coward, or lazy, or weak, or malingering, or have been screwed up as a child. *It wouldn't happen to me.* But think about it like this: if you broke your leg and it was never set properly and healed wrong and now you limp, can you blame the leg? Are the bones malingering? Stress hormones damage the software and the hardware, too.

My understanding, from talking to Dr. Boulanger and reading her book and others, is this: Extreme levels of stress chemicals can damage the neural pathways in the brain, which affects memory in particular. This damage has a disorienting effect, and people struggle to recognize their new selves and the new world. This disorientation leads to all the other problems associated with PTSD.

Where we run into trouble is that not everyone is traumatized by traumatic events. In fact, some people seem fine, or even appear to flourish in crisis or catastrophe. Some people seem resilient and strong—so the others must be cowards or weak. They bear some responsibility, right? The military deals with this problem all the time. Is somebody suffering from PTSD, or are they a coward? Society pushes this simple narrative on us. We want stories with a hero and a villain. We want happily ever after.

The problem of what society wants to hear is very much with us. CBS News reported that internal e-mails at the Department of Veterans Affairs proved that the VA knew that some twelve thousand veterans attempt suicide each year, with over six thousand succeeding in 2008, but the VA tried to downplay the numbers. Veterans were committing suicide at a rate four times higher than the national average. More soldiers commit suicide than die in battle.

The problem, of course, is that everyone is a personal tiny experiment of one. Everyone metabolizes stress differently. PTSD can manifest in thousands of ways, and has been diagnosed up to twenty years after the initial traumatic event. So you may think you're tough, that you passed through the traumatic event unscathed, but many years later something small happens, and now you start reliving that event, with all the subsequent disruption to your life.

Dr. Boulanger writes of a cop who survived a traumatic event and was driven to take greater and greater risks, to be a hero, for the next ten years. Everything seemed fine with him—until he experienced another traumatic event, albeit a lesser one. Then his life fell apart, and he started self-medicating with alcohol. It was fragmentary memories from the first trauma that caused the problem for him.

Some of the chemicals released during the traumatic experience, called endogenous opioids, can start to function like morphine. "Since opioids reduce the perception of physical and psychological pain, paradoxically, they lead survivors to seek out further danger as a way of coping with anxiety." *Adrenaline junkies* isn't just a pop culture term—turns out it's hard science. Maybe those soldiers who continuously re-up for more combat tours aren't just brave, but also addicts.

Audie Murphy climbed onto a burning tank to fight an entire

German company singlehandedly, while wounded, and became the most decorated war hero of World War II. He suffered from PTSD and called it battle fatigue—leading to insomnia, drinking, and nightmares. He attempted to bring the condition out in the open, to help others who were suffering in silence. The studies from World War II show that while at low levels of stress, those men prone to anxiety get stressed more quickly. Far from the front, at low stress levels, the naturally anxious were quicker to exhibit stress problems. But when exposed to the highest levels of stress, *everyone* gets PTSD. Nobody gets out alive. The greatest war hero of the "greatest generation" had it, complained about it, and tried to get it recognized so that others could get help. So it's fair to say that it's not just a recent invention, and nobody is calling Audie Murphy a coward or a malingerer.

Someone said that the Vietnam War was the first war we sent men into without God, implying that all the self-doubt those men experienced, all the PTSD and flashbacks and alcoholism, was indirectly caused by the idea of going into battle without being convinced that God was on our side. Without that divine mandate, which we had in simpler times, men questioned themselves.

Reading that the cause of catastrophic dissociation is something "unacceptable" to the mind, I thought of Dave Grossman's book *On Killing* and the idea that killing has become so foreign to us. We never kill our food or see death, whereas even a few generations ago you would have had a much more direct connection and understanding of it. You'd hunt your food, slaughter your own chickens and cows, clean up the bodies of dead family members and bury them yourself. Could it be that we are starting to send men to war not without God, but without an understanding of *death?* Are death and dying unacceptable to us because of our incredible longevity? Perhaps we *are* more susceptible to PTSD than a Viking warrior would have been, because seeing and confronting death for him was perfectly normal and acceptable.

How terrible would death seem after you've buried friends and family, children and parents with your own hands?

When I mentioned this to Dr. Boulanger, she wasn't convinced by my stunning logic. She said, "I have no idea how different our neurological systems have become, but if the Viking had the same startle reflex we do, than I suspect he lived in catastrophic dissociation much of the time. From my point of view, it requires a great deal of security to live *without* lopping off parts of one's consciousness."

In her book, Boulanger writes, "When I speak of adult onset trauma I mean to imply that someone has actually and precipitously been confronted with their own death or that of someone very close to them. This is the River Rubicon that those who survive massive psychic trauma have crossed. The die has been cast, '*jacta alea est*,' as Caesar said. . . . There is no going back, they have stepped beyond the limits of the familiar world." Boulanger is quoting Caesar on when he took his own troops toward Rome, facing either total victory or death.

She calls it "the secret knowledge," the space between two deaths. These people have faced annihilation, yet their biological death hasn't happened. This "intimate knowledge of mortality has robbed them of their citizenship within the ranks of the living . . . it is never clear that the trauma has been survived." There is no going back to ignorance; you can never regain the strength of innocence.

This is where the fascinating interplay of philosophy and biology lie in PTSD, a combination of chemical damage from stress hormones and some deeper damage from unwanted knowledge.

Dr. Boulanger told me, "This coming to terms with your own mortality, that you will die, that everything will die, it's not just the acceptance of it, but the extreme *suddenness* of it. The horror of that suddenness, that's the secret knowledge that people who have gone through trauma have." The denial of death is essential to life, and sometimes that veil is stripped away.

So what can we do?

In all the events that I'm thinking of, in all these apocalyptic scenarios, catastrophic dissociation will be the norm, not the exception. I don't care how salty you are: if zombies eat a family member, you're gonna dissociate. You'll have to, to survive. Unless, of course, you're a true sociopath, unable to connect to anyone, living comfortably inside your own fun-house mind of mirrors. Then you probably won't have a problem with PTSD.

"Is there any way for you to think your own way out?" I asked her.

"I hate to be negative about it," she responded, "but you really *have* to form groups. You can't do it on your own. You need someone else to validate your experience, even if it's their experience too. I hate to use the cliché, but you need to witness their experience, and they need to witness yours."

What she was saying is that this stress and damage—this shaking of your internal world—has, first and foremost, fucked up your sense of time. Your sense of the time frame of the traumatic event is damaged and toxic to remember. What you need to do is reestablish order—bring a narrative back. You have to talk it through, make sense of it, establish some kind of emotional control over the events, or else they will control you.

"It's not a bad thing to try and look forward in some ways—but you cannot deny or disavow another person's pain, or your own pain. You will become zombielike, divorced from your own experience," Dr. Boulanger said.

"I thought reliving trauma had negative effects?" I asked hesitantly.

"Oh, that is *such bullshit.*" She was angry and a little uncomfortable to be swearing, but she felt the need to convey the strength of her conviction. I was mentioning a well-known argument.

"We do not believe in trying to gloss over what is uncomfortable in life, mostly because *you can't do it*. You cannot erase memory. The military and society in general are often looking for a quick fix, but there aren't any. You talk about this, you start to build a narrative, and that brings all the memories. You establish reason and a sense of time, you give meaning to the experience. It's not black and white, and it's not simple, but you can get the sense of having some control over the experience, you can detoxify it. Or you will continue to experience all those symptoms. You will dream about it and dream the same bloody thing over and over. Or you will become numb, and be like a zombie."

Funny how she was the one who kept talking about zombies, not me.

I asked her about the signs to look for (in your family and yourself) in a postapocalyptic world, in a world where we are refugees from some disaster, some catastrophe that topples governments.

"I think you'll see enormous suspiciousness, alternated with bonding attempts. Tremendous wariness—the startle reflex and hyperalertness will be on display. There is a terrible price to pay for being highly stressed for so long: the stress hormones start to destroy you.

"I remember seeing someone who was being an absolute hero—and I use that word cautiously—working for the Red Cross after 9/11. I was working in the armory and helping people come to terms with the fact that there wasn't going to be a body." She sighed. "This guy, he was phenomenal, he was great, everywhere at once, and running on adrenaline, and probably somewhat dissociated from what was happening. I saw him three months later, and he looked like a ghost. It was horrifying." When you run on your afterburners, so to speak—when you run on stress hormones for too long—you create massive health problems for yourself, in the chemical balances in your brain.

"The problem is you won't see it in yourself. People withdraw, and you will too, and perhaps self-medicate with liquor and drugs. It's terribly, terribly, terribly hard for people to make the connection for themselves. I was a clinical director for a program for unemployed Vietnam veterans, and I would do evaluations, and when I told some of them, 'You have PTSD,' some were relieved, because they had a connection between their estrangement and their experiences. But more often, people would deny it. They don't want to make that connection, to be unheroic, or not tough. Sometimes it would take many years; much later they would reach out to me, having come to terms with the fact that they had PTSD.

"You'll see people withdraw, you'll see the thousand-yard stare. People will be short tempered, you'll see numbness, a flattening of emotions. But remember, you're talking about a postapocalyptic world here. Even if they don't have PTSD they're going to be depressed!" Her voice rose.

Good point, I thought.

When I asked her about what a layman could do—could we help each other by "witnessing" with each other?—Dr. Boulanger became wary.

"I find it so . . . hard . . . to advise people to take on the role of witnessing. We have to be aware of everything we are not witnessing, of all the ways we shortchange someone by not fully attending. The best thing would be an outsider. Someone from the outside, who can resonate with their experience. It's not about normalcy, but rather '*I hear what you are saying, and it is as terrible as you say.*' Listen without doubting, without denying."

She was obviously somewhat uncomfortable with giving her blessing to a bunch of amateurs doing hack psychotherapy. I could understand that.

"What I would say is that if people can share their experience, it's helpful. When they're ready. It's very hard, because often people feel that they are too much of a burden and don't want to impose, or that what happened to them was minor compared to what happened to others. Or too major. Both ways, they are isolated.

"Natural leaders will emerge, people who can help, but they will also burn out."

She thought for a moment.

"Pay attention to each other. Not denying, not doubting. And also, have ongoing work to do. Plan for the future and work for the future while you talk about the past. Forward motion is important."

In her book, Dr. Boulanger uses the term *the Real*, a term associated with Jacques Lacan, a groundbreaking psychoanalyst and psychiatrist in France who came to prominence in the 1960s. She writes, "To Lacan, the Real is that which always returns to the same place; in other words, it defies exploration, it cannot be altered or signified, it stands for itself and by itself, a point of endless return. . . . Trauma inhabits the Real."

The Real cannot be put into words. "Events that constantly fail to secure a place in social discourse—slipping out of the conscious awareness and defying memory's attempts to register them, leaving instead a gap where understanding might be, or a sense of confusion where clarity might be—belong to the Real. The Real is at work in every act of genocide that is overlooked, every war whose combatants find no socially acceptable avenue in which to describe their experiences and so are condemned to silence."

Dr. Boulanger, at the end of her book, calls the idea of bearing witness and creating a narrative "an act of insubordination against the Real that can never entirely subdue the Real, but it does oppose the forces of the Real, the gaps and evasions necessitated by horror, with a subjective voice that continues to question and to strive for understanding."

I love that. I stand insubordinate to the Real. What is anything we do but an act of insubordination against the Real? What can anyone do but oppose the Real, and strive to understand, for whatever brief moments we have?

We're moving. We travel now, and we work together. We share the load. Some days my wife sets traps, and we all gather water together. At first I built the lean-to, but now she builds it, and she builds a far tighter one than I do.

It's hard for a three-year-old to do chores, but he tries. We make games of it. His talking, his resilience, has brought her back.

We tell each other stories at night, sometimes, stories we lived through together. It's amazing that two people who lived through the same event could have seen it so differently, or remember it so differently. Did this happen? Did that? We sometimes ask the boy to be the referee, in jest, a task he takes with the utmost seriousness, and when I see the first faint ghost of a smile on my wife's lips, I feel like a massive weight has slipped off my shoulders.

The truth is, none of us will ever be the same people. Those people are gone. But we are still here.

More than anything, the need to move has galvanized us. The truth is apparent: there aren't enough calories out here for us. We won't survive the winter. Tomorrow we head back toward the road.

11.

THE ULTIMATE ABORIGINAL

It's cold. The dark of night has drained away, although the sun hasn't risen yet.

We're gathered in a deserted gas station, strangers. My wife and son are close by me, but as for the rest, I don't know them. I make a quick head count in the gloom: there's eleven of us, huddled in sleeping bags and rags, around the edges of this old travel center.

I'm not sure where the others came from, or where they were hoping to go, before they ended up here on Interstate 50. We've run through almost all the water here; we have a day left, maybe two.

Our impromptu refugee camp has no leadership or organization. Suspicion and fear are clear on the faces around me. Last night, one of the men accused another of stealing. They stared at each other, even made some threats, but the accuser was too weak to fight, and the accused didn't seem to care what anyone thought. We waited to see what would happen. Eventually, the accuser lost his strength and retreated to a corner. Slowly, we all turned away. Maybe I should have said something, but I don't know who is who or what is what.

There's a guy who gives advice, who seems to think of himself as "in charge," but he's a construction foreman, and I'm not sure he knows anything about survival out here. There's a woman who seems to know the area, but she's very quiet.

I walk out and take a look around. The mountains ring us; the rough country stretches away; the road is flat and empty, littered with a few derelict vehicles. Utter stillness. It's a pretty bleak picture, and I know from the maps that there isn't much out there. Still, we're going to have to risk it. The moon is fading from the sky, and the western horizon is glowing with the promise of the sun.

It's going to be a hot day.

Prescott, Az

—When I had asked John McPherson about other survival experts he liked or listened to, he frowned and mentioned Cody Lundin. I believe his words were "Lundin's worth a shit, I guess," which from John was glowing praise.

I had seen Cody's Web site and, more recently, his burly hippie presence on the TV show *Dual Survival.* He's maybe six foot two and 220 pounds, built like a linebacker, but he wears his long blond hair in braids almost to his waist, with bits of ribbon woven in. Native American silver jewelry, a massive lion-claw necklace. You get the picture.

His most character-defining trait, however, is bare feet. Cody goes everywhere barefoot, from the Arctic Circle to the equatorial jungle.

In his books, Cody boils survival down to its essential, scientific elements. I watched his show with my wife and found it surprisingly enjoyable. His partner on the show is Dave Canterbury, an ex-military Rambo type; they have to survive together, each representing a different survival philosophy. On one episode, Cody was walking around on a snowy island in Nova Scotia barefoot or in socks, and Dave was disgusted. Cody explained that it wasn't merely that he had calluses on his feet, but that he had somehow changed his body on a cellular level, finishing with the priceless "My mitochondria will kick his mitochondria's ass!"

I knew I had to check this guy out. He runs classes out of his hometown of Prescott, Arizona, and I wanted to learn some desert survival stuff, what with global warming and all. I called up an old friend, an ex–UFC fighter named Rory Markham who happened to be between gigs at the time, and asked him if he wanted to come along, as boredom mitigation. Rory was fired up. "That sounds awesome, and I'm bringing my throwing knives," he said.

"Okay," I muttered, not exactly sure if this was wise or even legal, but I'm used to professional fighters in general and Rory in particular— they're a little nuts, that's just the nature of the beast. I snatched Rory from the Phoenix airport and pressed on to Prescott, winding up through the desert. We had registered for Cody's nine-day Ultimate Abo course, and we were going to be late.

We dropped down through Prescott, a curious, if not unique, western mix of rural ranch subsistence and high-end Arizona sprawl, the town itself cute as a button. As we pulled into Cody's school, we could see the other students already packing up, everyone in tan nylon and drab boots, broad-brimmed hats, Nalgene water bottles dangling from belts. They all looked desert ready and watchful. We were late, unprepared, and dressed like city slickers, outsiders.

Cody walked out, barefoot and just as advertised—big, wearing the same clothes he wears on the show, Dutch-boy braids to his waist.

We hustled to pack up, and Cody called us over for a rushed meeting. I soon discovered that this was the default speed. Cody pushed a grueling pace with his students. Feeling a little frantic was normal for the whole course.

Cody warned about the upcoming rigors, how we had signed up for one of his toughest courses, and that we had to prepare to "go back a thousand years in time." He glared at us. Sunglasses were forbidden, because he needed to be able to see our eyes at all times. "What I'm seeing now is you, topped up, at a hundred percent." He fixed each of us in turn with his baleful blue eyes. "The eyes are windows on the soul, and also on your health. If you're crashing, I need to be able to see it."

We hastily strapped our packs together, piled into the two vehicles that would ferry us into the wild, and took off. Soon we had shaken civilization, swooping over curving, washboard dirt roads, pursued by a thick fog of road dust. We dropped into the Arizona outback like ships going over the edge of the world.

Cody's destination in the desert is a secret. That's a condition of all the press he's done, the countless articles in *Backpacker* and *Outside*. Even though it's on public land, he doesn't want an inundation of backpackers and day hikers tearing it up. But there is no danger of me giving up the secret here; I couldn't keep track of where we were headed.

We finally parked, hidden off the road, and gathered up our gear for the hike down into base camp. I asked Cody how long the hike was, and he smiled. "Long enough that you'll be glad when it's finished."

We drank water and set off, single file, traipsing behind Cody, who had actually put on sandals for the hike, as he was carrying a heavy load.

Having fought fires in Arizona, I had an experience advantage over everyone else. I was familiar with this kind of heat and work. A hot-shot crew of twenty hikes in a long line with packs and tools. Memories rose up: the clink and clack of gear, walking through the scrub desert. I knew how to pound water and stay hydrated—by the time you felt thirsty it would be too late. I muscled down water at every opportunity. Sipping won't cut it; you have to force swallows down.

Rory and I were both overloaded with supplies. Cody required two wool blankets of everyone, and I had also brought my own stove and coffee.

The walk was perfectly pleasant, a nice mellow stroll downhill, the arid desert welling up around us. We dropped down into a valley on a slight trail, then came to Cody's base camp, which consisted of just a little clearing with a rough lean-to and a clean, neat fire pit. It was something of an anticlimax, although some folks (including Rory) threw off their gear and gasped. A decent hike would have been about three times as long. But again, I was used to this kind of thing.

Cody eventually called us in to talk. We sat in a circle under the shade of a juniper and he informed us of group and camp etiquette, bathroom techniques, and how to keep the camp clean and minimally impacted. We talked at length about peeing and pooping, because, as Cody said, "Lack of sanitation is the number-one cause of death in the world."

"You want to minimally impact not just for environmental reasons, but for safety—if it is a bug-out situation, you don't want to leave signs that people have been here. If people are looking for you, you don't want those folks to find you."

A bug-out situation meant the end of the world, with the government fallen, cities in shambles, and complete societal collapse, forcing folks to flee crowded areas. Cody was talking about the presumed law-lessness and desperation of starving people.

"Leaving no trace is not just ethically the right thing to do, but the safe thing—there are dangers in being traced."

Rory surreptitiously raised his eyebrows at me. *What's up with the paranoia?* But paranoia was a world I'd been living alongside for some time. I knew where he was coming from.

"I don't care about profundities," Cody said. "That's your business. But this will change your life. You will never be the same."

Cody let that sink in, then continued, talking about Mother Nature. "She is the real teacher here. She'll let you know what you need to do. Survival is ninety percent psychology, it's a mind game. So get along, be respectful.

"The mountain men that were out here, they could do everything, they had the skills and the tools and the knowledge. But guess what? The average mountain man died at thirty-five, because *he did everything alone.* It wore them out quick. Being alone sucks. It's dangerous. You have a tribe here, and how hard this trip is depends mainly on how well and how quickly your tribe comes together."

With that, Cody asked us to introduce ourselves and talk about what we wanted from this course, why we were here.

Every disaster movie has an uncertain band of misfits from all walks of life coming together and clashing and surviving, and we had it, too. There was a theater actor from Chicago, a distinguished retired airline pilot, a young Airborne soldier still in the army, a mother with her adolescent daughter, a deep-voiced cook preparing for the end of the world (he had spent his life savings on preparation). About ten people overall. Everybody covertly eyed everyone else, because these strangers were going to become our forced intimates.

I sat there and looked around, wondering whether I could depend on these people for survival. If we were the remnants of humanity hiding out from postnuclear mutants out here in the Arizona desert, who would be competent? Who would want to be in charge? I knew Rory was as solid as they come, but as for the rest of these jokers . . . only time would tell. I'd probably solicit the airline pilot's opinions. Because of his experience reading clouds, he turned out to be an excellent weather forecaster.

Some people were there to test themselves, just for personal satisfaction, and others were concerned about the end of the world. A serious young man, preparing to immigrate to Israel, wanted to toughen himself up. A woman was looking to build confidence after a "traumatic experience." The airline pilot actually choked up when he spoke about what would happen if the supermarkets were gone, about nobody being ready for the end.

"The supermarket is an illusion," Cody said. He had written something similar in his book *When All Hell Breaks Loose*: "The majority of people composing our modern civilization are standing on one leg. They lack stability and balance in times of change. They have become unduly dependent on the illusion of infrastructure surrounding them. Pull the plug or turn out the lights and all hell breaks loose in their world, for they have no backup plan, nor do the majority care, or even consider the need to have a plan."

⸺

Cody showed us how to make fire with the bow drill, something I was already tolerably familiar with after my time with John McPherson. I felt like an old hand as I made my hearth and drill, as I sized up a bow. Cody uses a bow as long as his forearm, maybe half as long as the bow that John uses in Kansas. The difference is simply due to climate.

Cody said he had a friend in the Canadian Northwest who used a drill that measured armpit to fingertip, a longer bow for the damper climate.

As twilight fell, Cody put some pressure on the group: he wasn't going to make fire, so if we didn't get it, well, we'd eat our food cold tonight. He was content to let us fail. People got stressed, and that was intentional, too.

Not quite understanding his plan, I decided to just do it. It took me a few tries, as I hadn't made a good bundle and blowing the fire up was harder than I remembered. The ability to make fire is by no means a given—you have to do everything right, from cutting the notch to making the bundle. It rewards the patient and precise, and punishes those in a hurry. But because of my long days with McPherson, I got fire. While it's a stretch to say that McPherson would have been proud, he might have felt satisfied.

But after the fire was going, I realized I had screwed up—I had stolen the magic from those who had never made fire before. I had to be careful not to steal that joy of discovery, that sense of accomplishment, from anyone.

The night was cold, and I was chilled even though I had brought a sleeping bag. Incredibly, I discovered that Rory had never even been camping before—he was a complete city boy. This blew my mind, and I apologized profusely, because this was no way to start camping. Camping should be fun, with tents and warm sleeping bags, with big fires and a cooler full of beer, maybe grilling *carne asada*. Rory, in the rush to pack, had left behind the sleeping bag I brought for him, and he froze in his wool blankets. The night began warmly, but as the land cooled and the moon rose, the temperature sank like a stone. I could feel that he was on the edge of snapping. Later we would discover that the temperature had dipped into the forties. The moon was so bright the first few nights that you could read by it; it outshone the thousand twinkling stars.

In the crisp cold morning, someone blew on the embers and the fire came up, and everyone huddled around in the easy camaraderie of shared suffering after surviving the cold night. I watched the sun creep down over the cold cliffs that ringed the valley and sipped my instant coffee.

Cody's authority over the group was unquestioned. We'd signed up for his course. He told me later that this was an important part of managing a group in the wild.

"I lay down the law, right from the get-go. Here's the 'island rules,' here's what to expect. I take the instructor role of alpha—you can't have those roles reversed, or else it's a mess," he told me. The huge survival advantage of a group is its ability to accomplish a lot of work in a short period of time. But jobs have to be delegated. Over the first few days, Cody showed us how to do it, allowing us to find our roles. He would hand over control for the last three days.

We ate breakfast and started our day, with a few volunteers making water runs to the artesian spring nearby, where cold water bubbled straight out of the earth. It was clean and didn't need treatment, according to Cody. I was shocked—I had thought that almost all water in the United States was contaminated with *Giardia lamblia*, a protozoan parasite spread most commonly by cow waste in streams. *Giardia* infects the small intestines, and as it reproduces it spreads out and blocks the absorption of nutrients, so your body tries to rinse it out with diarrhea. It's one of the most widespread parasites in the world. According to the SOLO school, "one in six people have giardiasis worldwide," although 50 percent may be asymptomatic. It usually only kills malnourished kids, so it shouldn't kill you. But in a survival situation, it can weaken you to the point where something else might. So ordinarily you need to treat your water, usually by boiling or filtration or iodine.

Near the spring were Indian ruins, perhaps several hundred years old, and the remains of a cowboy cattle station from the 1920s. A creek runs year-round along the bottom of the valley, but a freshwater spring is more precious than gold out here. It's the main reason for Cody's secrecy.

Cody took us down to the shade of a massive cottonwood tree and we talked about flint knapping, another skill that John McPherson had taught me. We set to work breaking rock to make sharp, discoidal knives. I was already a little tired and hungry. Cody wanted us to get used to working through the hardship, to swim through the extra layer of mental fog caused by privation. This approach differed from John's, which was more about mastering skills under ideal conditions.

As we worked, Cody talked at length about survival psychology. The real key to survival, he said, is a group's ability to jell, their chemistry. Could we jell? Looking around, I felt cautious optimism. I was happy to see that our group had some good workers. Whether or not we really jelled would be tested later. For now, we had plenty of people willing to work hard on our mutual tasks, and that was a great sign.

I asked Cody what he'd be concerned about if he were in a situation without a clear leader. He laughed. "A lot. I'd worry about the person that's obnoxious and wants to be followed, sometimes with no experience or clue. They could take control of the tribe, which could lead to injury or death. And when people are too scared to make a decision, and they pass the buck, that can compound the problem. *Loudmouths* and *sheep*, those are the two extremes, and the danger comes when you have both. Sheep are easy: just lead them. Loudmouths are the challenge. Give the sheep something to do, anything—'You sit here and break up firewood and watch the fire.' More adventurous sheep? 'Go scale that peak, and use this signal mirror.' The main thing is, someone has to take leadership role."

I find that the best way to take the leadership role is somewhat obliquely—you can't come in and start bossing people around, because you don't have the authority to do that. Instead, lead the discussion toward the problems. Let people volunteer to solve them. Instead of ordering people around, let them come to the right conclusion—and pick your battles. If there's something important, fight for it. When you have a better understanding of the problems and solutions in a survival situation, then leadership falls naturally into your lap.

You have to have enough knowledge to sniff out the frauds, and understand that just because someone is confident doesn't mean they know what they're doing. And vice versa, a great survivalist might not have the people skills to manage a group—nobody is going to listen to a raving asshole, even if he's right. Cody talked about the dangers in "strong personalities." If your group has no clear leader, you can get into dicey situations.

His show, *Dual Survival,* illustrates the problem; when Cody and Dave, the Rambo type, disagree about what to do, there isn't a clear leader. They have to either find ways forward together or avoid each other. Dave sometimes does things Cody wouldn't let a student do. But trapped in television, Cody can only excuse himself from the decision.

Cody shook his head at the needs of TV, the need for the producers to have action and excitement. "They always want us to kill something," he said. "Because watching people conserve calories is boring." It's like anything on TV, whether cop show or beauty pageant: what's represented has only an oblique relationship to the truth.

I pondered the conundrum of Cody. Despite the braids, he was no hippie. He went on a long tirade about the silly *faux*-Indian shit people do for tourists, the fake spirituality, how much money he could make if his name was Little Wolf. He wasn't making fun of the Indians themselves but rather the commercial spirituality that some people wanted, eager to be bamboozled by mysticism.

Cody does speak of nature as "her," and he refers to a woman's menstruation as "her moon" (as in, "If a woman is on her moon, then tell me and we can pack the used pads out"), but aside from some idiosyncrasies, Cody mostly speaks in terms of physics and hard science.

And there is something else, some edge. He is a naturally well-built guy, but when he took his shirt off, it was obvious that he spends time in the gym. There was something going on under the surface. Rory saw it too. "He's a little paranoid. There's something to it, dude," Rory muttered to me.

Another Arizona morning, dry as a bone, the sky one unbroken sheet of blue. There was the morning hush over the camp, then the quiet murmur of voices as the early risers blew up the fire from last night's coals.

That hush never lasted long. Cody pushed a ferocious pace—we were always on the move, learning new skills, trying to fashion new equipment, with never enough time to *quite* finish anything. We were making the primitive stone-age gear we would need in order to survive the last few days.

"Hunter-gathering tribes evolved and revolved around containers. You have to follow the food," Cody said that second morning when we reconvened under the cottonwoods.

"The bigger the pot, the more meat in the pot and the more embroidery you get. Civilization has to do with food supply, with surplus. Where things are hard, the decorations and art stay minimal. The Yavapai, the indigenous tribe to this area, their stuff looks like fourth-grade pottery class. They never had time for more, and you'll see why after you experience how hard it is just surviving out here."

We set to work cleaning out the indigenous gourds that Cody had brought to make water canteens. "Any culture that has any contact with the modern world, they get a hold of a steel pot." You can cook in a gourd by putting hot rocks in it until the water boils (we did this later, to cook river clams), but it's a pain in the neck. For long-term survival, put a steel pot in your go bag.

The cottonwoods fluttered above us. I have always loved cottonwoods. Their leaves shimmer like fish scales in the breeze. They are magical in the desert.

"Cottonwoods actually breathe, they respire," said Cody. "They survive in the heat of the day by breathing out a mist of water vapor. That's why it is always so much cooler underneath and around cottonwoods. It's called transpiration. That electric green color of the leaves, that means the stomata respire water vapor. You can make a still with a plastic bag, but you don't get much water out of it, just ounces a day." He demonstrated how you can fasten a large trash bag around a big, leafy branch to collect condensation.

"Any leaf with a large surface area out here means that the feet of the plant are in the water," Cody continued. "Now, you might not be able to get to it, but there is water under there."

I thought of Antoine de Saint-Exupéry, who, after crashing his plane in the Sahara, wrote:

Do not blame me if the human body cannot go three days without water. I should never have believed that man was so truly a prisoner of the springs and freshets. I had no notion that our self-sufficiency was so circumscribed. We take it for granted that a man is able to stride out straight into the world. We believe that man is free. We never see the cord that binds him to wells and fountains, that umbilical cord by which he is tied to the womb of the world. Let him take one step too many . . . and the cord snaps.

"Looking for water out here is dangerous," Cody said. This was the desert, and water was scarce. Cody talked about looking for a multitude of clues, not any one magic thing. Cast your net wide, perceptually—another example of situational awareness.

"For instance, trees like the cottonwoods are a good sign, anything with that electric green riparian leaf. Songbirds, honeybees, going downhill are all signs to take note of."

I had been through the Kimberly region in western Australia, one of the last great wilderness areas in the world, and remembered thinking it was a land of hidden knowledge. Aboriginal society, what little I learned of it, seemed to consist of hierarchies of secrets. As a boy became a man he was introduced, step by step, to the secrets of the world. And surviving in that environment certainly requires knowledge. You have to know where the water is, because you don't have time to find it.

"What about local knowledge?" I asked.

"Yes, local knowledge is best," Cody said with a tired grin. But local knowledge isn't always an option; the locals might be hostile. Or absent.

Rory demonstrated his lack of local knowledge by going "tits-up" that day. He was out in the sun, with no hat, working hard. He got a headache and a mild case of heat exhaustion, and even started vomiting.

The desert heat is so deceptive that you really have to stay on top of it or it can bite you. I knew enough to bring a broad hat, wear light, loose clothing that covers your arms and legs, and stay out of the sun. We're just not acclimated to being outside for the whole day. Rory had thought he could suntan a little bit; he wore cotton T-shirts and he had brought two small, cheap, plastic army canteens, maybe half the size of a Nalgene bottle. So he was struggling to stay hydrated right off the bat. If you ever start thinking that you're ready to live off the land, about how much fun it's going to be, do yourself a favor: spend twenty-four hours outside. You can sleep in a sleeping bag, but not a tent. Just feel how exhausting that exposure is.

Rory's dogged, furious determination, his tendency to ignore small pains and push on—a boon to his training and fighting—was a liability here. I could see his lack of SA. His "head-down" mentality was a weakness.

"Your body is not compensating for the external hot temperatures, so your core temp has gone up," said Cody. "There are three terms for this lack of compensation: heat cramps, heat exhaustion, and heatstroke. And that's in succession of severity. So heatstroke, in the field, you probably won't live through. The others are very common, though."

I knew Rory was embarrassed—who wouldn't be? I gave him a little shit anyway. It's always better to get a little shit than have everyone overly concerned and caring. But I made sure he put my hat on, and Cody had him soak his T-shirt to cool his body temperature, so he recovered quickly. We had the water and the group to manage it— but I could see how dangerous heat exhaustion might be if you were alone.

That evening I gave Rory the sleeping bag so he could get a good night's rest. I wanted to try out the wool blankets, and they sucked. I could feel my body heat seeping out into the chill night air.

The days began to blur together, with barely a moment's rest. Cody said, "We're five to eight percent behind right now." He drove hard, and everyone was responsible for tasks: weaving straps for our primitive packs, getting the bow drill to work, or finishing a rabbit stick, a shaped throwing stick that *might* stun a rabbit, if you were extraordinarily lucky.

Someone caught a scorpion that was wandering through camp, and showed Cody. The sting wasn't fatal, Cody said, but would be pretty painful.

I started singing a Scorpions song, "Winds of Change," without realizing I was doing it. Cody looked at me strangely.

"Why are you singing their pussy rocker ballad?" he asked me. The Scorpions are a heavy metal band, and I was singing their one, soft rock, breakout hit.

"Because I'm not a metal guy," I said. "That's the only Scorpions song I know."

"Well, that says everything we need to know about you, doesn't it?" Cody said as he turned away.

"Are you a metal guy?" I called after him.

"Hell yeah, I'm a heavy metal guy," he murmured, as if to say, *Are you calling me an asshole?*

I was starting to get a picture of Cody, but things really became clear a little later, when he was talking about changing his life. He started off discussing self-sufficiency.

"I love freedom," Cody said, "and self-sufficiency *is* freedom. But they don't want that, because self-reliant people are hard to control, they're bad for the economy.

"Things started to change for me when the cops busted in and arrested me at my mom's house, a guns-drawn raid. *Bam*, they slammed me facedown on my mom's floor! I was supposed to do thirty years."

There was a deafening silence, and Rory and I exchanged a look. *Thirty years?*

"In prison you really learn to conserve and hoard your resources, to guard what you have and stretch it out."

"What were you in for?" I ventured in the silence. Cody smiled. "Dealing *drogas*," he said, making light. He moved the conversation onward, but Rory looked at me, and I could hear what he was thinking. *Thirty years?* Thirty years is no joke. What, was he in a cartel?

Later, Rory hissed at me, "I knew it, dude, I knew he was paranoid for a reason."

It explained his look to me, finally—his strange combination of badass and hippie. He had lived on the streets; he *didn't give a fuck* about fitting in; he was a death-metal hippie with a nose ring and long blond braids, and he was a barefoot scientist. If you didn't like it, who cares? He'd gotten into weights in jail, and when he had time in Prescott he "trained five days a week,",which meant he was lifting like a bodybuilder.

I was beginning to understand the barefoot thing, too, just from watching him move. He had toughened up his feet, sure, but it also slowed him down immensely. Being barefoot makes you *deliberate*. You have to be more aware of where each foot goes. In the wilderness, in boots and gaiters you crash and smash through everything, barely stopping to see where you are. Being barefoot, you can't do that. You have to slow down, and that itself is a massive survival advantage. Patience, precision, and persistence: Cody harped on those things as essential survival skills, critical mind-set stuff. Be deliberate. Slow is smooth.

On the final night before we were to head out into the last days with purely primitive gear, I saw another inkling of what Cody was all about. I could tell he was tired, and he had admitted to us that he was exhausted, between teaching and the shooting schedule for his show.

He had us do a "hippie thing," which was talk about our experience so far and how we thought it was going. His eyes flashed with a tiny, flickering excitement under his tiredness, because part of why he still teaches is because he loves *sharing* the joy that the wilderness and the struggle bring. He cares about the gift of the soul-changing experience.

"I could take you guys camping with tents and food and we could practice those primitive skills and be a hell of a lot more comfortable," he said, "but you wouldn't get the *rawness*."

I know exactly what he means. I have it tattooed on my arm in Latin: *Mundis Ex Igne Factus Est.* The world is made of fire. Your soul is forged in hardship, in privation. There is nothing worthwhile that comes easy.

Cody was happy with this group; he was happy that we had worked together without drama. We all flushed with pride. Who cares if he said that to every group? It felt good.

We went around the circle, and the actor from Chicago teared up: "In a way, I'm closer to you guys than my own family . . ." He trailed off. In that moment, it was true. A little privation and humans bond, flying together like magnets.

The next morning, as we began to gear up with our primitive backpacks and fill up our gourd canteens, the young soldier, Airborne, was goofing off and dancing around with his canteen on and the knot slipped. His full canteen slammed into the ground and cracked, and the water spilled, staining the dust. Cody looked up, grim faced.

"You're dead, right there. That's how quick it can happen."

As the young soldier stared, crestfallen, Cody said, "We'll help you, and you'll see how much teamwork can extend survival time out here. But these last three days will shatter any illusions you might have about living off the land." Again, this showed the strength of a team—you can dissipate a loss over a large number of folks.

Cody was extremely serious about our gear list, and didn't allow any food or contraband—he actually watched us pack up and turned out everyone's pockets. Bringing food or a steel knife would endanger the experience. You'd threaten the rawness, not just for yourself but for everyone. Cody wanted this rawness for a lot of reasons, the main one being that experience is a good teacher.

"Unless you feel pain in the field, unless you draw blood, unless you get rained on and shit on and are really out there, I don't care how well you can do a bow drill. Because you will get shocked in the real situation." Cody was talking about how stress would make these simple skills so much harder to use—he wanted us to be aware of the "pucker factor" of being deep in the wilderness, without help, and without the recourse to modern gear. This context was important to him. "There are a lot of people out there with survival training that are going to be corpses because they don't know what they think they know." They've learned their skills in a safe, suburban setting, and out here, under stress, it's a whole different world. He *wanted* us to sleep badly, to be hungry, to be exhausted.

We headed out into the unknown. Cody wouldn't help us decide which way to go. We had to stay near the creek—water was the only thing we were sure of. We had iodine to treat it, and seeing as we had absolutely no local knowledge, it really didn't matter whether we went upstream or down, because we weren't going far, maybe a mile or two. So I didn't get involved in the argument about which direction to go. If something important came up, I would get involved. In a real survival situation, you always go downstream—downstream leads to people. Unless, of course, you are worried about people, in which case you might go up.

We had only the stone knives that we'd made and rough packs made from willow sticks. Our wool blankets stood in for buckskin.

We made camp and gorged on prickly pear fruit. The product of the local cactus, prickly pear is a small crimson fruit shaped like a grenade with tough skin and prickers. You get stuck plenty by the quills, but it does have a sweet, pearlike flesh. We found a couple, and then dozens. Prickly pear became our staple.

That night, Rory, the tough-luck kid, chipped a molar on a mesquite seed and rocked in agony. The whole top half of his tooth had cracked off. The pain must have been excruciating, but Rory took it like a champ. This time, his training worked to his advantage. He had come a long way in terms of adjusting. I was impressed with his flexibility.

The next days were for us to hunt and gather: no more classes, no more Cody projects. It was delightful, even though we were slightly stupefied by heat and hunger. We had been on short rations at base camp, just a breakfast and dinner meal and very little protein, but now we were officially starving, which affected everything. Luckily, I had been down this road before, as had Rory, who had lost twenty to thirty pounds over a six- to eight-week period at least twenty times in his fighting career.

I could feel that *line* that Cody was talking about—the need to conserve, the edge of survival. When everything you do has a caloric price tag, you'd better buy stuff that pays you back. For instance, I wanted to hike and explore, to wander up the creek and climb the cliffs on the far side, away from camp. But my body struggled. I was quick to get a head rush. I felt weak and wasn't interested in taking notes. My fingers felt like nubs around the pen. It was okay to go for a long walk, to go exploring, but you'd better bring back a bandanna filled with prickly pear or find a place to set traps, something. The hunger was hard on some, and the complaining notes increased a few notches. As expected.

That night I snuggled up to Rory in a desperate attempt to stay warm and listened to his Chinese water torture snores—he's one of those guys who snores a little differently every time. Cody had helped him by putting a ball of pine pitch on top of his tooth to protect the nerve; later Cody told me that because of that incident, he started carrying a little dental emergency kit. It's not the first thing that comes to mind, but dental problems can be crippling, particularly in a grid-down scenario.

When we woke up in the predawn gloom, all of us coughing and sputtering, still shivering in our blankets, he muttered to me, "I was dreaming that I was in prison and cleaning with Pine-Sol, and my hair was falling out." I burst out laughing loudly against the low murmurs and crackling fire.

It was clear that a group this big had advantages and drawbacks. We could get a lot done, because everyone would work and divide up labor quickly. But there were also a lot of mouths to feed. We were going to strip this area of prickly pear in another day or two. There was already some muttering about a *certain someone* who seemed to be eating more than his share.

I spent the morning wandering, enjoying being alone. I set some traps and explored a bit, but I could feel both the danger of burning unnecessary calories and the risk of injury.

In the afternoon, we hit the creek, and Cody showed me how he crawfishes. The crawfish are an invasive species, so it was open season on these miniature lobsters. I could barely see them in the murky brown water. Cody would shuffle upstream, his bare feet stirring the mud and flushing them forward, trying to herd them into the calm shallow spots where they could be grabbed.

The fifteen-year-old girl, finally hungry, came into her own and transformed into a crawfish-snatching machine. Her young eyes made me feel blind. But all of it was hours of labor for mere mouthfuls of protein.

Rory had discovered some clamming spots, and he spent the entire afternoon hungrily clamming, coming back with bandannas-full. The clams were the size of a thumbnail.

Cody killed a rattlesnake that was in the high grass right by the water's edge. "He warned me, he was being a good snake," said Cody as he held the snake tightly by the head. The fangs were still deadly, and the snake could bite reflexively even though it was dead and pretty bashed up. Cody cut the head off with his stone knife and dumped it into a red ant hole. The snake body, adrift and rudderless, was a dense, taut cord of muscle that we skinned and ate. The cooked meat was white, and some, predictably, maintained that it tasted like chicken.

"Wild food will really make a big difference," Cody said. "It has such a high ratio of strength and density that even a handful of those clams can turn things around."

I was just drifting off into the deepest and best sleep I'd had all week when somebody shook me awake. Rain was incoming.

The monsoon season had been closing around us, and we had seen plenty of threatening thunderclouds, but so far we'd been lucky. Those storms had passed by.

Our luck was up. Here it was at last, bearing down right on top of us with thunder and lightning. We all got up, grumbling, fervidly praying for it to miss us, and sullenly clambered into our fifty-five-gallon trash-bin liners, the only modern accoutrement Cody had allowed us. He had shown us the proper way to wear a bin liner, with a small hole torn for your face. Wearing a trash bag is a science. You don't just tear any old hole in it, or it will come apart. You have to put your head in one of the bottom corners, and then carefully fashion holes for the face and arms. We stood in the darkness as the rain began to pound down and the lightning and thunder crashed and rolled. There was the flash, the strobe, the harsh light jagging the landscape, and then the gentle return to wet, hissing darkness.

We stood in our gleaming *burkas* in the dark, trying to hold our wool blankets up around our waists under the trash bags. I could feel Rory's anguish next to me, his seething resentment, but he took it. He wanted to snap—snapping would have felt good and had worked in the past—but he didn't. He took the punishment. There was nothing else to do, nowhere else to go.

I was actually delighted. A little lightning and rain was a fun change; a little misery would just make us appreciate when it stopped. I was happy for the rain, and even happier that it only lasted an hour or two—eight hours of rain would have shagged me. The monsoon with its boiling thunderheads continued to roil over us, but it rained only sporadically.

All our traps came up empty on the last day. We hiked all the way out, first back to base camp and then back to the trucks with all our gear. It still wasn't much of a hike, but it was certainly a little tougher than it had been on the way in because of our hunger. Some of my companions were shattered from the events, and somebody else went tits-up, but we made it out to the cars. I realized, almost sadly, that I had turned into a guy for whom this isn't really a big deal. Some of the magic, the sense of discovery, was gone. This had become sort of what I do.

We climbed into an ancient Suburban and drove out in a dreamlike haze, flying fast over the dirt roads. The sky was cut with bars of light and dark, and we could see massive white curtains of rain down on the plain. I felt exquisitely balanced on the knife edge between two worlds, in the bubble between being and becoming. No one talked. We just rode, maybe tired or maybe caught in the eddies between worlds.

That night we all ate at a grill in downtown Prescott and the food was almost indescribable, a riot of tastes.

I've been at sea for some thirty days, and you smell land far before you see it, a powerful rich perfume. I had a similar feeling landing in New Zealand after five months on the ice in Antarctica, stepping off the plane into night, into rain, into a warm breeze—all the things that hadn't existed for five months. The food at this grill was something like that, every flavor powerful and nuanced. Just tasting spices, after nine days without any, made all the difference in the world.

I glanced around at my new friends, my fellow survivors. Some I liked, some I didn't, but that was hugely unimportant. I could and had worked with all of them. *A team*, I thought. That's the best tool for survival. You want an organized team, with specialists on hand to cover the skills you haven't mastered. Like a military unit, but more well rounded. What's the best thing to have in your bug-out bag? A doctor or a mechanic. The numbers to stand watch, to divide up labor, and to fight if necessary.

Terrence Des Pres says in his book *The Survivor,* about people who survived Nazi and Soviet prison camps, that "survival could only be a social achievement, not an individual accident."

For a long time after the Holocaust, the popular conception of life in the camps was that survivors acted like children, dependent on their captors. In a terrible, extreme circumstance, it was every man for himself. People still think that in a survival situation, it's going to be *every man for himself,* that somehow this is natural. A war of all against all. We see this assumption in almost every postapocalyptic tale.

Des Pres writes, "Far otherwise, primary aspects of the camp experience—group formation, 'organizing,' sharing and giving of gifts—are evidence amounting to proof that in man social instincts operate with the authority and momentum of life itself, and never more forcefully than when survival is the issue."

In other words, the more social bonds you form, the better your chance of survival. Primates have always banded together in the wild for increased survival chances. Cooperation is precisely the survival strategy with highest rate of success, and has been selected for by evolution. "Group formation in defense against predation is common from insects to primates, and protective strategies often depend on intricate systems of communication and mutual aid," Des Pres writes. "The more pressure from without, the more 'solidarity' from within. . . . We can pretend we owe nothing to anyone, but survivors know they need each other."

We make camp. The setting sun paints the world around us a torrid red, the canyons bathing in orange. The night is coming. The sky far to the east is already purple, without a wisp of cloud between us and the icy cosmos. No sheltering sky.

The routine of setting up camp is reassuring. Everyone knows their job. Tents and shelters spring up, and cold rations are handed out. We've developed a pretty good system, we've turned into a real tribe over the last month or two . . . but it seems like that's over now.

Tonight we'll have no fire—tonight we're scared. We had thought we'd moved beyond fear, but it turns out you are never beyond fear. Fear can always find you.

I sit in a small circle with my wife; Adam, a professor; Danny, a lawyer; and Jessica and Sarah, sisters from

Sacramento, both nurses and worth their weight in gold. We make the decisions for the group. The others have no interest in the big picture.

We've done pretty well so far, I think—we've covered some ground, we've managed to keep finding water in radiators, in gas stations. We are a big group, and we usually drink a place dry in days. Then, finally, we reached the Blue Mesa Lake, and more freshwater than we can even use. But there are other problems. Although we've found a lot of dead bodies, there are still some locals out there, alive, and this is their home.

There are a lot of mouths to feed, and hunger is starting to affect us. We start later and later each day, and things seem to get bleaker by the week. Our bullets are nearly gone, to be saved for dire circumstances, or a deer.

Then, today, a shadow fell across our little band.

We stumbled into an abandoned campsite and found a pile of bones alongside the fire, picked clean and scattered. Human bones. A dozen skulls, most with blade wounds hacked into them. And worse.

A burned-out cookpot, with an assortment of bones in it. A terrible relic.

There had been rumors of cannibals. The girls from Sacramento had heard that a gang down from the Rockies was hunting and eating people, but we all thought it was just that: rumor. Rumors run wild in this new age, without broadcast news. Every stranger you meet has a new theory, as well as stories of carnage and horror.

Now we have proof, and this camp we stumbled into isn't that old—a few days at most. When I felt around in the ashpit, it was cold, but barely. They might have been gone only a day. We left in a hurry.

Now, for the first time, there is disagreement. Some want to head back toward civilization. Their reasoning is that law and order must have reestablished itself somewhere. There would be safety back there, somewhere.

I disagreed. I want to get deeper into the wilderness, into high ground. My wife agrees—we saw the alien robot spiders in Los Angeles, but we know not everyone believes us. Shit, I probably wouldn't believe us.

In the end, they've all decided to head back. It's a hard thing for me and my wife to go against the grain. We've gotten used to the comfort of numbers. But I have to do what I know is right. We'll stand watches in the night, then separate in the morning.

12

MY FRIEND, MY FRIEND, HE'S GOT A KNIFE

We're looking for food. This quest occupies every waking moment. The landscape has grown continuously quieter, more desolate. Months have gone by, trickling almost unnoticed through our fingers.

Against my better judgment, I've led us into a small town. We watched it for half a day, stomachs rumbling, and I didn't see any movement. Finally, our hunger drove us in.

The broken buildings lean in on each other, bird shit stains the concrete, crabgrass runs in rivulets through the pavement. It's quiet.

Glass crunches underneath our boots, and I glance over my shoulder at my wife, who looks wary. It's quiet.

Too quiet.

A high-pitched whistle, almost like a bird's, chee-chee-chee, *echoes off the canyons of concrete, winds away down the alleys. That's no bird, that's a warning—they are calling each other. The call comes again, from another place—they've spotted us.*

I pause, listening, hearing the thud of my heart, the breathing of my son, who's riding in my backpack. He's learned to be quiet. He's almost too big for the backpack, but he's still only four—he can't hike hard all day. He does half days, and he doesn't complain.

The machete is heavy in my hand, and the grip is uncomfortable. I hear a scrape on rock somewhere behind us—we're boxed in, a classic ambush. I should never have brought us this way, but it's too late now.

With muted footfalls, the wraiths slip out of their holes. There are five of them, wrapped in black rags, with red-rimmed eyes, humanity long fled. It's been less than a year since the world collapsed; can they really have fallen so far, so fast? What happened here? What happened to our brotherhood of men?

But the answer burns in their eyes: hunger is the only emotion left in those skeletal faces. My machete stands between us and a gruesome fate. They fan out in front of me, tire irons and shanks in their fists, weapons that have seen horrid use.

A sinking, bitter taste floods my mouth, and my mind races— how do I keep myself from getting flanked? Who do I hit first?

Vancouver, Ca

—I've spent a lot of time training for mixed martial arts: boxing and kickboxing, wrestling and Brazilian jujitsu. I'm comfortable in a boxing ring, getting punched in the face. I can relax wrestling at full speed with a bigger, stronger guy, and I can (mostly) avoid getting smashed. MMA is a competition-tested amalgam of fighting styles, and I am about as well trained as an amateur is going to get.

Preparing for the apocalypse has made me aware of the limitations of MMA: I'm practicing sport-fighting, under controlled circumstances, with a referee or a coach watching, and *I'm always ready for it.* Training in the gym, we know what's coming. Nothing springs out of the shadows before you've had your morning coffee or at the end of a long night. In the ring, nobody has a friend behind you with a two-by-four. It's not the real world.

Steve Rodriguez, a former police sniper, told me that in the real world, "there will always be more than one, and there will always be weapons involved." That simple sentence haunted me. Steve also introduced me to the twenty-one-foot rule.

In 1983, a cop in Vegas named Dennis Tueller wrote an article called "How Close Is Too Close?" for *SWAT* magazine. He had actually timed an "attacker" rushing a police officer from different distances, forcing the officer to draw his gun and fire. Tueller made a startling discovery: he found that when the attacker started his rush from less than twenty-one feet away from the officer, the attacker got there before the officer could fire. The average time for an officer to draw and shoot was 1.5 seconds, which was usually enough time for the attacker to cover twenty-one feet and hit the officer. All the stress factors— skyrocketing heart rate, flood of adrenaline—made it difficult for the police officers to act in time. Something like 12 percent managed it, according to the article. Tueller was initially concerned with legalities— that a shot from twenty feet would probably not be considered self-defense, which could mean prison.

Here's the shocking truth: *up close, a knife is better than a gun. I* had heard policemen say that but never quite believed it. What would

I rather have in a fight? Please. But when you factor in the "combat paradox," then it starts to make sense. Stress only helps gross motor skills—stab, slash, or bash. Stress hurts the finer motor skills, like drawing, aiming, and firing a pistol. Safeties? Jams? Reloads? All fine motor. The gun requires distance. Up close, it's all about the knife. The knife requires pure gross motor skills, so you won't forget how to use it. It's effective when you're on autopilot.

Almost every postapocalyptic film has the hero fighting his way through hordes of bad guys, zombies, or mutants with a knife or a sword. I should really be able to do that, for when the bullets run out.

Eskrima, arnis, and *kali* are all terms for martial arts from the Philippines. Eskrima involves fighting with sticks, which makes it a good skill to learn in preparation for Armageddon. First of all, the stick can be exchanged for almost anything—a knife, a machete, a tire iron, a coffee mug, or just a tree branch. The improvisational aspect fit into my burgeoning survival philosophy.

Historically, the strategic value of the Philippines has led to constant invasion from other countries with different technologies and warfare styles, and so the art of eskrima was and is constantly evolving. The Chinese, the Malays, and the Japanese came through, and then the locals faced the Spanish rapier and the Portuguese cutlass. In Palau, the name for Filipinos is "people of the knife."

The Philippines were under Spanish colonial rule for more than three hundred years. Think about that—for longer than the United States has existed, Filipinos were a subjugated people. This had a major effect on eskrima and the mentality of *eskrimadors*. Eskrima was forced underground, and that secrecy permeates the art to this day. In the southern islands, the savage Moros resisted the Spanish successfully for the duration of the colonial occupation.

The Moros are Muslim Filipino tribesmen who fought with knives and *bolos* (broad, leaf-shaped swords). Their terrible proficiency shocked Americans (who had bought the islands—and their problems—from the Spanish) during the Philippine-American War of 1899–1902. Vic Hurley wrote in 1936 that "the Moro was a soldier, sailor, fisherman, pirate, slave-trader, pearl-diver, navigator; he was a composite portrait of competent savage. Piracy was his profession. Murder and rapine were his lighter amusement. The history of the Moros is a history of continuous warfare. War was relaxation. To die was an earned privilege." Maybe Hurley was laying it on a trifle thick, but you get the idea.

The marines fighting in the close-packed Philippine jungle would empty a .38 into a charging Moro and still get beheaded. This led directly to the implementation of the "1911" .45, because the soldiers needed knockdown power in a handgun, something that could blast the Moro off their feet. Or so goes the myth.

I wandered through the eskrima world in Los Angeles and Vancouver until I found my way to a guy named Mark Mikita, who turned out to be a revelation.

I first attended his class in Vancouver, in an open room like a traditional ballet studio, thronged by a large group of students, mostly stuntmen and -women. Mark is tall, lean, rangy, with a big grin and pale blue eyes. His hand movements are not so much quick as smooth and immediate: he knows exactly where to be. When he moves with a knife, he is *infinitely* dangerous.

He lectured like a college professor, a good one—encyclopedic, animated, and exhilarated by the subject. "This is *martial* arts," he said. "Martial means war. This isn't about competition. It's about winning. I arrange the circumstances, no matter what they might be. Real martial arts, if we're enemies, I don't challenge you to a duel with a stick and knife (the classic eskrima pairing of weapons). Real martial arts is me following you, unseen, for days, and then sniping you from a roof across from your house when you come out the front door. That's martial arts."

Here's my guy, I thought.

"There's this idea that people are really *fast,*" said Mark, his voice dripping contempt. "I do this all the time, I line up everyone at the seminar with their hands against their thighs. When I snap, they clap. As soon as they figure out what's happening, it sounds like *one* person clapping. Young guys, old women, everyone is essentially the same speed. It's not about speed, it's about being *sooner.* It's about shortening the distance, about not telegraphing anything—controlling what the other guy perceives. Allow me to arrange the race, and I'll beat Usain Bolt in a footrace—I make him run fifty yards, and I run ten feet. Martial arts is about arranging a short race. Professional boxers are extremely hard to perceive. They don't telegraph their punches, they're very sudden, so when you spar them it feels fast."

We started drilling with hard plastic knives. Mark would often pause to lecture on what the knife should be doing—and it literally turned my stomach. It was disgusting. It was horrific. This was by far the darkest place I'd been on this journey.

"You don't just slice," he said. "The old Filipino guys, the guys who had fought in intertribal warfare, they train to cut and slice *along* the arm, to lay whole sheets of flesh off. If your opponent looks down at his arm and sees his bones and muscles exposed, a flap of skin hanging to his knees, he's no longer thinking about you at all. You have turned his mind inward."

I shuddered.

"The knife is a piranha under the water. Take a UFC champion like Chuck Liddell and cut off half his face, and he's gonna struggle to stay focused."

I felt queasy. Was this really where I wanted to go?

"Kicking somebody's ass, that's about humiliation. In a fistfight in a bar, people target the face, the seat of personality. You bloody them up, but it's about dominance. There's an ancient basic survival component to this—if there's six guys in my tribe, it takes all six of us to hunt a mammoth. If we fight and I cripple you, now I've jeopardized everyone's survival. So there's an evolutionary part of not really hurting someone in the way we are capable of.

"There's all the social conditioning we go through as children— don't hurt anybody, play fair. But in warfare, you don't do that. With the knife, I slash and lay open your face and you reach up and feel your teeth, you can't concentrate anymore. And I'm still going. The knife is a buzzsaw, tearing you up. That's why the knife is infinitely superior in a close combat situation, because there's nothing you can do to stop it."

"Do you have nightmares?" I interjected.

"I sleep like a baby," Mark said, and grinned. "But students sometimes do have nightmares from this stuff. It's real and it's horrible, horrible stuff."

As Mark talked and drilled us, I started to see the carnage that could come from the knife—tendons snipped, hands and fingers sliced, thumbs lopped off, the cold steel seeking arteries, transecting muscles and doing irreparable harm.

I could suddenly see that if I had a knife, it would nearly negate an opponent's ground game (his wrestling). With a sharp knife in my hand, I could easily roll with a jiu-jitsu black belt (a guy who would normally just toy with me) and carve him to pieces. All that boxing I had done, all that MMA training—it wasn't useless, but the knife came along and changed it in a terrifying way.

"Let's go back to the stick," Mark said, and swung a stick forehand at me. "This is *a priori* knowledge: you're born knowing how to do this. Put a stick in anyone's hand, a knife, a sword, and they'll swing it like this."

Mark had me stand at what he called single-tempo distance, where I was out of range and it would take one action—a step—to get into range. The term comes from fencing; Mark studied with Edwin Richards, an Olympian in 1964 and one of the prominent fencing coaches in the United States. In one international tournament, Richards won all three weapons categories, epee, foil, and saber—one of the last fencers to achieve this feat. Mark studied with Richards for fifteen years. Fine distinctions of range become part of the training when weapons are involved. Mark held up a Thai pad for me to strike. "Now, come forward and brain me," he said. "Just come and hit."

I stepped across the floor and smashed my stick down onto the pad, which made a satisfying *blam*.

"Did everybody see that?" Mark asked, smiling. Many of his students nodded, murmuring. "That's the *classic error.*"

He had another new student do the same thing, and apparently got the same result. "Did you see it?" he asked me, grinning ear to ear.

"The classic error is when you bridge the distance without the strike coming. You step forward and the weapon goes back, to build power for the swing. Essentially, for that split second you're leading with your face."

Mark demonstrated the difference. He stepped forward and his arm went back, chambering the strike, then he hit the pad. But his face and head were traveling forward and exposed for a moment as he came into range, before his blow was on the way.

"Now, the solution is to start your strike *before* you come into range—so that as you bridge the distance, you lead with firepower."

And now Mark overemphasized the correct way. He stood still, prepared the strike, and then stepped forward *as* the strike came down. And now you couldn't take advantage of his being open, because when he was open he was still out of range. When he came into range, the blow was already coming at you and you had to deal with it.

We drilled with padded sticks, and it was fascinating how quickly my reaction time began to tighten up and my focus became sharper. It wasn't that I was moving *fast,* I was just seeing deeper into the future of my opponent's action and acting in time. Usually, I had to slow myself down and actually wait for him to be in range.

I knew that this drill was a way for Mark to reach people like me, people with a lot of martial arts experience who think they know what they're doing. It's a way for him to say, *Look, there are layers within layers to the stuff. You think you understand, but there are always deeper places to go.*

In a stroke of luck, Mark eventually moved back to Los Angeles and opened a school about ten minutes from my house. Again, it resembled a dance studio, with full-length mirrors and even stretching bars. It was a macabre dance studio, though, with weapons of every kind hanging on the walls—a real jousting lance, various broadswords, rapiers, long blades, and countless shorter knives. He had rubber guns in ten different models, from a .45 to an AK-47; Western and samurai suits of armor. A real skull and a model of the spine hung on the walls, along with two huge anatomy posters detailing the muscular and circulatory systems. Mark could talk like a doctor about anatomy, about the horrific vulnerability of a human body to his thirsty blade.

I asked Mark what he thought of the twenty-foot rule, and he smiled. "Well, I know you've already read about the stress, and the likelihood of missing the shot, but there's even more to it than that. If I can close the distance, then I can do more damage with the knife in the same amount of time. We're standing face to face, you shoot and I cut. You have a hydrostatic shockwave in front of the bullet, and often that wave pushes things aside. Things like veins and arteries are designed to flex. The knife transects everything, it's all bleeding out. I can open up an eight-inch-deep, fourteen-inch-wide wound with this four-inch knife. I'll scribe your spine from the front." The knife is intimate—you have to be close, and at close range, the knife doesn't screw up, doesn't run out of ammo, can't jam.

One of the great advantages to sparring, in boxing, and "rolling," in jiu-jitsu, is the traditional concept of *randori,* the ability to fight without permanently or seriously injuring each other. It's different when someone is actually trying to hurt you. With weapons, the sense of urgency climbs off the chart. I could feel myself tightening up, becoming more desperate. I became hyperaggressive in my counteroffense—because I might have to be to survive. Weapons really change everything. Mark liked to joke that the Ultimate Fighting Championship should be called the Penultimate Fighting Championship. I started to realize that MMA, this thing that I had thought of as the be-all and end-all of hand-to-hand combat, was really just another form of sparring.

Mark is an intensely cerebral guy, and his study has been *intelligent.* I felt lucky to have found him, because at fifty, Mark seemed to me to be entering into some kind of profound, deeper mastery. He was still incredibly fit, but it was clear from old photos and the way he talked that he had been a superlative athlete in his world. Now his mind was expanding. He read, he studied, he pondered and examined his art like a scientist.

Mark told me that of all his teachers, his own father had made the biggest impression. "He questioned everything. He really forced us to think for ourselves. Even as kids, we learned the alphabet the regular way, and then out of order"—Mark recited the out-of-order alphabet he'd learned so long ago—"just because it was arbitrary and he wanted to prove that to us. So we'd do that in school to annoy teachers." He laughed. I'll bet that worked.

Mark grew up in a military family. His father was in the army for five years and the air force for twenty-five. "My dad had fought in the Philippines during World War II. He was there with MacArthur in 1944, and he had seen the Filipino guerillas. He saw them volunteer to walk point for the army and hunt the Japanese in the mountains, and he saw how skilled they were with *bolos* and sticks. They would get into scrapes with the marines, and these little guys would kick the shit out of the big marines. So he led me in that direction, and in 1971 I found my first eskrima teacher, a Filipino gunnery sergeant named Santos.

"I could see right away that this was an art based on common sense. There's no stylistic mumbo jumbo—here comes a guy with a weapon to kill you, and here are some ways to avoid that. 'Whatever works,' he would say. We'd be training and I'd ask him should I be left foot forward or right foot forward? And he would say 'Sure,' which was frustrating. I wanted to know which was better. Santos was always saying 'This is good,' and later eskrima teachers would say the same— make it work. You don't have to get back to 'ready' position, and needing to might get you killed.

"People will talk about knife-fighting skills, and they'll get hung up on figure-eight movements, patterns—just techniques. If you really want to talk about knife fighting, it all comes down to anatomy. I don't have to be strong, I just have to be accurate and know where the targets are, and be able to get at them. I don't waste time plowing through meat, I go to major arteries and I shut him down."

He demonstrated a point by taking his real skull off the wall (Mark had studied real cadavers with a student of his who was a neurosurgeon). "The skull has so many vulnerabilities," he said. "The occiput, supraorbital plates, the foramen magnum. The spinal cord is exposed right here, so I put you into forward flexion and slide my blade down that part of the skull and I cut right through the spinal cord; it turns off the lungs, the whole diaphragm. Your knees would collapse, your heart will probably stop. I find the spinous process and the slide the knife through. It takes *no strength,* but I do need a very sharp knife. And the *willingness to use it.*

"In a close-quarters fight with weapons, you don't have a lot of time; there's a very limited window to get business done. You go after the periphery, and that starts the process. You pull defenses away and then start seeking with the scalpel. There are specific targets: subclavian arteries, the aortic arch, the femoral artery, the popliteal artery—whenever arteries and veins have to go around joints, they are forced close to the surface. It takes accuracy. You need to switch from hack-and-slash to surgery. You've got a tool that is totally destructive to everything. You put your hand up and I cut your fingertips off, and as you pull back I follow—right to the carotids, an extraordinary, superb target. Twelve point five percent of your blood volume runs through each one. In eight pumps of your heart, all the blood in your body is gone through a cut carotid in a six-foot geyser of blood."

He shook his head. "You can see why it's often a lose-lose situation with a knife. A knife fight should never be competitive. If he has a knife, and you pull a knife, you both should run away. If we're both equally skilled, we're both dead."

Mark continued, "Numbers get thrown around, that a weapon is present in seventy to ninety percent of street altercations, but most martial arts schools don't train much with weapons because it's really hard to deal with. The best way to deal with a knife attack? Don't put anything out there, run away. If you can get your shoe on your hand, or take your shirt off and wrap it around your arm to block with, that's fine . . . but just run."

He paused, and turned to me for emphasis. "Listen, if you train every day with me for five years, and somebody pulls a knife on you and you run? Then I've succeeded."

I started to come to understand the stakes and the dangers, and I kept training—because there might come that moment when I couldn't run. Mark and I talked at length about "the interview," where you assess an opponent, he assesses you, and you both lie to each other like crazy. You bait; you try to get a reaction.

"We know well you can't afford to trade, with weapons. And this is even worse in a grid-down scenario, there's no help coming, no emergency room surgeons. So the most important thing to control is the distance. Whoever masters the distance will win the fight. The dangers of the weapon mean you almost never, ever commit to something— the lunge is suicide. You would commit to the big crushing blow only when the enemy is defenseless and stunned. You target the hands. *Eskrimadors* call it taking the fangs from the snake."

Another reason why eskrima is a great self-defense art is that you can be be completely nonlethal. If a guy comes at you with a knife and you break both his hands with your stick, he's probably going to leave you alone. And also, he'll live.

"But you have to retreat and assess. This is critical: maybe you slashed his wrist but hit his watch! So in a real fight, in a real doomsday-type scenario, I'd use the distance—which gives me time—and take tiny clips, here and there. I start taking bites out of his periphery. If he's bleeding from a dozen little cuts, I keep him moving, make him chase me, and now he's pumping blood out and things get bad for him. Imagine the worst cut you've ever had in the kitchen. If you've got a few of those on your belly, on your neck? Your mortality is leaking out. All those thoughts about you kicking my ass are gone. I'm attacking your anatomy, but also your psychology."

We trained in class to work on that "interview" process, sparring with padded sticks. We went after hands and stalked each other through tiny shifts in distance. *When am I in range? Can I draw him in? Can I cover distance without him realizing it?* The speed, focus, and clarity that you have to bring are exhausting.

I tried to imagine a real encounter—maybe in a burned-out building when I was trapped and trying to protect my family. A machete against another guy with a machete. Or a tire iron. I wondered if I could do it.

One day, a top student of Mark's and I sparred with the padded sticks for *hours*. We really went at it—trying to cover the distance, trying to protect ourselves while at the same time seizing the opponent's stick, looking for openings, blasting feints at each other's hands.

Patterns quickly emerged and repeated. We danced around, out of range, or we crashed: there wasn't much in between. That space in between, where all the damage gets done, was where you might only have a split second, and that's where the fight would probably get decided. You didn't have to take his stick, just kill it for a beat, entangle it for a split second. If he grabbed me, I could use that—his hand on my wrist could be seen as me grabbing him, too. As we began to tire, we crashed more and more often, and more clumsily.

I was bigger and had a longer reach than Mark's student, and maybe I was in better shape, but he had a lot more experience with this drill. We went back and forth, and the tension built. Even with padded sticks, you could still get hurt, so we were going "light touch" to the head. Then he caught me, *bam,* on the side of the head, a little too hard.

Now, in MMA gyms where I come from, you often spar *as hard as the other guy wants*. If he wants to go light—and try new techniques, and mess around—I'll go light. If he wants to bang, I'll bang him back. There's a little bit of the tough-guy attitude there, but human nature is what it is, and if somebody hits you, you hit back. I crashed, caught his stick, and, as he reached to try to free it up, cracked him on the head, *blam!* Definitely in violation of the light-touch rule.

Mark broke us up. He'd been watching, letting us ride the line of going too hard—because it was good place to train, a place for us to push each other.

"Did you see what happened when you got mad?" Mark asked. "You came straight to him. You were aggressive but also really vulnerable, because you were so hot to pay him back. You put yourself right in harm's way, there. If we're sparring, and I have a great counter to a side kick? If I really, really want you to come at me with a side kick, what do I do? I hit you with a side kick. And sure enough, then you come back at me with a side kick, and now I've got what I want. I programmed it into you. You can't lose control and get mad, because this isn't boxing—you can't take one to give one. It's a cliché, but *men are like steel, useless when they lose their temper.*"

I felt the flush of shame. I had not been in control. Anger is the easy way: it feels good to let go and collapse into rage because of the endorphins and pleasure it can bring. But that's not the man's way; that's the boy's way. The chump's way. If you're playing for mortal stakes, the cold clear mind is essential. Anger is just too dangerous.

I asked Mark what the perfect knife would be for the apocalypse.

"It depends on the job, on the circumstances. Sure, it'd be great to have a razor-sharp sword. But that's not always feasible. You would want three or four knives, different tools for different tasks, but you can't be hung up on them. They're just screwdrivers, just tools. And the tool dictates the style, where the knife goes and what it does. The one important thing is that they be razor sharp, and a combat knife *cannot* be used for anything but cutting human flesh." Right. I knew the reason for that was so that you wouldn't dull your combat blade on everyday use, but it still sounded scary, medieval. The thirsty blade, only used for killing.

I set out to find the best series of combat knives I could. The Internet knife world is a bonanza. I found my way to Cold Steel, a manufacturer that takes pride in its testing and has a great selection. The biggest and baddest knife it makes is the San-Mai Gurkha Kukri. A kukri is a curved short sword favored in Nepal; the Gurkha were Nepalese British soldiers from the old days of the British Empire; San-Mai refers to the steel composition, with a core of hard, high-carbon steel and more flexible steel on the surfaces. The Cold Steel catalog shows a burly knifesmith slicing through fifteen one-inch cords of manila rope with one chop. It's a heavy knife, seventeen inches long, and I could cut your leg off with it. The kukri is a perfect weapon for killing zombies, which is probably why Milla Jovovich carries two in the *Resident Evil* movies. And she kills a *shitload* of zombies with them.

I found another short sword, called the Junglee—the odd brand name is Urdu for "from the jungle." It's lighter and faster than the kukri, almost as light as a stick. It can't compare in quality to the Cold Steel blade, but it's also a sixth of the price. The kukri is a hack-and-slash weapon, while the Junglee is all speed and reach.

Mark said, "Those are good choices, and they show you that with a weapon like this, you really could fight multiple opponents because you can do so much damage so quickly. And the grip needs to be so tacky and rough that it's uncomfortable, because blood is like motor oil; it's super-slippery stuff." The details you have to think about. Mark told me it's good to practice stabbing cardboard boxes, to see how good your grip is.

In the end, I bought a Spyderco Civilian, the same nasty, serrated, hooked folding knife that Mark sometimes carries. It is a terrifying-looking knife, which serves a self-defense purpose all its own. "I've pulled that knife out and cleaned my fingernails while guys were threatening to kick my ass in a parking lot," Mark said. "Amazing how suddenly the fight goes out of them."

The Civilian scared the shit out of my wife, because it is obviously, despite the name, a knife for killing. It held a horrid fascination for me. I was lying on the couch watching football and idly practicing opening the knife one-handed when I slipped, and the knife *bit* me on the thumb. That's the only way I can describe it. The blood flushed and streamed down my wrist. I felt an electric tingle, and the hair on my neck stood up. And my cut was a little accident, hardly more than a scratch—it was hard to imagine what a real slash might feel like, the horror of it.

The Civilian tucks into the back of my pants and looks like absolutely nothing. It's almost invisible. I started carrying it, and instantly my perception changed. I didn't realize it at the time, but I was carrying it illegally. It's legal to carry one in most of California, but not in Los Angeles County.

Being armed, even with a legal knife, makes you pay a little more attention. You take a little more responsibility for your actions and your surroundings. This is a common feeling about "concealed carry," the general term for carrying a concealed pistol. "I feel like James Bond" is a common sentiment, but there's more to it than that. I thought about what Tiger McKee had said about preparing every morning to use the weapon. If you think you may encounter a situation in which you have to use extreme force, you have to make the decision beforehand. In the moment, you won't have time. If you dither making moral decisions when somebody is trying to kill you, you'll get killed.

Carrying the knife changed the way I saw the world, too. I'm not saying I no longer feared any man, but I certainly saw things differently. I was at a local supermarket and I ran into an absolutely giant guy, a famous pro wrestler, exploding with steroids, maybe six foot five and probably 320 pounds of muscle and tattoos. I was watching him, so he eyeballed me a little, but all I saw was flesh and targets. I wasn't even a *little* worried about him. I knew I would just carve him to pieces. The knife would take and keep taking. Once the fight started it would go fast.

As I got back into my car outside, I paused. Had I gone too far? Was I really that blasé about carving another human being up? Did I really need to be studying how to kill with a knife? Was I becoming one of those paranoid dudes who find each other on the Internet and no one can take seriously? Next up: conspiracy theories.

Sure, of course, it's all for self-defense—that's what we tell ourselves. But is some part of it also about being better than the other guy? The same drive that had led that pro wrestler to steroids and into a cartoonish, Incredible Hulk body had propelled me deep into the study of killing with a knife.

A very real danger when it comes to weapons is losing your temper, giving in to anger, escalating a situation. The laws in the United States are predicated on "sufficient use of force to deter the threat." There is no difference between the knife and the gun, legally. Using a knife would be deadly force, and I would need to be able to prove in court that my life was in danger. A parking lot argument, a road rage incident, something silly like that, could escalate into a situation where suddenly I'd ended a life, and put myself in jail for twenty years.

Mark liked the Jeff Cooper quote, *"Knowledge of personal weapons and skill in their use are necessary attributes of any man who calls himself free."* Mark would elaborate on that to say, *"Skill in their use* engages every aspect: can you control your temper and make the right decisions under stress?"

It went back to the very foundation of martial arts, which is self-control. "Being tough and capable is good, but if you can't control it, you'll put yourself in prison," Mark said.

I eventually put the Civilian away and went back to wearing a Leatherman Wave multitool, which is not only legal but far more useful. I use the pliers all the time. And in a pinch, there's a sharp knife on there.

The Shocknife is a training tool designed by a Canadian company for police and military use, and it's pretty cool. I had gotten hold of two of them. They look like large, clunky plastic knives. They don't cut, but when you press a button, a shock races around the blade. They also buzz and crackle and flash blue, and the noise is almost as alarming as the shock. They make the air crackle with the promise of pain.

To spar with them, I faced off with Ari Calvo, one of Mark's longtime students. We put on fencing helmets to protect our faces and eyes. As I stood across from Ari, I suddenly felt that *this was stupid.* In terms of tactics and strategy, being equal like this is just dumb; it's a no-win situation. We had discussed this aspect of combat training, and I'd read about it, but now I felt it.

The implausibility of the confrontation was half the lesson, right there. We tentatively edged closer to each other, darting and jumping. As we engaged, there was a lot of cutting at hands and wrists. Very often, a lunge ended with both of us dead, knives buzzing into each other's masks, chests, armpits. If I lunged and hit Ari's face mask, I would often catch a stab a half-second later in my own body.

The pain was real but no worse than a sharp bee sting, even with the knives set to their highest level. The idea of pain was much worse. Adrenaline is a hell of a drug. Facing that crackling, snapping blade, my skin crawled to stay away. I twisted and leapt and contorted to keep that blade away from my flesh. Mark was laughing that he had never seen us bounce around quite so much. Ari tired first, and he started just taking the stab into the chest to stab me back. Mark stopped us—sparring was over.

"You see the danger of this? The dangers in the drill?" Mark broke in. "This is why you can only train with these knives a little bit, as exciting as it is. Because the minute you start to accept that it is just *training,* that the blade isn't really dangerous, the drill becomes the disease. This is true for almost any drill: you have to use it very sparingly, or it can become dangerous to you."

I understood that this was the deadly disease that Mark was fighting in teaching weapons, a paradox: you can't train full out. Any training drill you do that is safe for your partner is the opposite of the real situation. I never want to lose the terror of weapons, the skin-crawling aversion.

"Like Richard Pryor said," Mark muttered, "If a guy pulls a knife, you run . . . and if you can't run, fly!"

Mark was by far the deepest student of weapons that I had ever met, and he could very quickly take a conversation about nearly any facet of combat into deep technical places. I have, quite literally, hundreds of pages of notes from my study with Mark, and that was just scratching the surface.

There is one technical concept I will address, because it is so essential to any understanding of melee weapon combat. Mark calls it "line," and it sort of makes sense and sort of doesn't. I'm only now starting to understand what it means.

Mark would often wax poetic about how the old Filipino masters understood eskrima so well that they could be nearly unbeatable. One of his great teachers will remain anonymous, because, as Mark said, "Many of the old time *eskrimadors* prefer anonymity." (Perhaps this is a holdover from the centuries of Spanish subjugation of the Philippines.) "He was untouchable. He was four-eleven and in his mid-eighties, and he could destroy me every time. These old masters have been studying the art and training for sixty years or more. You would see guys come in, young strong guys with a ton of skill, who would have their sticks sizzling like buzzsaws, and it made the real *eskrimadors* laugh. They call it *amarra,* which just means exercise, twirls and whirls, and it looks good; but these old guys could come straight inside, *take the line,* and kill them.

"Line could be described like this: when we're playing pool, I want to sink a ball without giving you a shot, and if I can't sink a ball, I make it so neither can you. I also set it up so that when you try and sink a ball, you are forced to give me a shot."

Line means a direct line between my weapon and you—your head, your legs, whatever my target is. Whoever has line has the offensive initiative. They have the option to throw a shot that will land before the counterattack will land. *Closing the line* implies much more than simply blocking one particular strike: You don't just close line, you also *take line.* You arrange the circumstances in your favor. In boxing, when a right-handed fighter fights a southpaw, both guys try to keep their lead foot outside of the other guy's, because if you have the outside foot, then your jab has line; it has the advantageous position and comes over the top of his. If you can constrain him to a few options, then you have easy attacks, counters, and snares. You have a short, direct line and he has a long way to go—you run a sprint and make him run a marathon. If we're fencing, and my blade is inside of yours, I block your blade to the outside of my body as I run you through. I have line.

"You know it when you feel it," Mark said. "We're primates; we've been swinging clubs since before we had language. It's *a priori*. You can tell when he can hit you and you can't hit him."

Hitting a fastball in major league baseball is considered one of the rarest abilities in sports. Many great hitters can read the pitcher's body language and "feel" where the pitch is going. Of course, that makes sense: the ninety-mile-an-hour fastball covers the distance between mound and plate in milliseconds, so fast that the human eye essentially can't pick it up, because the nerves don't have time to communicate. But people hit major league fastballs all the time. How? The batter has a wealth of experience and is picking up a thousand little cues from the pitcher, so he can swing at where the ball is going to be. He sees into the future, essentially. And he does it without thinking, because thinking would be far too slow.

The more experience I had in the blazing speed of drills with Mark, the more I could see into the future. I could feel where strikes were coming and what the next steps were going to be by a thousand cues. If I tried to think about anything the pattern would fail, and I would be dead.

The study of weapons and hand-to-hand combat is a wonderful, powerful thing. Most, myself included, find it freeing, heartening. And the results are sometimes counterintuitive. For instance, a lot of police departments haven't wanted their officers to train in martial arts, because they think it would make them more likely to beat people up. But the result is the opposite—the more comfortable you are in a physical altercation, the less likely you are to go to deadly force right away.

Learning martial arts relaxes you. If I have a stick, and a guy pulls a knife on me, I won't freak out and go right away for my gun and shoot him—instead I'll bust his hands up if he comes near me. If someone jumps on me, I won't panic and freak out, because I've been doing jiu-jitsu and wrestling. If you perceive a fight as something more or less normal, then you can operate calmly.

Getting good exercise while learning valuable, perhaps lifesaving skills kills two birds with one stone. The seriousness of knife training is a good counter to the relaxed nature of everyday life. It's so easy to go through days and months without getting really stressed. However, your body is like a car. If you don't ever take your car out on the freeway and open it up a little, you're not doing the engine any favors. It's too easy to drift through modern life half asleep, and training to fight keeps an edge on you that just feels right. It helps keep things in perspective. Sure, maybe you missed that promotion or got a speeding ticket, but hey, you didn't get your spine scribed from the front, so things can't be that bad.

The destroyed city looms around us. The five cannibals have boxed us in. They are twenty feet away and closing fast. We will fight or die right here. I retreat quickly, moving back into a corner by a Dumpster. I know they won't fight well together—they'll fight as individuals, so maybe I can make that work.

I smoothly slip off the backpack with my son in it, and I feel my wife catch it as it slides off my shoulders. And then, quick as thought, out come the machete and the savage six-inch kitchen knife, razor sharp. I've got nothing to do at night but sharpen my knives.

Two of them are closing in. I leap to one side, and for a split second, I'm only fighting one of them. He's swinging a tire iron at me with a big powerful swing, but I've had time to prepare while he commits; thinking is over. I drop-step underneath his swing, and my machete, almost of its own accord, takes the angle and whicks cleanly through his wrist. The tire iron and hand sail past me, spraying blood. He howls and clutches his wrist, staring, the world forgotten. I blast him with a push kick, a memory from my muay thai days. He stumbles into his friend, and now I'm out and moving, walking quickly, keeping them from flanking me.

I attack the closest, bringing the fight to him, making him react. I cut high with the machete and he blocks with his club, but my move is just for show. As I take another step toward him he sees too late that the real danger is underneath. The kitchen knife licks out, caressing his chin. As he goes down and I step out, the machete spins around the blocking club and bites deep into his neck.

That's enough for the rest of them. They scatter, and the one without a hand stumbles after them, keening. They were looking for something to eat, not a war. They melt away, as quickly as they'd come. I stand for a moment, panting, waiting, ready to fight and die. Gradually, the silence penetrates my mind. They're gone. Time to move.

13.

THE PURSUIT OF PROTEIN

We've gone deep into the mountains. The high ground called me, the hills beckoned with safety, and we've pushed on, higher and higher, climbing into the wilderness of what used to be southern Colorado. There's plenty of water, but the nights have grown cold. After a few days, I no longer worry about pursuit. We pass empty farmhouses, ranches without cattle. Some of the houses are burned. We move from pavement to a smooth dirt road.

Then, one morning, a couple of days' walk from the last paved road, we find it: a small white trailer and a rough campsite, tucked away near a stream. I watch it for an hour from the cover of trees. Nothing. It feels abandoned.

"Let's check it out," I say. My wife comes with me, and the boy. At this point, our unspoken commitment is that if they get one of us, they get all of us.

I creep across the road, machete in hand, and gently pull on the door. With all my might I resist the urge to call, "Hello?" The door is intact and pulls out with a hiss.

As I climb inside the gloom, I can tell it's safe. It's so still. There are bodies, locked together in the corner, and from a brief look I can guess what happened. A family of four came up here to get away from the zombies, and one of them brought the infection with them. Now even the zombie remains are decaying and dried, and the rats have been at them.

The trailer is a treasure trove. There's camping equipment, winter clothes, sleeping bags . . . our rags and blankets are tossed aside in something that feels like delight, like gratitude. Even better, I pry open a locked box to find a long, gleaming hunting rifle with a scope. There's only a single box of bullets, but each shiny round holds the promise of life.

I step outside, as my wife and son continue to ransack the trailer, and consider the sky. It's gunmetal gray. We're deep into fall, the air is freezing cold at night, and I can smell the damp scent of distant snow. Normally I would make us move off the road, but we won't last through the winter without shelter. Snow will close these dirt roads soon, which will shut down everything but survival. Maybe we can hole up; maybe that's the smart gamble now. But we'll need food.

What can I hunt up here?

Southern Co

—The sun slanted heavily into the canyon, cutting bars through the trees, on an unseasonably warm October day as I followed Don Yeager up the trail into the wilderness, into thin air. Sweat sprang out all over my body. One hour ago I had stepped out of the car after a two-day drive from sea-level Los Angeles, and now, after three uphill steps, I was blowing heavily, my pulse thudding in my ears. We were climbing from nine thousand feet, and I felt the oxygen debt rise like a red tide. All the old clichés about hiking at altitude came back to me, *it's like breathing through a straw.*

We pushed into the timber, tall dark spruce and regal aspen gone bare for winter. Don could hear me gasping, so he set a forgiving pace. At the top of each steep push, each little hump, he stopped, looked around, and found some detail to point out or murmured a brief story, politely ignoring my shuddering breath. Every corner had a tale: the place his dogs had flushed out a mountain lion, a place where his son Kip had hunted.

Finally, we reached the top: a wide meadow of grass and sage, bright sun, wind, and the whelming awe of open spaces. We walked quickly across the open field, keeping our profile low, into a parklike "tree island" in the middle of the meadow that was fed from an underground spring. A heavy down log makes a perfect seat, and Don and I settled in.

Before us stretched a vast panorama of southern Colorado: canyon, meadows, steep hilly mountains, snow-capped peaks close at hand. Somewhere over there were the Continental Divide and the headwaters of the Rio Grande. Don is a lifelong hunter and a former soldier. He had served as an instructor in the marines' Combat Hunter program, and he knew how to pick an observation spot. We had breathtaking command of the entire landscape.

Don raised his binoculars, compact, powerful 10x42 Swarovski's attached to a harness around his chest, and began to "glass" the far side of the valley. His motions were smooth, born of a hundred thousand repetitions. I followed suit with my borrowed binoculars, and the far meadows and benches leapt into sharp, shimmering relief. I explored the edge of a far-off meadow for a long moment, then lowered my binos and stared at the epic grandeur.

My legs ached and I was coated with rapidly cooling sweat, even from that short hike. In a flash I understood something wonderful about glassing: I was hiking without hiking; here, from this vantage point with good binos, I could explore a good portion of this whole valley without moving. Part of the drive of hiking is curiosity: What's around the corner? What's over that hill? Now I could peek into hollows, study downed trees, and look over rugged cliffs without moving my burning legs. It wasn't far from flying.

Don lowered his binos. "Not yet," he murmured. In the silence, my breathing started to regain equilibrium.

"I spend a lot of time up here," Don said. I had seen the calendar on the wall of his gunroom, marked with a check for every time he hiked up into the mountains; Don was sixty-five, but most days had two check marks. This is a big part of what Don does, and an essential part of who he is.

Don Yeager is the son of Chuck Yeager, the iconic pilot immortalized in *The Right Stuff*, a World War II ace and the first man to break the sound barrier. Don's round forehead is similar to his famous father's. He has crisp white hair and a weatherbeaten face, most often wreathed in a big grin. Even at sixty-five, his vision was much better than mine, as we quickly discovered. He and my wife, both progeny of fighter pilots, have 20/15 eyesight or better, while my vision, never wonderful to begin with, began a slow dive off a cliff about five years ago. Don is slender, with a neat military bearing and mustache that are slightly at odds with his West Coast friendliness.

The light began to slant more steeply, and a warm glow bathed the valley. At the "magic hour" that cinematographers love, the mountains were suffused in the rich amber of sunset, and solitary clouds streaked incandescent pink against the sky.

It was two days before rifle hunting season opened, and we were waiting for elk.

The elk loved the magic hour, too. That was when they would emerge from the trees to feed in the open. Dawn and dusk: that's when you hunt elk up here in the mountains. The Combat Hunter manual that Don had cocreated, to teach hunting skills to marines, referred to this time as the *mesotopic*, when the low light "can result in inaccuracies in visual perception, making marines most susceptible to attack during this time." The elk took full advantage.

"Well, they should be out here, they were out yesterday—but there are no guarantees with elk, I'll tell you that much," Don murmured. His voice was a comforting combination of country and California from the sixties of his youth. Sometimes a "dude" would sneak in.

"Elk, above all other animals, you hunt on their terms. You develop an enormous respect. Those fat-asses who hunt from four-wheelers don't have any respect or understanding, and they don't deserve it.

"When I got back from Vietnam," Don said, "I didn't hunt for a long time. I was tired of the killing, the death. I hunted birds, a few deer . . . but I didn't want to kill anything with a rifle. So I picked up a bow maybe thirty-five years ago. I didn't know anybody to hunt with, so I taught myself. It took me five years to kill my first elk."

I knew Don was feeling confident; he had told me over the phone, months earlier, that I would be bringing home hundreds of pounds of elk. "So I should buy a freezer? Is that a jinx, bad luck?" I had asked.

"Hell, yes, buy a freezer," Don had laughed over the phone line. Now, he was urging caution.

"Elk are weird. You'll find out. Just because you see them some place one day doesn't mean they'll be there the next day. They really travel; they move all over the place within their range.

"It makes hunting frustrating. You'll think you know where they're going to come out, and then they won't. Or they'll be too far away, and you can't get near them. You gotta walk a lot, without getting in a hurry—because if they see you, you're screwed."

The sharp senses of the elk were one of Don's favorite topics. He had stories of getting caught by the elk and having to freeze like a statue for ten or fifteen minutes, frozen in a walking pose, because if you do anything to spook them, they're gone.

"They're incredibly wary, and they have a real deck of cards for detecting you. Not just the senses, but the herd means there are a lot of eyes. And their eyes bulge out from their skull, you'll see . . . their motion detecting at their periphery blows me away. I've been a half-mile away, crossing a field, and the sun was on me, and then *bam*. One of them looks up, staring at you, and now you're playing the statue game. And the kinesics of the herd means that if she continues to look, pretty soon they're all staring, and now you're blown.

"The old saying is *'Elk hear you three times, see you twice, and smell you once.'* What that means is, if the elk see you or hear you, they'll run, but they might not go too far. But if they smell you, they're gone, for miles. Nothing will drive elk out like smell. You really have to understand and hunt the wind." Hunting the wind means keeping the elk upwind of you, so your alarming smell is carried away from them. It's easier said than done.

We glassed, breathing deep in the gorgeous clean air.

Suddenly, I heard a high, long, whirling sound, ending in a scream. It was inhuman and hollow, pure and lyric, like a humpback whale's song crossed with a red-tailed hawk's screech. Treble is what carries in the mountains. The sound echoed with some of that sense of space that a loon's laugh carries; it could be miles or it could be a thousand feet. I knew what it was without being told—the bugling of a bull elk. The hair on the back of my neck tingled.

We were in the tail end of the rut, the elk mating season. The rut runs on the elk's hormonal calendar, which in turn is driven by necessity. Winter is a starving time, when the elk have to outlast the cold on stores built in the summer and fall. The cows need to be impregnated at the right time, to carry all winter and give birth in the early spring, so that the newborn calves can grow enough to survive the following winter. During the rut, the bulls clash, compete for females, dash their famous antlers together, and bugle. The rut had been going on for a month, and had peaked maybe two weeks ago.

"The sound in the morning is really clear, when the air is moist. Humidity transmits sound better, like foggy mornings on a lake. The vibrations travel better."

We paused, glassing in the hush.

"There they are," Don said, and I aped his posture, following his angle.

Like magic, like ghosts, they had appeared in a distant meadow with heads down, grazing. They had dark legs and underbelly with a tan body. A flush of joy went through me: *eureka!* I had been reading and thinking about elk so much that to actually see them was a surprise, but also oddly familiar. My imaginary picture shook, then jelled with the real.

More elk kept appearing, until Don estimated that there were maybe a hundred animals moving through the high benches of sage and grass. What had been an empty meadow was now dotted with elk, plain as day, bold as brass. Their movement was deceptive: they seemed stationary, heads down, grazing, but they covered a lot of ground and were vanishing when I checked back.

"Sometimes you got to haul ass when you hunt elk," Don said in the deepening gloom. "I usually hang back and wait for the wind to quit, but when the time is right, you have to go get them before they get out. Once they get into the timber, you'll never get close enough. You run a lot when you're hunting elk; there's a ticking clock."

As he said this, the elk were vanishing, fading into the trees.

As true twilight descended, the elk were gone. Like a magic trick, like the tide. Somewhere in that magic hour of falling light, maybe forty-five minutes, maybe more, was my window for shooting an elk, and then it would slam shut.

Is hunting what makes us human? David Petersen, Don's favorite thinker on hunting, writes in his book *Heartsblood* that "to hunt is to *be* human." He means that humans have spent many millions of years of their history hunting, and only about ten thousand years farming, so hunting was and is our natural occupation. He quotes famous anthropologists and riffs on archeological dates to prove his point.

Petersen uses this as the basis for a ringing endorsement of bow hunting, a pursuit that he loves and finds incredibly spiritual and *natural*. But even a layman like myself had to wonder: when were the bow and arrow invented? Primitive hominids that predate *Homo sapiens* probably would have found a bow and arrow a technological marvel not far removed from the space shuttle. The persistence hunt is a far more *natural* way to hunt, and I have to wonder how Petersen would feel about trying to run down an elk.

From talking to Daniel Lieberman, the anthropology professor at Harvard and exponent of the barefoot running/persistence hunt hypotheses, and from reading his book on the evolution of the human head, I started to glean a picture. The stone spear, the bow and arrow, even the persistence hunt are all merely *symptoms* of the real change. The real change was internal: the birth of strategy. The persistence hunt was strategic. In colder climates, where it was harder to get animals to overheat, other strategies evolved, such as chasing animals into mud or off cliffs, as the Plains Indians did.

All these hunting methodologies are symptoms of a larger brain, which goes hand in hand with the consumption of the easy protein and rich fats that meat provide. A big brain is a serious energy drain. About 25 percent of your metabolism when sleeping goes toward maintaining it. But its advantages are obvious, enabling the ability for what is sometimes called *speculative hunting,* which means to track an animal and imagine what it has been doing, where it's going, and *how it feels.* The South African game tracker and author Louis Liebenberg has referred to this very ability as "the origin of science."

As Professor Lieberman was quick to point out, successful foraging (as opposed to hunting) also depends on problem solving and memory, so a bigger brain would also lead to better foraging. The human brain has evolved to catalog and study and problem-solve, not just to learn tracks, scents, and minute details of animal behavior.

Lieberman urged caution. "It's a neat idea that hypothetical deductive thought processes that hunters use are the ones we use when we try to solve a problem. But hunting is not the only problem that humans solved—it is an important one, but I suspect that it's a bit more complicated than that. Foraging, social relations, predictions, and manipulations probably all play a role."

Our "natural" state is to be a deep student of our environment. That's the essential precondition of survival. Primitive man would have lived in tension, a profound student of his surroundings, or he wouldn't have lived at all.

If you had a yard as a child, you probably remember it with a startling intimacy. You *knew* that yard: every inch, every bush, each step on the tree you could climb, the whorls and knots in the branches, the bare dirt spots, the sandy gravel, the soft grass. It was deep, profound, intimate local knowledge. You intuitively *knew* what was happening around you at all times. Primitive man would have felt that way about a much larger stretch of ground, but it was still "his" territory. This very ability is really what allowed *Homo sapiens* to expand and succeed the way we did.

These various factors, working together, are what make us human. Art and science (as well as less noble pursuits, like entertainment and sports) were born in the pursuit of protein and survival.

Don has a wondrous spread, nestled right in against a federal wilderness area. From the couch in his living room, we could glass elk with his spotting scope. The house was immaculate, with warm wood and high ceilings and giant racks of antlers. He practiced an old-fashioned hospitality—my house is yours. He'd agreed to serve as my mentor for about a week—not for money, but for friendship and for a love of the hunt.

Don's son and daughter live on the property in houses of their own, both with kids. Francie, his wife, has a greenhouse and gardens, and egg-laying chickens run wild, although she complained that a mountain lion had been preying on them—she lost a couple this year. If anybody was in a good spot to ride out the apocalypse, it was the Yeager clan.

Kip Yeager, Don's son, is a rangy, stoop-shouldered former marine grunt, a veteran of the house-to-house combat in Fallujah. Don, with a father's pride and subdued awe, regaled me with stories of Kip—he'd gotten his first two elk when he was twelve, and had been guiding professionally at fifteen. I stayed in Kip's boyhood room, which was decorated with the skins of a mountain lion, a black bear, and other animals Kip had shot or trapped as a youth.

Both of these men are hunters and outdoorsman first, warriors second, in the vein of frontiersmen. They aren't big, buff, muscle-bound soldiers. They are the older model, thin and wiry and strong as hell, guys who chase elk for weeks above ten thousand feet. Kip had just finished a successful bow hunt. He'd stalked a particular bull elk for two weeks before getting the shot he wanted.

For all their martial prowess, the plain emotion emanating from both Kip and Don is warmth, friendliness, camaraderie. Don hugged me when he met me; we'd had enough phone conversations that we were already friends. And Kip wears a permanent massive grin, which only faded when he talked about some other outfitter's unethical behavior.

This wasn't confusing to me. I had seen it before with professional fighters. The better the fighter, the more mellow the man (and, in Thailand, the better the Buddhist). The ego gets burned away. These are both men who have well and truly gone to war, and yet they are almost incredibly warm.

Don talked freely about "his" Vietnam. Although he'd been drafted into the infantry, Don always took point and asserted control of his destiny as much as he could. He felt that the war was worse for the guys who felt powerless, like the men who had been shelled heavily by artillery.

When Kip was returning home from his third tour in Iraq, his third "pump," Don calculated the angles and times and realized Kip would be flying overhead, so he went out and glassed the plane. Kip called when he landed and said, "*I flew over our land!*" Don said, "*I was out there.*" He'd been out there, watching for his son to come home from the war.

At midday, when the elk would be hiding in the trees, Don and I went out to shoot. Don was graciously allowing me to use his rifle, treating me like one of his own children, albeit a rather old and awkward one. Kip had shot his first elk at twelve, as had Dru, Don's daughter. I was the "slow" son who gets to go hunting at thirty-six.

The rifle was a bolt-action Remington Model 700 hunting rifle with a stainless steel barrel and a synthetic stock. The bullets were 7-millimeter Magnum; the scope was a basic Leupold. Don had had the rifle for twenty years, and had spent less than eight hundred bucks on everything. He told me that a lot of hunters spend ten times as much.

We went out in the harsh sunlight to the side of Don's property where he had a target set up and, a hundred yards from the target, a shooting bench. The bench was a massive steel desk (which Don had cut from the roll cage on a bulldozer) with a rubber pad covering the top.

I needed to shoot a little bit to acquaint myself with the weapon, and also we needed to zero the gun's scope. Zeroing the scope simply means calibrating the aim. Don and I had different bodies, and the way we held and looked down the scope created different angles, so he would have to see where I was shooting and adjust the scope accordingly.

The idea was to be as absolutely accurate as possible here, under controlled circumstances. Then, in the field, as error began to creep in, hopefully we would have enough accuracy built in to still make good hits. I sat in the chair, over the bench and the rifle, and carefully wound myself in behind the gun.

"Now find the target. You need to figure out how to best find the target through the scope. It's hard, and takes practice. A lot of hunters, they'll see an elk, throw the gun up, and now they can't find the elk. So practice finding it. I pick up my head and look over the top." In hindsight, I should have practiced this more.

I practiced dry firing first, working the bolt without bullets in the gun. I could still hear Tiger's voice in my ear: *ppprrreeessss*. The gun going off should surprise you. Don said to picture the trigger as a thin glass rod that you will break if you're not careful.

"Your sight picture shouldn't even move when you dry fire. Match the crosshairs to the target. When you shoot your group of three shots, every shot is the same."

Now I could feel it and remember. Shooting a gun is really about the trigger, not about aiming. Anyone who can see can aim. It's like steering a car; little kids can steer fine. The real trick is in pulling the trigger without disturbing the rifle, just as when you're driving a stick shift the real trick is managing the pedals.

Kip wandered by and told me, "In sniper school, they teach you that your body is the most stable at the bottom of your breath cycle. So prepare yourself, let out the breath, and when you finish, touch it off."

Don continued, "You want to train your brain, when you're shooting at an animal, a lot of guys will look at the whole thing and just plunk the crosshairs in the middle. What you want to do is pick a spot, a tiny spot on the animal, and hit that exact spot. Aim small, miss small. Elk are very tough animals; they'll get hit and haul ass."

I slid three of the long, lovely gold-and-silver bullets into the rifle. I worked the bolt, pulled the stock to my shoulder, and watched the crosshairs float around over the target. I took my time, buried the crosshairs dead center, and exhaled. I tried to "touch it off," as Kip had said. Through my ear protectors I heard the crack of the shot and its booming echo, and the rifle bucked in my hands.

After I shot three, we all walked up to take a look. I felt some trepidation, but it turned out I was shooting decently: an average grouping, maybe two inches left of center and a little high. As long as the hits are close together, that's good, because it means the bullets all going the same place. You can adjust the scope and the sights to get you centered up.

Don explained why the group was high.

"The rifle is zeroed for three hundred yards, which means it's supposed to be dead on at that distance. So at a hundred yards it will be high, and even higher at two hundred yards, because the bullet is still climbing; and then at three hundred it drops back down. I'm going to try and keep you from shooting over three hundred yards, because if you do, then you have to start aiming higher—hold on the top line of the elk's back. At four hundred yards you've dropped maybe six inches, but at five hundred yards, you'll drop twenty inches. It's like throwing a ball, the bullet drops in a ballistic curve."

Don was talking about the basic problem with shooting over long distances—the eye and the scope see in straight lines, like a laser, but the bullet travels like a thrown baseball, in an arc.

I fired maybe twenty or so shots before Don called it a day—he didn't want me to bruise up my shoulder or develop a flinch. Compared to how much I had been shooting in Alabama, we hadn't even gotten started. But later that night, my shoulder was bruised up.

As opening day of the season approached, Don and I continued to hike up the mountains and glass for elk, right before dawn and right at sunset. Although the midday was unseasonably warm (seventy degrees at times), the nights were in the twenties, and the mornings held onto the icy edge of winter. I still couldn't quite believe that I was going to do this, hike up there and kill an elk. Don and I talked incessantly as we hiked about hunting, about elk, and about survival.

As we talked, I tried to employ a technique that the SOLO school's Bill Kane had explained for acclimatizing yourself to high altitude: breathing out through pursed lips to create a little back pressure. I tried it without much success. Acclimatization takes time, and sleeping at altitude acclimatizes you as well as anything. After three days you start to produce more red blood cells in response to the increased demand. When you hike all the way up Everest, your body adjusts gradually, because the ascent takes weeks or even months. But if you landed on top of Everest in a helicopter, you'd be unconscious in three minutes and dead in ten.

Don told me about how the marines' Combat Hunter program had started. He'd been part of a group that was trying to help marines function better in Iraq, using hunting skills.

"We went down in this big group. There were officers from other countries, inner-city marines who'd been in gangs. They divided us into groups and gave us a scenario: You guys are inserting into the heavy jungle in Panama. Walk to these coordinates at night, set up observation on a hillside near where the bad guys are stashing drugs— just a scenario. Triple-layer canopy jungle, no GPS. I said, 'Okay, we can do that.'

"But then all the groups met up and discussed it. Every other group says they have to wait until daylight, it's too dark . . . one of the British guys says, 'It's darker than a dog's gut.' " Don laughed at the turn of phrase.

"Well, this is what I did in Vietnam. I traveled at night with a map and compass and a hundred guys behind me. If I went off a hill and rolled to the bottom, a hundred guys rolled down behind me.

"I told them my group did it, and they gave me a hard time—'How did you do it? That's impossible'—until finally I said, 'I wish you guys had been with my CO in Vietnam and told him that this was impossible to do, because you would have saved me a lot of bruises and cuts . . . we did it all the time, walk all night and hide all day.'"

Don shook his head and grinned at how the world works.

He moved on to our more pressing concerns: where to shoot an elk.

"I used to take precision shots to the brain. But you can fuck up and blow their jaw off, and now what do I do? In addition, I found that killing them like that, they don't bleed. Sometimes, it makes the meat really tough—some spasm, some chemical release. So I try for a lung shot, a double lung shot if I can—it allows them to run and bleeds them out."

Don was a lifelong hunter for food; he wasn't hunting for a trophy set of antlers (although he'd done that, as well). One of his paramount concerns was preserving the flesh, the good steaks and the best cuts. With the razor-tipped broad-head arrows, that isn't a concern, but high-powered rifle bullets can destroy meat.

"You are probably throwing everything away that the bullet hits. The hydrostatic shock blows the layers of muscles apart and it fills with blood, like jelly. It's all totally blood-shot and just a mess. You end up pitching it. I don't take three-quarter shots because you end up chucking a shoulder."

Don wanted me to understand where the organs were inside the animal and envision them in three dimensions as the animal moved. The perfect placement of a shot is right behind the shoulder, at the top of the crease at the back of the foreleg.

"Be patient, don't take a bad shot, let her turn," Don counseled. "The bad thing is if you hit the stomach, the first big chamber is where all the food is, and after a night of feeding it's huge. It's full of densely packed grass and will stop a bullet. Generally, they'll run, lay down for a minute and you think, *Oh, it's dead,* and then it gets up!

"My policy on elk is, if it stops and it's still standing, shoot the thing again. Don't quit shooting until it goes down. If it's running, let it run. Stay on that animal. If you lose it in the scope, then pick up your head and go over the top. Don't shoot another animal, that's how people get in trouble. I've seen elk with their hearts and lungs blown out, pumping blood out their sides, run two hundred yards. It's amazing."

If I only wounded an elk, Don's main concern was tracking it. For Don, the ethics of hunting required tracking; but also you are legally required to make a reasonable effort to track the animal. Of course, what that effort means varies from hunter to hunter. Don was full of stories of tracking wounded animals all night, for hunters he was guiding. Tracking until flashlights and headlamps ran out of batteries. Wearing out clients until they were crying, "You take the rifle," begging to be let off the hook, having tracked miles and thousands of vertical feet.

"Some guys will track for three days, some guys won't track fifteen minutes," Don said.

—

I woke in the dead silence of the deep woods, eyes open in the ink black. I could hear Don moving around upstairs, and I knew what that meant. Rise and shine, up and at 'em.

My body flooded with tension, stiff on the bed. *We're going hunting, and I'm going to make the shot.* I hit the switch, and yellow light flooded the darkness.

The glass eyes in Kip's perfectly preserved mountain lion skin stared blindly into space. Kip had gotten that mountain lion at the same age I had been playing Little League baseball.

Don quietly handed a cup of coffee through the door while I dressed. Then he vanished into his preparations. I mentally ran my checklists, gaming various scenarios: I get lost, Don gets hurt, a fast storm. The WEMT daypack guidelines urged supplies for three days. Don, the master, packed light, just a small camouflage hunting fanny pack, so I tried to lighten up too. Just water, a snack, camera, binos, knife. I threw in a rain shell, just in case. We wolfed down a quick breakfast of home-laid eggs and toast.

Wearing headlamps over synthetic Windstopper hats, we darted through the door, out into the cold, clear night. It was six in the morning, with sunrise projected for seven thirty. We needed to be in position before the light came up. Don knew from long experience that the way to hunt this area was to strike surgically. The longer you were up there, the more your scent spread out and contaminated the area.

It was cold and dark in Colorado at nine thousand feet, an hour before dawn. October's chill was strong in the air. The bright, sparkling moon and stars seemed close, maybe a mile or two off. In full camouflage I followed Don up the trail, clumping in my new boots over the dirt and gravel. He set off at a decent pace, across his property and up into the wilderness.

"It'll happen fast": Don's words rang in my ears. I felt pretty good, all things considered. I used to dread pressure situations; as a little boy, I hated baseball and football for the gnawing fear they inspired. I guess all that self-inflicted stress inoculation over the years had worked, because I was enjoying myself. Also, I was completely reliant on Don, comfortable in the hands of a master.

We stayed on the old trail until it petered out in a dry streambed of boulders and grass. We paused and heard the ghostly bugling right overhead. We were down in a dell, a deep pocket of timber, and above us were the benches. *They're up there.*

Don murmured, "I think we can turn off our lights now," and we hiked in the lightening gloom through the dell. The bugling continued, some of it right up the mountain from us, some of it across the fields to our left. A thrill every time.

Don stopped to mutter, "We'll come up this way, and be ready, because things can happen quickly. Just cross your fingers that nobody opens fire, because they're gone if that happens." He was worried some other outfitters could have come in earlier, or even last night, to ruin our hunt. Apparently, in other parts of Colorado, there are hunters all over each other, blaze-orange behind every tree, gunshots, elk running to and fro, heated arguments about who shot what.

We started up a steeper slope littered with rocks and low grass, and instantly I was panting. Stalking when winded makes for a kind of claustrophobia. You have to take small silent breaths, but what you desperately want is huge noisy gulps of air.

The elk sounded close, right over the next ridge. "Get your heart rate under control," Don murmured. "This is going to be pretty fast." We kept climbing, picking our way around boulders and sagebrush. A few hundred yards ahead, I could see the bench level out. The elk were somewhere over that rise.

We were near the top when the rifle (slung over my back and jutting up a few inches over my head) snagged a dead branch on a fir and snapped it loudly. Don looked back quickly, as if to say, *Okay, who brought the new guy?* He whispered, "You can carry that down now, be ready to shoot." He watched me chamber a round and flick the safety on, carefully. Could this really be happening so fast?

We carefully peeked over the rise, in good cover of trees, and saw them. Flashes of grayish white, too far away, and already moving back toward the trees.

"C'mon, let's move," he whispered, and then he was gone, darting across the open ground crouched low, a small rise shielding him from the elk. I jogged clumsily in his wake, trying to stay low, rifle in hand, backpack jouncing.

"C'mon, Sam," muttered Don. *Move it, dumbass,* I thought. We scuttled through a small copse of trees, and I crouched behind Don, bringing my binos up.

"Oh yeah, there they are," he whispered. "Get some deep breaths, start slowing yourself down, and let's find a good place to shoot from."

Oh shit, I thought, *I'm not ready to shoot.* In my mind, I had imagined elk hunting as a slow, comfortable process—sneaking into some well-hidden spot, setting up a nice prone position with back-packs, carefully picking out the animal at a hundred yards, and mak-ing the shot. Don took off his daypack and gestured for me to take it. "Slide it up there," he said, pointing to a small, rocky rise. "Go out there and make it happen."

I crawled out of the cover onto the rise, tossed the daypack down, and laid the rifle carefully on it.

"Stay down," Don hissed from behind me. I awkwardly settled in.

The elk looked large in the scope, but they were all facing away from me. Their heads were down, feeding in the grass. One or two were facing sideways, but I couldn't tell what they were: spikes (young males) or cows?

We held a whispered conference, Don invisible behind me and glassing the same herd. He floated over me like my conscience. I felt a little desperate—this shot was far, on the edge of my abilities. We talked about a big bull sitting regally on the grass with his large crown of antlers.

"Don't shoot that bull." *No problem there.*

"The cow all the way at the right, that's a great cow for sure," he said. *All the way at the right?* I looked and saw the one he meant, but she turned away from me. I had no shot, just an ass. She was already almost hull down. They were all dropping out of sight behind grass, and. I felt a twinge of despair.

"Over to your right, there are two cows together. You've got a great broadside. Let me affirm that's a cow . . . you see what I'm talking about?"

I stared down the scope, helpless.

"No, no," Don hissed. "Way over to your right, way over." He had come around behind me to check what I was looking at. I pulled off the scope and looked with my naked eye, then reset my whole body, and *now* I saw what he was talking about. I was too scope focused. You have to pull your head out of the scope and look *before* you settle in. I hadn't seen the whole herd. There were three or four elk in broadside—still a long shot for me, but no longer impossible. We discussed, in hushed whispers, which one to target.

I settled in prone and felt decent, not breathing too hard, focused down the scope and across the field. I picked the elk almost at random: *that one,* you're mine. Don used his range finder and reported three hundred yards. Which meant I just had to hold my aim perfectly on the elk's center mass.

I dithered uncertainly. Was now the time? Part of me wanted to quit, to try and sneak around through the woods for a closer shot. This was too risky. This would be my fourth-ever shot at this range.

"We gotta make something happen, we're running out of time," Don said—not nervous, but factual. There's a ticking clock to elk hunting, and he was feeling the seconds stream by.

"I'm gonna cow-call, and she'll turn. Do you have her?" He had a plastic diaphragm in his mouth already, a piece that could be used to call turkeys or, with a little practice, elk.

Down the scope, the crosshairs drifted, moving with my breath. Did I have her?

"Now, this is a make-or-break move, so they're going to turn and look, or they'll go. So check the head for horns, and then forget the head, find your spot, and hold dead on. Three hundred yards."

"Okay," I whispered.

"Is the safety off?" Don asked.

"Yup," I answer, and instantly Don cow-called—a high-pitched squeal, almost like a puppy getting its tail stepped on.

A different elk picked up her head, not the one I had in my scope.

I waited, and time stretched, elastic and mindless. Don called again. Still my cow didn't look up.

Then she did. Press. The sight picture disappeared as the rifle leapt in my arms.

"You got her, buddy!" Don's voice was in my ear. "Nice fucking shot!"

Relief flooded my system, and I laughed and started to stand, without the gun. "Reload," Don said sternly, and I fell back down and clumsily worked the bolt.

"She's down . . . okay, she got up," Don said with a note of tension in his voice. I was blind, just listening to his voice. "She's running, hang on. Fuck, you knocked her down . . . get up and watch, get ready to shoot again, use your binos."

I clumsily stood up. I had no idea where she was or what was happening.

"There, she's stopped. Hit her again."

I found her in the binos, standing stock still, much farther down-field. I looked around wildly, found a tree stump, and tried to get a steady rest on it, fumbling around with the rifle. I couldn't get a good rest, and I fiddled and diddled, trying to get an arrangement of bracing that would allow me to make the shot.

Finally, Don said with some heat, "Sam, put the safety on, come around behind me, and go up on top, slither up there and kill her. Go go go, we don't have all day!" I know he was worried about losing her. If she was wounded only mildly, she might run for a mile, somewhere into the timber, and there was a chance we'd never find her.

I followed orders, slithered up to a perfect spot, and couldn't find her. "Way to your left, Sam. Look with your eyes and not the scope."

There she was, and when I got back on the scope, she was perfect in my site picture, a perfect broadside. I carefully took my shot, and this shot rang loudly in my ear. I realized I hadn't even heard the first one.

"She's down, buddy. Nice shot." I worked the bolt, ready to shoot again, but she was down for good.

"You hit her real good that first time, right in the lungs, and if we'd sat here she probably would have gone down, but never trust it— if the elk is standing, shoot it again."

I stood, a little shaky, and Don hugged me. "You did it, man!" He was laughing.

Don was already glassing the other herds of elk, watching to see what the shot did to them. He was thinking about the other hunters out there, what they might do, based on how the elk were reacting.

Don lowered his binos and looked at me. "Your problem was, you were trying to see everything down the scope. Use your eyes, then the binos, then, after you've figured out what's going on, you get down on the scope."

Don and I walked over to where I first hit her, then tried to track the blood spots to where she fell. It was extraordinarily difficult. Don only found a few spots of blood, and even with him pointing I could barely see them: faint red dots, maybe a centimeter across, sprinkled on a single aspen leaf the size of a silver dollar.

She hadn't bled much. Don speculated on the various things that could have happened between the two shots, and he ended on, "Of course, you might have missed her with the second shot, and she just fell down at that exact moment. That's happened before."

Finally, we approached the elk, a massive, burly, beautiful animal. Her stomach was as huge and round as a fur-covered barrel, and I walked in amazement around and around, reveling in the touch, the feel, pressing her hooves with my fingers, looking into her eyes, her long velvet ears, her wide mouth. I sat by her and rubbed her fur.

Don showed me how sharp her teeth were. She was a healthy young cow, and we looked at her teats. They were not full of milk, so there wasn't some calf out there bawling for its mama, which was a salve to my conscience. I snapped some pictures, close-ups, wide angles.

"CSI Colorado," Don said.

"I suspect foul play," I replied, and Don laughed.

There was only one bullet hole. A tiny red dot. Maybe a trifle high, but really, a perfect double-lung shot. Was that the first or the second shot? How could I have missed with one of those? But suddenly, I *knew* with absolute clarity what had happened. That second shot was long—nearly four hundred yards, longer than any shot I had taken before. At four hundred or five hundred yards, you have to aim high. "At four hundred yards I would aim right for the top of her back," Don had told me earlier, in order for the bullet to drop into the elk's center mass. But I hadn't done that.

Don had given me range for the second shot, but it hadn't sunk in. I made a perfect hundred-yard shot on an animal that was closer to four hundred yards away. The bullet had, probably, passed directly beneath her, a clean miss. And somehow, she'd fallen at the exact same time. Which was great, because I hadn't spoiled any more meat with bullet mash-up. But I did feel a twinge of failure at not computing that shot, and as I relived the moment over and over, I realized with some small satisfaction that at least I would never make that mistake again.

Don and I talked a little bit about stress. As a combat veteran he was very familiar with the Cooper color code. Condition Red, Condition Black. "Sometimes you have to pull yourself in and out in a firefight—I've done it."

In hunting it's referred to as buck fever. Both Don and Kip had stories about guiding hunters into perfect spots to make fairly easy, hundred-yard shots on big bull elk, whereupon the hunters get confused, don't shoot, miss wildly, or wound several animals by accident. "There are guys without experience who go right up into the Red, and that scares them and they can't function," Don said. "Tunnel vision, sweaty palms, fast breathing. If you go up too far, and are bouncing on the Black, you just check out. You can't do anything. Kip sees it all the time, he guides more than me. He sees horrendous misses, stupid misses—easy shots, forty, sixty yards—guys jerk the trigger, they fill the scope with the animal and just start cranking away on the trigger."

This had all happened so fast, I could see how easily buck fever could grab hold of someone who was unprepared, without a calm voice like Don's in their ear. I had never taken a shot at four hundred yards before, and when I had to, I missed it clean. The interesting thing, in hindsight, was how impossible it was to "snap out of it," because I hadn't even realized I was in it.

Don had mentioned that exact thing happening, a miss and the elk falling simultaneously. He had so much experience he *knew* what was happening all the time. It seemed like precognition.

I had expected to feel sad—but instead I felt absolutely nothing. Not a twinge of guilt, not *sorry for killing this beautiful animal,* nothing. A mild, pleasant joy at a job well done, at not disappointing Don or making his life harder; a sense of mild satisfaction and wellbeing. I had felt sad upon seeing other animals killed in the past, but I had no sadness in me now, not a single drop.

Part of the reason, I think, is that in some way I wasn't really the hunter, Don was. Don made all the decisions, he held my hand and led me around, he pushed and prodded me into the right space. I was just part of the rifle, really. True hunting would be me, alone, making the decisions, trusting my own judgment, finding my own way. This was just training. Don was showing me how to hunt, what a hunt could look like. He sometimes talked about testing oneself, hunting the elk up here on their terms, but this had only been a test for Don. Could he go hunting with this weird rifle that had feet and didn't shoot that well? This was Don's kill, Don's responsibility, and Don's triumph. I had just been a handicap, like the weight on a race horse.

This was a necessary step, a part of the apprenticeship, but I wouldn't be a hunter until I did the whole thing on my own. And this wasn't for sport, this was survival training. If it comes down to me and my family or an elk, then morality and ethics won't play much of a role. You won't anthropomorphize Bambi when you're starving.

Don and I turned to the real work, almost an anticlimax. We had to skin her, get the meat off, and pack it down the mountain. The meat needed to cool, without the hide, quickly. It can sour if the hunter takes too long to properly dress out the animal.

Don talked me through the whole process and made me do most of it. In a real survival scenario, you would eat almost everything, including the guts. Indeed, when we came back a few days later, the spot was picked clean; even the hooves were gone. Don told me that meant that a black bear, getting ready to hibernate, had come around. Nothing gets wasted in survival situations.

Don and I packed out two loads of meat, maybe seventy pounds each, and left the two massive hindquarters in cotton bags to cool under the shade of a fir tree. We went back for them later, in the midafternoon, with empty frame backpacks. We hung the meat to finish cooling in Don's massive "cool room," a refrigerator kept at about thirty-five degrees. Don has a large work shed full of freezers, and he usually processes seven or eight elk a season.

Later, Don talked to Kip, who was having a hard time with some clients who had brought their own rifles and weren't shooting very well with them. One of them couldn't hit a target at a hundred yards. Don came in and said to me, "I told Kip how you made a double-lung shot at three hundred yards, and he just said, 'I knew he would.'"

Don smiled. I'll admit, that was pretty satisfying to hear.

—

Nothing changed for Don. He still went up glassing in the early mornings and evenings to look for elk, to watch what other hunters were doing. I stayed on a few more days and went with him, furthering my education.

It had been seventy degrees at midday on the day I'd shot my elk, and Don and I had gone back up in T-shirts and shorts to pack the hindquarters out. Two days later, as we hiked up the same trail to glass, first there was rain, then sleet. We could barely see anything, but we could hear the elk in the frigid mist, their mysterious, sonorous, squeaking bugles.

"All over Colorado there are guys hunting, and maybe one percent are hearing elk bugle right now. You're getting spoiled," Don said.

On the benches the snow and clouds came whispering in, shrouding the landscape, hiding the panorama. The near hills vanished like whales in a misty sea. The wind came squalling, then howling, and biting, and now the snow suddenly, shockingly came down hard and thick. It was a stark reminder of the big wild, the reality of the mountains. In a slightly different situation—if you were up here and expecting it to be like yesterday, seventy degrees and sunny—then this surprise could be deadly.

The elk appeared out of the woods like ghosts, somehow surreal yet wholly natural. There was an empty field; then, for a strange, hushed moment, there were elk; then, as the light changed, the field was empty again. All in silence, broken only by that mysterious singing, the keening bugle.

Part of the attraction of hunting elk is that they touch us with the *wild,* reminding us of the mystery and magic and bigness of the open spaces. Just like dolphins for a sailor. The dolphins always remind me of the vast blue sea, the unknowable spaces underneath me. I have seen dolphins come play in the bow wave hundreds of times, and yet every time comes the rush—the sea is huge, and I perceive so little.

On my last morning, I left with Don early, for one last glass. We went up the hill in the dark, as always. It was cold, but the ice and snow of the previous morning had melted and the storm felt like a dream. I had finally begun to be acclimated, my respiration loud but normal, and Don took me on a hike all over creation.

It was eerily quiet that morning. I felt, in my bones, that the elk were gone. The landscape felt empty, vast and still. The silence was overpowering.

"I think they're gone," I said to Don.

"Sometimes they move on, just like that," Don said thoughtfully. But he wasn't convinced. He thought they might still be around here somewhere. As usual, Don's instincts were right.

We walked back into the canyon, into a hidden, dense area of aspen that Don had nicknamed Oz. We followed a game trail, easy hiking up to the top, then wound our way back into the deeper, higher canyon, a turn that had been invisible to me at lower altitudes. We were on one wall, and across the open stretch of air to the other side was a massive aspen grove, acres and acres of trees. And now we could hear the elk bugling, lowing, moving through that timber. We couldn't see them, but we heard them as they moved higher, toward a spring that Don knew.

Don and I stood there, stomachs growling after a long hike before breakfast. It was cold, our breath fogged the air, and we waited for a long moment in our camouflage, listening. Twigs cracked, elks bugled, the unseen crowd moved upward.

Don grinned at me. The trip was over.

The crack echoes off the hills, then again, like distant thunder. I'm not too worried about the sound; it's been months since we've seen another person. Still, if there are people out there, this might bring them. Can't be helped.

The elk herd vanishes, darting into the woods, but one is left behind, running, limping, plunging to earth.

"Nice shot, honey," I tell my wife. She smiles as she works the bolt. I pick up the brass; we won't leave anything out here. My son is already running into the field, his sturdy little legs pumping. He loves this part. He's going to hurl himself on the elk and act as if he killed it himself.

We've been killing and processing an elk a week, making pemmican. I had fashioned a kind of half-ass cold cellar that seemed to do a little bit in the way of refrigeration. Of course, if the snow stays we won't have any problems keeping things frozen. I just hope that the elk stay long enough, too. Pretty soon we'll be buried in snow, and we'll start the long, slow race against starvation until spring.

As my son karate-chops the dead elk, my wife and I begin to quickly and efficiently lay out our tools for butchery. But only one of us will work; the other will stand watch with a loaded rifle.

The gray winter sky threatens more snow. A lot more.

14.

A WORLD LIT ONLY
BY SEAL OIL

The wind is all teeth, biting through clothing, penetrating all the way to the bone. My breath billows like smoke, like a soul departing. Under the wind, I can feel the deathly silence. The Earth is buried under five feet of snow, never to thaw. It's been three or four years since we've had a real spring.

Our footsteps crunch in the snow. The sound is nearly obscene. I follow a slender figure, shrouded in rags and layers like a Bedouin.

We wend our way through the box canyons of white, the square valleys of regular snow that hint at the city underneath. We pass, brief as a breath, across the thick ice, where sometimes the bones of an old car jut through. There is no sun, just low, heavy clouds. We haven't seen the sun properly in years, but it's not something you forget.

We bang through an old door and into an abandoned building, and move through the familiar darkness. This has been our home for several months, as we scavenged through this town for food and supplies.

My wife looks up expectantly as we enter the little room at the core of the building. A small potbellied wood stove crackles with life in the corner, and the candles gutter at our entrance.

"Cold out there," jokes my son, the Bedouin, as he unwraps. He's almost a teenager now, grown up in this cold world, and he stamps his feet and shakes snow from the layers of rags. My wife's eyes track in the dark to the sack he's been carrying. A sorry haul, several cans of beans, dented, ancient.

"That's it," he says, lightly. "That's the last of it." It's been snowing for weeks, and the temperature has hovered below zero for months. We've been holed up here, taking food from a buried supermarket—but finally it's running out.

"We're going to have to move," I say in the silence. Moving means outside, over that ice and snow, in the wind, for days, weeks.

"Maybe we should try hunting those dogs again," my son murmurs. There is a pack of wild dogs we've seen from a distance. Foxlike, they run from us; anything alive has a reason to fear man's hunger.

"Maybe," I say thoughtfully.

What happens when the world freezes over? Whether caused by nuclear fallout, a meteor, or climate change, an iced-over Earth is a grim possibility. Glaciers have covered the world before. Our ancestors survived the Ice Age. Could you?

I've been cold. I worked a season in Antarctica, at the South Pole Station, where the pay was bad, but the working conditions were straight-up dismal. A fair portion of the workers were kids like me, goofballs looking for adventure and a free trip to the bottom of the world. The grizzled veterans called us "one-season wonders," but really, who was laughing at whom? It was the job site from hell. The only positive was that when you were drinking a beer outside, the beer got colder.

The cold was a live thing. You could feel it sniffing around the edges of your gear, snaking its way through your clothes. At night I slept in a Quonset hut that was supposed to be heated to sixty degrees but was probably in the high forties, and the cold seeped up the metal bed legs. A six-pack of unopened beer left on the floor would freeze and explode overnight. Of course, the sun never went down, it just circled the horizon in a maddening oval, so who was to say what was night?

The first week, the temperature hit 70 below zero, and with the windchill it was something like 119 below. That's serious business, right there. So I knew and loathed the cold, but I didn't know much about cold weather survival: how to build igloos and snow shelters, how to read the sea ice.

I started nosing around and found exactly what I was looking for: the Nunavik Arctic Survival Training Center, or NASTC, in northern Canada, near Hudson Bay. When I called, the coordinator, a pleasant-sounding man named Mario Aubin, said he had a sixty-year-old native on staff who spoke English and could teach me about seal hunting and sea-ice survival. The arrangements seemed a little casual. They normally train small-plane pilots, oil-rig workers, or members of the Canadian military, especially Search and Rescue technicians. I signed up.

The casualness persisted. I never got a real itinerary or gear list. I flew into Montreal on faith that there would be a connecting flight from Montreal to some tiny town in Nunavut, and that in that tiny town an Inuit man would teach me how to survive in the snow.

After a full day of flying in small planes, town-hopping from

Montreal over a sea of ice, and listening to the burble of *Inuktitut*, the Inuit language, we landed at my stop, *Puvirnituq*. In Inuit, *Puvirnituq* means "the place that smells of rotting meat," and no, I'm not kidding. The town is at exactly sixty degrees north latitude. I watched the tiny airport approach through the window of the small jet with some trepidation: I hadn't heard from Mario in weeks and I didn't have any contact information for the NASTC. Suppose nobody was there to meet me? It seemed like a very real possibility.

In the small terminal building, a forty-foot-square room with a dozen seats, a white man with a slightly furtive look made eye contact with me, then introduced himself, to my great relief, as Larry Brandridge, my contact here in PUV (which is what everyone calls *Puvirnituq*). Larry is a powerful man, medium height but obviously strong, clean-shaven and fair skinned. Larry is a lot of things—Search and Rescue, an ex-cop, a very serious mixed-gas diver, and a commercial dive instructor—and he spoke professionally about the High Arctic, where he has been working for most of his life.

"C'mon, jump on the snow machine and I'll take you to the hotel," he said in his nasal Canadian twang, and I zipped up my Carhartt jacket in anticipation.

That snowmobile ride was a nasty shock. Thirty below was *gnarly* on that thing. I was wearing thin jeans and no long underwear, within seconds the tops of my thighs were burning. I had to shield my face with my mittens, the wind stripping tears from my eyes.

I knew that the short exposure time meant I was going to be fine, but I got a sense of how cold the air really was. The snowmobile created a thirty-knot wind. Let me tell you a little something about windchill: it's gruesome. Moving air whisks heat away, and its effect on perceived temperature is exponential. Being outside in negative twenty isn't a big deal, but if there is a five-mile-an-hour wind, then the air feels like forty below. The wind can't make the air colder than the ambient temperature, but it can make it feel that way because your body desperately tries to keep your skin warm. The more wind, the faster it strips the heat off your skin, and the colder you feel. But it's not just perception, because convection is a way for you to lose heat. So the windchill does damage.

The town reminded me of Antarctica, like McMurdo Station, but slightly less remote. *Puvirnituq* gets three Sealifts (deliveries from cargo ships) of supplies a year; McMurdo gets one. PUV is a big town for this part of the world, fifteen hundred to two thousand souls living in tight, contained, self-sufficient little government houses. The snow-mobile is how everyone gets around, but I saw a few cars on the iced streets.

The PUV hotel is utilitarian and comfortable, with a large cafeteria looking out over the frozen river that leads to the nearby Hudson Bay. Larry sat down to drink tea with me and have a welcoming chat. I told Larry a little about what I was doing, and he smiled bleakly.

"If the apocalypse hit," he said, "up here not much would change. For most of these hunters, they wouldn't even really notice until the gas stopped coming. Within a few years, they would start regressing to the old ways. Sled dogs. Life would go without much of a bump."

"What are the common survival problems you see up here?" I asked him.

Larry talked at length about the scientists and documentary film-makers who come up here, and how they want to *do too much*. They have a hard time being reasonable, staying within safe bounds. In an unforgiving climate like this, you have to know your limitations.

I had noticed a sign for the NASTC, with its motto, "You're only as sharp as your *panac*." Seeing as I didn't even know what a *panac* was, it seemed likely that mine wasn't very sharp. Larry explained that the *panac* is a snow knife, similar to a machete (traditionally made from bone, but now from aluminum). The Inuit use it to cut the blocks to make igloos, and in a pinch to do anything else that they need a knife for—clean caribou or gut fish.

"Aikimie will show you," he said.

My guides were to be Aikimie Novalinga and his young helper Ipeli, a distant relation of Aikimie's, perhaps a nephew. Aikimie spoke excellent English. He was a hunter, which is something of a job description here and something of a character trait, because, as Larry said, "These guys don't *go* hunting. They're always hunting, whenever they're out on the land."

If you are on the land, it means you're away from civilization; Larry himself had just come in from five days on the land training some cadets. He ended up lending me an extra winter parka they had given him, and thank God for that, because it was a true arctic parka—real Canadian goose down with a giant fur-lined hood.

Out my hotel window was a frozen wasteland. The sealed houses billowed smoke from tight, clean metal chimneys. As the light changed, the landscape shifted from hour to hour. I saw things in one place—a boat, a snowmobile—and then, a few hours later, the hotel seemed to have spun gently on an unknown axis so that I was facing a slightly different direction.

Whenever someone offers you a pair of wolf fur mittens, say, "Yes, thanks." Sure, I had paid two hundred dollars for a pair of Outdoor Research super-duper Arctic explorer's mitts at REI, but real wolf mittens? Are you kidding me? First of all, they were art objects—massive fur gauntlets reaching nearly up to my elbow. The fur was stunning: deep and rich, maybe two inches thick. Underneath was the raw hide of the wolf. The mittens weren't brain-tanned and had to stay cold or the fur would fall out, but I didn't think this was going to be a problem.

Simon Novalinga offered them to me. He is Aikimie's cousin, an Inuit with a weather-wizened face and a grin with scattered teeth. "I was born in igloo," said Simon. Though he has a heavy accent, his English is far better than my Inuktitut, and there was something mildly embarrassing about that. Here was a man from another time (born in a damn igloo) and here I am, the sophisticated twenty-first-century world traveler, bristling with technology . . . and he has to learn my language?

When Larry saw what I was wearing, he raised his eyebrows. "Simon must like you," he muttered. Or pity me. Whichever, I'll take it.

I was heading out on the land with Aikimie and Ipeli. I had met Aikimie briefly at the hotel. He was a jolly, round-faced, gasping man, with two blackened circles on his cherubic cheeks from repeated wind-burn or frostbite.

There is a tendency to ascribe mystical wisdom to Indians, to the elder Inuit, to any "primitive" culture, and I had to be on guard against this Noble Savage problem. It's just a gnat's ass from racism, and more than that, it's factually wrong. Before the white man came, the Inuit and other Native Americans starved to death all the time; they had warfare and rape and all the foibles of human nature (although, to be fair, nobody does warfare and devastation like the white man).

Aikimie warned me that he was not an Eskimo. *Esquimeaux* was the French interpretation of an Indian word for "the eaters of raw meat," which is how the Indians referred to their northern neighbors, the Inuit. The Inuit do indeed eat raw meat, but more on that later.

Aikimie had also been "born in igloo," which he said with some pride, but underlying the pride was a poignancy, a realization that the world had moved irrevocably on. Perhaps I imagined it. You have to guard against this proclivity to ascribe attributes you wish were true to cultures you do not understand. All the same, is there anything that could separate you more from the modern world than being born in an igloo?

Aikimie had worked for Air Inuit, had been a cop ("I quit because I got tired of arresting my friends, and I couldn't get transferred"), and had taught Inuit culture here in PUV for many years. He was, in short, the perfect guide for me.

On the first day, the wind was blowing too hard for us to head out on the land, which was frustrating, but I understood it. It was gusting up to fifty knots, which is a hatful of wind, especially on a cold day. So I sat around the hotel and talked to Larry, and he told me that outside of town the visibility would be down to a few hundred feet. He could sense my frustration, and he gently, obliquely explained Aikimie's reasoning.

"I think the most common mistake people make up here is that at some point, a little voice in their head says, '*You should stop,*' and they don't," Larry said. Maybe it's snowing and visibility is bad, and then your snowmobile malfunctions, or you have to dig it out. Larry called it a "path of mistakes."

I know what he's talking about. I once heard a lecture on decision making where they called it a "cascade of bad decisions," one leading to another. When you push the envelope in a hostile environment, a couple of minor mistakes can kill you. It's why high-altitude alpine climbers are dying all the time. They make mistakes just like anybody, but the environment is so hostile that the mistakes quickly add up to death. If your car breaks down on the way home from work tonight, it's an inconvenience. If Aikimie's snowmobile breaks down when he's three hundred kilometers from town, it starts to be serious.

One of the main problems is that when something does go wrong, the cold makes it that much harder to deal with.

Hypothermia is essentially a mental problem. The gradual cooling affects your mind, and only later does it really start to affect the rest of the body. Hypothermia makes you stupid. The WEMTs used to call it "the umbles": is the patient stumbling, mumbling, fumbling? That's serious hypothermia. As your brain cools, the blood in your brain flows sluggishly, your thinking slows, and your glucose levels drop. Common sense starts to go, as the brain vasoconstricts to reduce blood going to the skin. If you get as cold as ninety-four degrees Fahrenheit, you become severely mentally impaired, apathetic, unaware, forgetful. Most likely, you're going to make increasingly poor decisions until you freeze to death. It creeps up on you.

Your priority in the extreme cold is shelter—food and water can wait. Larry talked about the need to break the wind, and how quickly frostbite can set in.

"Frostbite can be superficial or deep," he said. "On the outer layer of skin, it's a sunburn, a windburn. Just cover it and it goes away. The Inuit will rub snow on it to reduce scarring, and you don't want to warm it too quickly." Deep frostbite is something else entirely, and can be life threatening in the field.

Aikimie somewhat grudgingly decided to head out the next morning. It was still windy, but the wind had dropped off to maybe twenty knots. It was obvious that Aikimie was still worried about his delicate guest.

We finished loading up the *qamutik*, the sleds (pronounced "homma-tick"). Aikimie had a big snowmobile, and he was pulling a big *qamutik* that held the majority of our supplies. I was on a smaller machine, a 350, with a correspondingly smaller *qamutik*, on which Ipeli was ensconced. If I got too cold, he could always take over.

The sun was out by nine, and at ten we drove out of town. I followed Aikimie by a few sled lengths. The snowmobile's two-stroke motor whined, tinny and high-pitched, and we zoomed down the hill and out over the ice. Within seconds I was adjusting my neck gaiters and goggles, trying to get myself covered perfectly. The wind sliced through, finding the weakness in my defense.

It was blowing twenty knots right in our teeth. Aikimie said something about the temperature being fifty below. We were doing anywhere from twenty to thirty-five kilometers per hour on the snowmobiles, and the wind was a ripping laser. The "apparent" wind must have been something like fifty or even sixty miles per hour. It was ungodly. Something was always wrong during the two-hour drive: my face, my eyes, my hands. In the fifteen minutes when nothing was freezing cold, I had to pee.

Being out here on the land reminded me that there is nothing intrinsically evil about discomfort. Modern man, terrified of discomfort, flees the tiniest pain. If anything feels the slightest bit unpleasant, we stop it. In no place on earth is that phenomenon more prevalent than Los Angeles, simply because we drive so much there. You're never uncomfortable in your car, sealed in a steel cocoon with climate control.

Being on the land also revealed the distinctions between discomfort and actual pain. What I felt on the snow machine was discomfort, but I *knew* I wasn't in any actual danger, not yet. I got a tiny strip of frostbite on my cheek, in a gap where I only had one layer of clothing. It was a minor annoyance, like sunburn. My core never even got cold, and my feet were fine.

The snowy landscape streamed by in a heady dream. I chased Aikimie's snowmobile across the endless white, the wind howling and tugging my hood back. The incessant whine of the machine was deafening. I was in a trance, diving over a lunar landscape. "Lunar" may seem like a cliché, but it was utterly appropriate: this was a child's moonscape, white and frozen and barren. Flat, gentle hills, small valleys. The tundra near the sea, frozen solid, the lakes and rivers indistinguishable from meadows except for being slightly flatter.

We stopped often because Aikimie wanted to check on me. He would clamber off his snow machine and I would pull up alongside, careful to give him room. It was a cold, hard ride, but I was into it—I wasn't going to switch over to let Ipeli drive and become a passive passenger. Aikimie had recently driven sixteen hours straight on the snowmobile, five hundred miles to another village to help with Search and Rescue. I could finish out this little two-hour drive.

The NASTC isn't just a training program for outsiders; it also employs and trains local Inuit for Search and Rescue. Many of them are ice divers as well as qualified parachutists, so they can parachute in, administer first aid, and survive for at least three days. Aikimie is part of that squad, and he told me about that long haul he had just done. They found the lost hunters just in the nick of time—one of the hunters was stripping off his clothes. "He lost a foot, but he was a lucky guy," said Aikimie.

I remembered from my WEMT course why someone might do that. The roots lie in the body's reactions to cold. It starts with vasoconstriction, which means the shrinking of blood vessels—they contract like a muscle. It's why your hands and feet get cold; the body reduces blood flow to the extremities in an attempt to keep the core conduit warm, heart to brain. Fingers and toes go first, sacrificed to the essential organs.

Eventually, the body gives up fighting the cold, and the vasoconstriction eases. Blood flows full strength back to the extremities, and you feel warm again; when you freeze to death, the last feeling is of a dreamy, warm stupor (sometimes you'll see this called "paradoxical rewarming"). That's why the SAR team had found that hunter stripping off his clothes, and why Aikimie said he was lucky, because that dude was close to death. The cold is a cognitive issue, first and foremost.

Interestingly, the best and most efficient way to rewarm is from the inside: with food, especially sugar. Kool-Aid mix is what the books recommend.

Bill Kane, my WEMT instructor, said, "For mild hypothermia, feed 'em, beat 'em, and heat 'em . . . mild exercise is good. But if person is too physically exhausted, then no exercise—food, water, get 'em dry. Warm fluid is not about imparting heat—twelve ounces of fluid at one hundred degrees into a hundred-eighty-pound person at ninety-three degrees will raise their temperature basically nothing. But what we're doing is putting in something that is already broken down into a liquid, and doesn't have to be warmed up to be digested. So it's faster, and warmth in the stomach and intestinal tract will coax a faster digestion. Warm sweet tea is great." People in severe hypothermia won't be able to digest solid food, and for unconscious folks, you just try to keep them warm and dry from the outside.

Certainly, we drank warm tea by the gallon. Chemical heat, the reaction inside your body, is critical. Got to keep the furnace going.

Aikimie climbed back on his snowmobile, and I marveled that he had his cheeks exposed. I had read about the Inuit metabolism, and Larry had warned me, "Don't try and match those guys, they handle the cold differently than you and me." The Inuit have a significantly higher basal metabolic rate than Caucasians, meaning they've got a warmer temperature; they run a little hotter.

Some interminable time later, Aikimie slowed ahead of me and stopped, and I carefully pulled up alongside. We shut down the snow machines, and he pointed ahead to a small, lonely cross on a minor rolling hill overlooking the rivers and lakes.

"My grandfather is buried there," he said. Apparently, this had been his grandfather's favorite fishing spot. He had been hunting with his friend in a boat, and a storm had come up and killed them both. Aikimie was full of stories like that, illustrating his incredibly tight family connections to the land, the generations tracing back over the snow.

Then, up ahead, a funny rock resolved into something else, a block, and I realized as we crossed another river that this was the cabin we were aiming for, at last. We pulled up alongside the tiny shack.

"Let's go warm up, have a tea," said Aikimie.

The cabin had a small foyer, like a closet, then the main room, which was about twenty feet square. I was stumbling like a drunk, delighted to be off the snow machine and away from that drone at last. Aikimie and Ipeli fired up the two small Coleman stoves they brought, and although it was still below zero in there it felt warm without the wind. Our breath fogged the room.

There was a tiny mirror over the stove, and I examined the frostnip on my cheekbone, outside of where my goggles fell, something between sunburn and windburn. In a few days it faded to a more clearly defined dark mark. "The girls will like it," said Aikimie.

Frostbite is caused by the water in the skin cells freezing and rupturing the cells. I had what's called superficial frostbite. The blood vessels had constricted for long enough that there was reduced blood flow to the area and some minor cell damage. The best way to warm mild frostbite is with skin-to-skin contact.

Real frostbite, deep frostbite, is very dangerous—the tissues are frozen, hard, and dead. Thawing can release bad proteins from the damaged tissue and give you a fever as well as intense pain. The worst possible damage happens when flesh is badly frostbitten, gets rewarmed, then freezes again. In any case, you're gonna need to surgically remove that area of flesh. In the field, without proper medical attention, you're knock-knock-knocking on heaven's door.

We ate *banac,* a kind of fried dough, salty and delicious, with our tea. By the time tea was finished the room had warmed to where we could no longer see our breath, and I had forgotten the struggle with the wind. Everything was peachy-cozy. The Great White North was a good time. There were long silences filled with the gentle hiss of the Coleman stoves as we melted more ice for water and sipped our tea.

Aikimie and I chatted companionably, albeit sporadically. I asked Aikimie whether the wind was normal for this time of year. He shrugged, as if to say, what does that question even mean?

"You can't trust the days," he said. He meant that climate change is happening so fast here that experience is no guarantee. The ice and the snow had been *months* late this year. "My ancestors said that some-day there would be a winter with no snow," he said, "and I didn't believe them." He laughed, because he believed them now.

After a while, we suited back up and headed out to check on some nets that were nearby.

Without a guide, I would have been instantly, horribly lost. This was a near-featureless white plain that Aikimie knew intimately. I could have followed the snowmobile tracks, but if it snowed or blew hard, tell my mother I love her, bury me under the ol' willow.

We went straight out over the ice to a board sticking up that marked the net. We were miles from Hudson Bay proper, but if you looked at a topographical map of the area you'd see it's dotted with thousands and thousands of tiny lakes and rivers. We were out on one of the little lakes now, one of Aikimie's favorite spots.

Ipeli pulled an ice chisel and a tool that looked like a long-handled sieve spoon out of my *qamutik,* and we went to work. The net was stretched underneath the ice, between two holes maybe 150 feet apart. A friend of Aikimie's had placed this net a few days ago, and the holes had frozen solid. To get to the net, we had to dig the holes out.

The ice chisel had a blade about two inches across and four or five inches long, a wood chisel welded to a five-foot piece of rebar. Ipeli shoveled off the snow, and then we took turns working on the hole, careful to not slice the rope. The chisel had all the weight of the rebar, so the job consisted of lifting it and controlling the fall, letting the weight and the sharpness do the work. Ice splintered and exploded under the chisel's edge. When the hole choked with ice shards, Aikimie took the long-handled sieve-spoon and carefully cleaned it out. This is probably all old hat to anybody who goes ice fishing, but it was new to me.

Swinging that chisel was hard work. Instantly I started to sweat and my forearms started to burn. Ipeli and I traded off, although it was clear that Aikimie thought I was going to slice the rope with the ice chisel, no matter how careful I was. My main fear was of going through the ice and sending the chisel straight to the bottom.

We got down about two feet, and taking a breather, I turned to Aikimie and asked him, "How thick is the ice here?"

"Oh, not too thick, maybe five or six feet," he said blandly.

Well, shit, Sam, that hole ain't gonna dig itself.

The nature of the beast is that if you're warm sitting still, then the minute you start working, you will sweat profusely. My hair was soaked under my hat. Sweating is one of the dangers of strenuous exercise in the cold. Alpine climbers sometimes get hyperthermia, not hypothermia—because of exertion and being too warmly dressed, they actually overheat in the freezing cold. Then, the minute you stop, all that moisture starts to freeze, which can get you going the other direction.

I was on my knees, smashing away, when I felt the chisel go through, but I was ready and held it. With a burble and black rush, the water came spilling up over the lip and then, with a sigh, regained equilibrium at the top of the ice. The five-foot-deep hole was gone, and now there was just a small circle of open black water. Magic. We carefully cleaned out the ice chunks with the sieve spoon, then trudged across the ice to the other hole to repeat the process.

Finally, with both holes clear, Aikimie tied a long piece of synthetic line to one end of the net and pulled the other end up. He and Ipeli had waterproof diving gloves to handle the net and the fish, so I took pictures as they hauled the net up through the hole and disengaged the fish, tossing them out on the ice to freeze. The fish came up alive and wriggling, flipping and flopping. They were whitefish, of good size, most of them over twelve inches.

Suddenly, it hit me what a massive survival advantage the temperature was here—these guys essentially lived in a freezer. Sure, there were plenty of drawbacks, but one gigantic plus was that meat spoilage was not going to be a problem. Nothing left outside in the winter could ever thaw. Fish, caribou, seal, whatever—you could kill it and throw it anywhere, and as long as the foxes didn't eat it, you could chew on it whenever you wanted.

It seemed like a bountiful catch to me, but I was informed that this was a mediocre haul, thirty or forty footlong whitefish. We didn't need the food, but it would go to the village larder, to Aikimie's family, or to Hunter Support—a program that provides food to those who don't have any, who are elderly or alone. The rapacious, endless quest for food is a given. Within minutes we had restrung the net under the ice, placed the boards back up to mark the spot, and were motoring home.

We settled into the cabin for the night, boots off, and Aikimie fried up a mess of caribou with onions and mushrooms. Eating when you're in the cold weather is like a job—you'd better do it and stay on top of it. Almost always, if your hands or feet start to get really cold, it's because you haven't eaten enough, or recently enough. At the South Pole, the cafeteria had extremely high-quality food, and in particular always a lot of dessert selections, such as chocolate cakes and dense, rich cookies. We used to joke, "It ain't breakfast till you've had the pie," but if you didn't eat enough, you'd suffer.

When I went out to piss, it was bitterly cold and the wind was howling in the dark. The northern lights were up, streaming across the sky, a ghostly swath of luminescence, amazing and delightful. They're hard to pin down, somehow changing shape without seeming to move, so it's as if you never quite truly see them. The scale always feels strangely off; how can they be so far away and yet move so fast? No picture or movie can ever do justice to the northern lights, because what is truly awesome is their scope, their vast sweep, bell to bell, horizon to horizon in gently twisting arcs, sinuous, calligraphic, paint strokes of light.

I "know" that the *aurora borealis* is caused by solar winds, ionization, and the Earth's magnetic field, but what does that mean? I can say the words, I can read the articles and take comfort in the fact that the scientists understood most of the phenomenon, but it is still awesome and awe-full, mysterious and ominous. Those lights stroke a mystic nerve.

I stumbled back inside, to life and warmth.

I asked Aikimie about seal hunting, and he told me the wind was wrong; it has to be blowing from the east to open up water. We were on the west side of Hudson Bay, where the prevailing wind blows the ice in against the shore. To hunt seals you need open water, so either you go out hundreds of miles on the sea ice (a very risky proposition) or you wait for a wind shift, which might open water up nearer to shore. The thing to avoid is getting caught on the ice, a hundred miles out, when the wind shifts.

The traditional way to hunt seal in the winter is to find blowholes in the ice—the spots where the ice is thin enough that the seals come to breathe. You find the blowhole, and because the sound of your walking to it would spook the seals, you have to wait patiently by the blowhole with your harpoon until the seals come back. Doesn't sound so bad, right? But you might be waiting for hours, motionless, silent, ready to strike, as the chill radiated into your bones. Aikimie had waited for five hours before, and he recalled his father waiting ten. A lesson in survival patience.

The importance of the seal to the Inuit dawned on me when Aikimie told me of the *qulliq,* the only source of light and heat in a traditional igloo. The *qulliq* is a stone bowl filled with seal oil or blubber, usually with a moss wick running the length of the bowl. If you don't get a seal (and you often don't) then you're shit out of luck in the realest way possible: no light or cooking for the winter, eating everything raw in the dark. You could survive, but just try to imagine it.

Aikimie warned me that starvation haunts the Inuit, even the experienced hunters. The threat never goes away. He told a story about when his mother and the other women, with the children and elderly, had been left behind for a month while the men were out on the land. They tried to catch fish, but sometimes they would go a week without success.

"They got so hungry they knew they weren't going to live anymore, and there was a big old dog they decided to kill. They had no gun, so they got a rope around his neck and three women tried to choke him. They were weak and running around and the dog was really fighting, and after an hour they killed him. That's why I'm here." He laughed. "If she didn't eat that dog I wouldn't be here."

This is a people barely a generation removed from real subsistence, and they make full use of the combination of incredible knowledge and understanding with modern technology—the snowmobile, the rifle—to hunt their fill.

Over the next week, I was introduced to the pure nomadic nature of the Inuit and what it means to survive in the North. We moved. We ranged constantly on the snow machines, always seeking food. When the weather was bad we were lazy, loitering in the cabin drinking tea for hours. When the weather broke, when the wind dropped to nothing and it was maybe ten below, we moved without pause until after sunset, checking nets, hunting ptarmigan and caribou.

I realized that just because this place *looks* wind-blasted and empty doesn't mean it is. There is grass under the snow, and rabbits, foxes, caribou are out there in the vast landscape, snorting and snuffling for the grass. In addition, there are birds, fish teeming under the ice, mice.

The Inuit culture is one of the very few that is all hunting, almost no gathering, and the igloo reflects this. The igloo is a critical part of the Inuit world (*igloo* and *kayak* are the major exports of Inuktitut to the English language). The Inuit can build an igloo in a short time, even half an hour, especially if one man is cutting the blocks and another is stacking.

"For a beginner, it will take two or three hours," said Aikimie. "Cutting good blocks is very important: clean cuts, and the right size. For the survival course, we first make a big igloo for everyone to sleep in, a six- or seven-man igloo. Then, the next day, we show how to cut blocks. It's hard to make an igloo at first. It looks easy, but it's hard."

As far as heating the igloo, Aikimie told me, "You have to not heat it too much, or it will melt, eh? You need to see the smoke coming out of your mouth, all the time. If you can't see it, you have to cool the igloo down." Dripping is common; that's okay.

Aikimie showed me how to cut blocks one morning before our day really got started. It was usually too cold in the early morning to do anything, so although we were up at six, we didn't get moving outside until ten. He took the *panac* and probed the snow in a few places—it had been cold and blowing for about two weeks, so the snow was old, hard, crystallized. "Some Inuit can tell just by walking on it," he said, "the feel and sound. Not me." He was probing to make sure there weren't different kinds of snow separated by a few inches, because the blocks have to be homogenous.

Aikimie hacked his way down, cutting an X and then chopping to make one edge of the first block, a flat edge maybe three feet across. Then he sliced in, four inches on a side, cut the back out at the full length of the blade, maybe two feet down, and sliced the bottom. He had a clean block three feet by two feet and four inches thick. He popped the block out with the *panac,* neat as a bastard, and lifted it free. The blocks were surprisingly heavy, maybe fifty or sixty pounds. Aikimie laid them in a circle around where he stood. You should never have to leave the footprint of the igloo to cut blocks: all the snow in that footprint can be made into enough blocks to construct the igloo. And that way, you're making the whole thing deeper at the same time you're building the walls. He sliced fast, shimmying the blade through the snow with deft flourishes.

He laid the first course and then, facing the 'door,' cut down into the first course at about 3 o'clock and cut through 12 to about 9 o'clock (with 12 as the door). He cut rising up from the bottom in a long diagonal through the half-circle, to even out at the top at 9. This created the slope for the next course, giving the whole thing an upward spiral. It sounds complicated but isn't. The trick is to cut good blocks, which is part art and part science. You need to have the patience, but also the feel. Your second hundred igloos are probably a lot better than your first hundred. I also could tell that there were a multitude of details that Aikimie was performing without telling me, without thinking about it, like putting the door opposite the prevailing wind, or cutting smaller blocks as the courses climbed.

Aikimie handed over the *panac* and I set up inside the ring, cutting blocks and popping them out.

The blocks were so heavy! I cut a few that were too big, and they nearly broke my back. They probably weighed a hundred pounds. Aikimie showed me how to lay in the second course. The most important thing is to start making the angle sharp, bring them inward, to *not* make a wall that goes straight up. That's a common beginner mistake. Because of the sloping angle Aikimie had cut, the blocks now began to spiral upward, and he bent them in at a sharp angle, used the *panac* to trim the edges, then banged them into place with a knowing thump of his mitt.

"It's only snow, eh?" he said. Meaning, you can't go whaling on it and tossing blocks around, they'll crumble, it's only snow. I tried to cut the blocks the way Aikimie had, slicing with the snow knife, mimicking his fishing motion, and then popping them out. I broke several for each one I got onto the wall. Sweat poured down my face, as I was now sheltered from the wind.

"I'm not going to have enough blocks in here," I told Aikimie, who was outside. He laughed.

"It's only snow, eh?" *We got a lot of that.*

Finally, I got to the thin keystone block, which is what holds the whole puzzle together and locks it in place. I finagled the block up through the hole, turned it, laid it flat on top, and, working overhead with the *panac,* shaved it down until it fell into place. Snug as a bug in a rug. The sunlight shone bright blue through the thinner snow.

There were a lot of chinks in between the blocks, so Aikimie and I cut little slices and stuffed the cracks, just like stuffing insulation in a building. We shoveled loose snow onto the top, and eventually we had a sealed igloo. Aikimie made sure I cut a ventilation hole—you need circulation. Apparently, an igloo can be too airtight, particularly if you're using a stove inside.

Aikimie told me I could pee in the igloo at night, right in the corner, and it wouldn't smell.

"Do you want to sleep here tonight?" he asked me doubtfully.

"Sure," I replied, with an uneasy twinge. How bad could it be?

That night, with some trepidation, I slept in the igloo. Ipeli helped me set up, laying down a base mattress of willow branches, gathered and tied tightly together, maybe an inch thick. This was to help keep the heat of my body off the snow, to prevent me from melting into it. It's the same reason they build pipelines and buildings on stilts over the ice or permafrost.

I had my zero-degree sleeping bag, which I didn't trust at all, so I borrowed an extra bag from Aikimie. He didn't like the all-nylon backpacking bags that outsiders always bring north; he used heavy, down-filled cloth bags.

It was already dark when I finally crawled into the igloo. The warmth of the day had faded and the bitter cold was back, along with the wind.

You always put your hood up when you enter into an igloo, to avoid getting snow in your parka as you crawl and scrape through the low entrance. I maneuvered the door block in behind me, leaving a little gap on the top, and then I lit a candle. I stared around at the flickering walls, but there wasn't much to do but go to sleep. I started to divest. I took the massive boots off first and removed the liners—if there was sweat in there, I didn't want it to freeze overnight. The trick is to bring everything that can freeze into the sleeping bag with you. Larry Brandridge had told me he uses his liners for a pillow, and I tried that. I placed my gloves (not the wolf mitts) inside the bags, in between layers. I slept in my medium and under layers, and threw the parka over the top.

I was hot. Who knew that the budget zero-degree Slumberjack bag from Gander Mountain would end up being an actual, honest-to-God, zero-degree bag? That plus the big down bag on top that Aikimie lent me meant that I was cooking. Outside the bag, I could feel the deep powerful chill on my face and hands. But I pulled down deep into my cozy nest, zipping zippers and warming my iceberg hands against my thighs. I stared up at the translucent darkness, the faint outlines of the snow blocks, the steady hum of Aikimie's generator a pleasant break from the snores that emanated from Aikimie and Ipeli every night.

I was far, far warmer in that igloo than I had been on Cody Lundin's Arizona trip with two crap army-surplus wool blankets.

At one point in the night, I awoke, listening. I heard footsteps walking around the igloo, right outside. Would Aikimie be out in the night to check on me? I doubted it. I was fifty feet from the cabin, like a little kid camped out in the backyard. I was willing to bet a thousand dollars that Ipeli was deep asleep. So who was out there?

The footsteps crunched closer, loud and plain.

"Hello?" I called, a weird sound against the silence. Nothing. Maybe a few more steps, then silence. I felt like a sucker for calling out—I remembered Aikimie saying that the foxes would come around at night, and they would sound like people.

There was, however, no way in hell I was getting up and getting out to check, so I rolled over and went back to sleep. If it was a polar bear, I'd deal with it when he broke through the igloo. If he didn't, live and let live, I say.

In the morning I lay deep in my nest and stared at the blue light seeping through the cracks between the blocks, watched my breath billow in heavy clouds, and thought about life in an igloo. Stultifying boredom was something Aikimie had touched on when he told me about being a small child in an igloo in the winter. His one toy had been a little bow and arrow. Then I tried to imagine a whole winter with no light and no heat, just the calories from raw frozen fish to keep you alive. Surviving off the internal furnace. I could see how it was doable: there were plenty of fish here, though the catch had declined from the old days; but *yikes*.

When I stomped into the cabin early that morning, Aikimie

rubbed his eyes, sat up, and shook my hand. "Let me congratulate you," he said, and I wondered if that was forced, a little rehearsed, something that the NASTC guys had told him to do when the paying guest survives a night in an igloo. I thanked him, but it was nothing. Spend a whole winter in an igloo and then I'll shake your hand.

A clearer picture was emerging for me of what it takes to survive here. You have to be mobile, and especially in the days before snowmobiles, that meant you had to have dogs. Dogs are the secret ingredient to life up north. Aikimie had grown up with dogs; his father and grandfather and ancestors had hunted with them. A dog team meant the ability to range and hunt and therefore survive. The Inuktitut word *qimutsiit* refers to one entity, the dog team and the hunter together—separately they are less.

The dogs aren't just for transportation—they are protection and early warning. They will gang up and fight off marauding polar bears.

"In the fall, when the ice is thin," Aikimie said, "the dogs know when the ice is dangerous. They're not gonna go. Even if it looks good to us, they'll know and they stop, so we have to go around on better ice. When we get caught in a bad storm, in a blizzard, the snow is so thick you can't see the dogs in front of the sled, but the dogs can take us home to igloos we built before. But we have to be quiet! We have to trust!" He laughed.

After we returned to PUV, Simon Novalinga agreed to take me out for a day's ride, overnight at his cabin, and then bring me back by dogsled. Larry Brandridge picked me up from the hotel with my gear, and he decided to come along on his snowmobile.

We stopped in front of Simon's house. All of the houses in town are the same cookie-cutter, cold-weather-sealed cottages. The Canadian government ships the materials here, builds the houses, and rents them to the Inuit.

We barged inside, and I shook hands with Simon and his grandson, Davidee, who was going to run the sled. Davidee was training to be a dogsled racer, like his father and his grandfather. A particularly impassive fifteen-year-old, he gave me an almost imperceptible nod, and that was about as far as our communication ever went.

I walked down to see the dogs while Larry went after his gear. It was a cold day, with a trickle of westerly wind over the ice. Larry had given me strict instructions: "Don't pet the dogs, don't get down on their level," and I didn't. They looked like huskies, big but not huge, wiry and scrappy.

A few little boys were down there with me, maybe five years old. One of them had a Batman logo sewn onto his black parka and a black cape sewn onto the back. They wrestled and played and teased the dogs, but were obviously respectful, wary of getting bit. These were not pets. Some dogs could be played with, but some had to be avoided.

As Simon and Davidee began putting on the dogs' harnesses, the dogs exploded in anticipatory barking, howling, and yelping. The harnesses, modern synthetic straps, fit snugly over the dog's head and put the strain on the chest. They were clipped in with small, ordinary metal clips like you might use on a regular dog leash—my first indication of the loads involved. These dogs weren't pulling thousands of pounds of pressure a piece, so the loads weren't huge. But the sled could get going and have its own momentum, so you had to be careful. Simon warned me about hanging on and being dragged: if you fall, just fall and let go.

There was no briefing, no instruction. I saw Larry holding some dogs that had been hitched up, so I went out and helped as Simon and Davidee brought more dogs out one by one, howling. It was organized chaos. The dogs were after one another, growling, yapping, sniffing, a few on the loose. Thin, orange, nylon three-strand line with an eye splice was clipped into the back of each dog's harness, and the lines all met at one point in a fan formation, where they were attached via a loop of sealskin—much stronger than the nylon, Simon assured me—and tied with a slipknot.

You may have seen the southerly "tandem" or "Nome" hitch for sled dogs, where they run in a long line, two abreast. That's for areas below the tree line, for running on trails. The fan hitch is for the far north, since the varying-length leads allow each dog to pick its own path over the ice. And the dogs can choose what dogs they want to run alongside. Probably most important, if one or two dogs go through the ice, the rest can pull them out.

Just as the cacophony peaked, I saw Simon coming with the last dog, his leader dog, a big black male with a thick mane. His name was Kakkinuk. The dogs truly went nuts, and I saw Davidee running for the sled, so I jumped and stepped over the lines and dashed for it, piling on. A sudden surge of speed threw me against the back of the *qamutiq*.

There was abrupt silence as the dogs raced forward and the sled whooshed over the ice, gathering speed, like a racing dinghy filling sail. The dogs fanned out in front of us in a loose, twisting group. The harnessing system allowed them to crisscross and tangle as much as they wanted. The fan was simple and effective. The howling and yowling was over, and now the only sounds were the swish of the runners and the tramp of dog feet. Davidee broke the silence in calling to the dogs, trilling to them, encouraging. Like a cowboy moving cattle.

I settled in for the long haul. This was a short trip, only ten kilometers, but it would take about two hours. The sled streamed on, moving between three and five miles an hour, over the open ice.

At times, Davidee would post a leg over the side, grip a handle, and jerk the sled, turning it a few degrees. At other times, he would nimbly leap off and run next to the sled for ten or twenty seconds, his boots pounding, his arms swinging wide for balance. He would do it when the sled slowed, taking his weight off and giving the dogs a little lift, allowing the sled to build up some momentum. As it passed him, he'd dive back on.

Aikimie had told me that good drivers can make themselves light for the dogs, and here was a pretty simple way to do it. Get off the damn sled and run.

I'll try that, I thought. I leapt off and started sprinting, and suddenly realized the egregious error of my ways. I was wearing Sorel minus-one-hundred-degree boots, which fit loosely and had only a few eyes and a loose nylon lace—definitely *not* meant to be run in. Imagine sprinting over snow and ice in loose-fitting platform shoes, trying to keep up with a dogsled? Four miles an hour may not seem like much, but it will leave you behind in a hurry. I nearly ate it, and dove desperately back onto the sled after four or five steps, landing heavily on the fur-covered wooden platform.

I caught my breath, heart pounding at the near miss—that would have been the ultimate embarrassment, to go down while running alongside the sled. Who knows how long it would take Davidee to stop, or would Larry or Simon come back and get me, even greater humiliation?

Davidee leapt off and sprinted again, running ten, fifteen, twenty seconds before leaping adroitly back onto the sled. If he fell, how would I stop the sled? I asked him, and after some confusion he silently showed me the brake. It was a two-tined fork of rebar, curved and attached by a synthetic line to the front of the sled. Davidee mimed pushing it into the ground. *Okay, sure,* I thought, I can do that.

Finally, a strange outcropping of rock in the distance took on a regular form, and we pulled up on Simon's cabin, a small rectangular shack with some even smaller outbuildings, covered in snow, buried for the winter.

Davidee threw the brake over and stomped on it, and the sled dragged to a stop. Simon and Davidee quickly worked to separate the dogs, and we set up the chains that would hold them for the night and keep them from fighting. The dogs were relaxing, sated from the run, accustomed to the routine. It was amazing to think that they would stay out here, that they would curl in little balls, backs to the wind, and lie down in minus-thirty-five-degree temperatures to sleep the night away. Later they'd be fed, two frozen fish and a chunk of lard for each.

Larry, Simon, and I sat around drinking tea and eating *banac* while Davidee went straight to his bunk, in the back of the cabin, and went to sleep.

Simon had far less English than Aikimie, and we often struggled to be understood. He seemed older than Aikimie, as well, but he was smiling and in excellent spirits.

"Be happy: if you want to sing with the dogs, sing to the dogs, be happy. Do it," he said. Larry grinned at me. *I'll give a shot,* I thought.

Inside, we talked about dogs for hours. Simon stressed the importance of a good leader dog, how good Kakkinuk, his leader dog, was.

"Leader is very, very important, without leader they cannot run," he said in his rough English. "They run crazy, all the time—but with the leader, run straight."

The leader dog is selected because he pulls in a straight line, and he is the one that really understands the verbal commands from the sled driver. The leader dog is the only dog that ever comes inside, as a puppy, because having a good relationship with him is important for driving the sled. Simon even mimed dragging the little puppy through his jacket, out of one arm and then the other, to teach him right from left.

He was prepping his dogs for the big race that was coming. The race was from Puvirintug to Salluit, around three hundred miles.

"How long will that race take?" I asked.

"One week," he said, "if weather's good. If bad, could be almost two weeks. They can pull forty miles a day if the weather's good. I drive fifty miles to my nets, never stop, eight hours."

We talked about building a sled dog team. "If you have no dogs, you have to get a female," Simon said wisely. "If someone gets me a female, then we can work on making dogs." I couldn't argue with that.

"Greenland has good dogs," Simon said. "My dogs are from Greenland."

When I asked him why his dogs were from Greenland, he said, "In the sixties the RCMP shot the dogs." He was talking about the Royal Canadian Mounted Police.

"Why did RCMP kill dogs?" I asked Simon.

"So Inuit has to buy snow machine!" he said, and laughed.

The Canadian government denies that there was ever a "cull" policy, while the Inuit elders remember mass slaughter of dogs. The Canadian government dispatched the RCMP to investigate itself, and the Mounties found no evidence of a conspiracy. So the Inuit, feeling ignored and disparaged, created the Qikiqtani Truth Commission, or QTC. What emerges is a bleak picture of culture clash, misunderstanding and miscommunication, racism and poverty. A story as old as the Americas. The QTC seemed to come to a pretty fair conclusion, that there was no conspiracy but that the southern government was trying to make the far North more like the South, with little understanding or concern. Mainly, they forced the Inuit into living in a dozen small towns, as opposed to hundreds of tiny, spread-out settlements.

Between 1957 and 1975, there was a steep decline in dog population. While there was disease and some Inuit killed their own dogs when they moved to the settlements (as they were required to), the drop-off suggests that thousands of dogs were killed. The police used a host of reasons as excuses: the dogs were dangerous to kids, they carried disease, they were wild. But those all revolved around cultural issues, because the Inuit didn't keep the dogs chained, letting them run free instead (they would chew through rope quickly, and where was anyone going to get that much chain?). This had never been a problem in the far-flung family units, but as the Inuit moved into the settlements the government created and forced them into, it became an issue for the white administrators and policemen.

The Ordinance Respecting Dogs mandated that dogs could not run loose, and could be in harness only if they were muzzled or under the control of a person over sixteen years of age. Often nobody bothered to explain the new rules to the Inuit, who couldn't really understand why their dogs were being killed.

Simon and the other Inuit who have dogs today in PUV take them out to nearby islands in the summer. Each dog team gets its own little island, and the Inuit leave them there for the whole season, dropping off a load of fish once a week. If they make it, great. Sometimes a few of them don't. These aren't pets.

The loss of the dogs was incredibly destructive to the Inuit, because without that mobility, they couldn't hunt, and most could not afford a snowmobile. Even today a snowmobile up there is expensive, maybe fifteen thousand dollars, and fuel is also extremely pricey. The settlements don't have anywhere near enough jobs for everyone, and the food sold in the stores is bad for the Inuit—diabetes and obesity are rampant today. If you were Inuit, it would be hard not to see a conspiracy to make you dependent on the white man. And in a way, they are right: it is kind of an unconscious conspiracy, a conspiracy of human nature, of bureaucracy.

Aikimie and I had discussed the issue carefully, out in his hunting lodge. "I wouldn't want to go back to the old days, not anymore," he had said. He meant the old days without the snowmobile, without gas and Coleman stoves. That's the real problem for the Inuit. They're caught between worlds right now, especially the young—they have the Internet, they have MTV, but an airline ticket to Montreal costs three thousand dollars and there are no roads. Jobs are scarce. The Nunavik people still don't govern themselves, although the Canadian government had been forming committees to explore that possibility for years, and handover is always imminent. They can never go back, and the way forward seems bleak.

Simon got up and went out to piss. Larry and I sat companionably, drinking tea, and after a while I ducked outside too.

The night was glooming down, bitterly cold and clean, the darkening sky and blue ice almost purple in the twilight. Simon was down by his dogs, chattering away in Inuktitut with admirable volubility. He didn't talk to me like that. I could hear the rising gutturals, the alien rhythm, the odd cadence of Inuktitut.

I came down and stood next to him, pretending that I wasn't freezing my ass off.

"What are you telling them?" I asked. We were filled with the relaxation of the day being done, of all the chores and work finished.

"I'm telling them they are good dogs," he said.

Up early, bathed in the cold blue light of the predawn bouncing off the ice and through the windows, I heard Simon hacking and coughing as he got a kettle going.

I debated whether or not I should ask to drive the sled home. Would Simon let me? Would it be overreaching? Did I not know some mysterious detail that would wreck us? I lightened my pockets so that I could run more easily and strapped my clunky boots down as tight as I could.

We eventually suited up and got going, after much tea drinking, some chatter, and some long, thoughtful silences.

Again, the familiar chaos of the dogs—they were barking and howling, ready to run from the moment it became clear we were harnessing them up. The night before, we had fed them two fish and a block of lard each. One meal a day. Simon said he can run them every day for a week, and then he has to rest them for two days.

Simon began harnessing up. The dogs were going mad, more agitated than yesterday, spinning and barking, and the lines seemed to get tangled—but you could see the genius of the system, because no matter how the dogs crisscrossed each other, the fan was so simple it sorted itself out. You just had to make sure your legs were clear.

Things were getting wilder and wilder, and I finally looked up to see Davidee running for the sled and Simon attaching the lead dog, Kakkinuk—it was time to go. I leapt clear of the singing lines and pounded heavily back to the sled. Davidee was trying to get the knot untied from the anchor. He was in the rear, so I jumped in front, thinking, Fuck it, I'll drive, I can do it.

"Push," Davidee called. He needed me to push back against the dogs. They were already running, and Davidee needed some slack. I set myself and heaved backward, not sure if I was doing anything, but then Davidee got what he needed and we slipped free and were *away*. The dogs fell silent, *becoming* what they were meant to be, a pack on the move. The sled rushed, and the snow whirred under the rails.

I was driving, and I jerked the sled a little, not because I had to— the lead dog ran directly onto our track and we were heading perfectly in the right direction—but because I could. *Hey Ma, I'm driving a dog team.*

It was a real, in-the-bones thrill. Elated, I called to the dogs the way the cowboys I had worked with in Montana called after the cattle, "Heeeyyyy—up!" I tried to replicate the trillings and ululation of Davidee, in the backseat. I set myself, grabbed the caribou antler handle, and jerked the sled—barely effectively, certainly not as smoothly as Davidee had done it. But I was doing it.

I howled at the dogs, I shouted, I gave them a *"Mush, you huskies, Mush!"* and I lectured them on the importance of hard training: they had a big race coming up, this was just an easy run, two hours and they're home, let's see some action! Sometimes my voice seemed to surprise them, the deep strange English causing the dogs to look back at me, questioning.

Laughing and shouting, I looked at Davidee, and he gave me the only reaction I saw in two days, a brief smile that flitted across his face, a tiny ray of sunshine. "This is awesome," I shouted back at him.

Davidee and I took turns sprinting alongside the sled, letting it get up some momentum. I had tightened up my massive boots, but it was still touch and go. A couple times I had to dive back to the sled, and one time I nearly went down and ended up sprawled awkwardly across the struts and on top of Davidee. But I did it, I sprinted, every time he did, and sometimes when he didn't. Excellent high-intensity interval training.

We came up on Simon and Larry in their snow machines. Simon had an extra dog to put back into the fan. "Stop, stop," yelled Davidee at me, and I thought, *What? We're stopping?* I dug for the brake, got it out, and started fumbling it into the snow. I was too late, and we'd streamed past Simon before the sled stopped.

"No no, go go!" shouted Davidee. What? Okay, I guess we don't wait. We were about a hundred feet past Simon, and I yanked the brake out. But now the dogs were milling around and a nasty little fight broke out, three or four dogs in a whirlwind of snarling teeth and roaring. Davidee snatched the whip and leapt in, lashing around. The whip didn't seem like much, but it worked, bringing the dogs to their duty, and the sled surged forward. I guess that was why we couldn't wait. Once the dogs were running, they wanted to keep running.

Simon and Larry surged by on their Ski-Doos, and the dogs surged in chase. I watched how the leader dog straightened the others out; he bent to his work, trotting in that ground-eating trot, while the others would sometimes screw off, pissing on things, defecating, until the strings yanked them on. The leader dog was a rock.

We came up on Simon again, swishing over the snow, and this time I was ready and buried the brake perfectly, the metal prongs digging, and the sled stopped with the dogs all around Simon. Davidee leapt up with the lead, Simon clicked the extra dog in, and we were off again, smooth as silk. Almost like I knew what I was doing.

Coming into town, the wink and gleam of houses, civilization, the barking of other dogs at our team as we streamed by—it was very much like being in a boat coming into harbor. The view felt the same.

The dogs knew exactly where they were going, and as they pulled up to Simon I jammed the brake in—but it was scarcely necessary. I felt euphoric, and then I saw Simon's beaming face.

"Did you learn to make the dogs happy?" he asked. "I heard you sing to them."

I thought, Maybe I did. They made me happy.

I finish tucking the string around the strut of the sled, wrap it around my gloved hands, and pull, tightening down the lashings. That's it. I tie it off and look up to my son.

"The sled's ready. Let's go get the dogs."

He nods, and we walk out of the garage to where the dogs are yapping and leaping in the alley. A light snow is falling, and the air is still and cold, but without the wind it's almost pleasant. A winter wonderland.

We each grab a dog and haul them, tails wagging, toward the sled. They want to pull, because they know it means they'll get fed tonight. The leader dog leaps up onto my son but he knocks him away. "You're last, buddy," I hear him mutter.

We've got a long way to go, at least a week's travel, and hopefully we'll find some food. But at least we've got the dogs.

The snowflakes hang over the deserted city, frozen in the still air, suspended as if in water; the idea of time seems ridiculous. There is only the present. We live here now.

15.

THIS IS THE END

"Today might be the day I have to use my weapon," Tiger McKee told me. That mantra was part of his mental preparation for going armed. He prayed he would never have to (and Tiger did pray), but he was always ready.

As I learned new skills for surviving a postapocalyptic world, I began to feel a change in my own way of thinking. I was becoming more like the survivalists I met. Not paranoid, just prepared. Wise, savvy, even slightly superior to the unaware around me. Ready to use my weapons and knowledge. But even in my own head, I had to wonder at the distinction between paranoia and preparation, and the gray areas in between.

In boxing, they say, "Be first." Be first with the jab, be first with aggressive action, don't wait; beat him to the punch. He can't hit you if you're hitting him. Trainers yell it from the corner: "Be first!"

We all know disaster is exacerbated by human nature. In the summer disaster blockbusters, people usually turn out to be the real enemy—driven by fear, selfishness, stupidity, or plain old evil. In the comic turned TV show *The Walking Dead*, the living are the true horror, not the zombies. Mankind's worst nature will rise in the postapocalypse. People are dangerous and panicky. When the Big One hits, it's going to be social Darwinism, survival of the fittest, dog eat dog. If your neighbor comes to loot your house (and he will), you'd better "be first" with the pistol.

The English philosopher Thomas Hobbes wrote that without social order, without strong rulers, society breaks down into the natural way of every man against every man, *bellum omnium contra omnes*. Civilization is just a thin veneer underneath which rage our true, savage selves.

My own neighbor said to me, "During an earthquake, I'm worried about the *have-nots* coming over here to take from us." Common wisdom dictates that people (especially the poor) panic in a disaster and transform into unstable, frothing animals.

But what does the evidence say?

We all remember Hurricane Katrina, when New Orleans descended into utter lawlessness. People ran wild, killing, looting, and shooting at helicopters. The law of the jungle returned. Nowhere was this worse than in the Superdome, where some twenty thousand evacuees took refuge from the storm. Trapped in squalid conditions for days, without any police or government aid, the toilets overflowed and rape, murder, mayhem, and death reigned inside like the Four Horsemen of the Apocalypse. Reuters reported that there were hundreds of bodies in a makeshift morgue, and the chief of police, Eddie Compass, told Oprah that "they were raping babies in there." That's what happens in disasters: people become savages.

Except, of course, that it isn't.

When the National Guard finally showed up they brought hundreds of body bags, but when they finished the evacuation of the dome, they pulled only six bodies. Four elderly people had died due to exposure, one person had overdosed, and another committed suicide.

Of the nineteen thousand people searched as they left the dome, only thirteen weapons were found.

Who can say where a rumor starts? The police and local radio stations claimed they were receiving phone calls and texts about gangs and roving rapists and murder from people inside. It turns out there was no cell service in the Superdome. When you think about that horrific line, "They're raping babies in there," does that even sound like a crime report, or instead just a nightmare given voice, the sound of panic? And all the stories of snipers shooting at rescue helicopters were later retracted. People may have been firing into the air to get attention. But major news outlets, CNN and FOX, reported the "state of siege" in the city—massive gang violence, rapes, and murders—as fact, which in turn influenced how the police and National Guard acted.

Everyone was buying into the notion that civilization is just a thin veneer and that at any moment we can all revert to animalistic, Hobbesian behavior. The National Guard commander Brigadier General Gary Jones told the *Army Times* that the city was like Somalia: "We're going to go out and take this city back. This will be a combat operation to get this city under control." From the top down, the outside in, the view was that the survivors were dangerous and wild. And the racial element added a whole other element to the news coverage. Rebecca Solnit wrote in *A Paradise Built in Hell,* "It was as though a levee had broken and a huge flood of deadly stereotypes was pouring in."

This fear of the survivors made a difference—aid was delayed or not delivered because of the "security risk." Food and water had to wait for an armed National Guard escort.

"The vast majority of people [looting] were taking food and water to live," Captain Marlon Defillo, the New Orleans Police Department's commander of public affairs, later said. "There were no killings, not one murder. No bullet holes were found in the fuselage of any rescue helicopter."

There was looting, for survival, and there was plenty of petty theft, but there wasn't widespread violence. Disaster scholars, social anthropologists, and sociologists who have gone back and studied the events of New Orleans and other disasters—earthquakes, fires, and so on—find that mass panic doesn't really exist. It can flare up in crowded spaces where there is limited exit, like soccer stadiums or burning nightclubs, but otherwise it just doesn't happen in big-city disasters. Solnit writes, *"The basic notion is of people so overwhelmed by fear and selfish desire to survive that their judgment, their social bonds, even their humanity are overwhelmed . . . belief in panic provides a premise for treating the public as a problem . . . Hollywood eagerly feeds those beliefs. Sociologists, however, do not."*

Look at the earthquake in Haiti. The people of Haiti are much worse off, economically, than those living in any major city in the United States to start with, and they suffered a devastating disaster. And lo and behold, there wasn't a massive social breakdown—raping and looting, gangs roaming the street. Sure, weeks later there was looting—for food and water. But somehow, here in Los Angeles, a disaster would turn us into a marauding horde in five minutes?

Survivors of the 9/11 attacks on the World Trade Center recount how orderly the descent down the stairs was, how polite people were. In any Hollywood treatment there would have been old ladies getting trampled, guys in suits getting into fistfights. Instead, people waited patiently.

Journalist Amanda Ripley examines mass panic in her book *The Unthinkable.* After studying incidents where it happened (during soccer matches, rock concerts, and plane evacuations), engineers determined that group panic needs certain distinct, *extremely specific* factors to occur. First, people have to be tightly pressed together, unable to move freely; essentially, claustrophobia plays a major part. Second, people have to feel that they *could potentially be trapped*—not that they *are* trapped, which is different (group panic doesn't happen in elevators or submarines, for instance) but that they *might* be. Third, they have to feel totally helpless. And fourth, they have to have a sense of isolation, of feeling alone in a crowd. If all four of these factors aren't present, you don't get group panic. It doesn't just *happen* to a crowd during an earthquake. People don't just start screaming and running around in circles, trampling babies and old women. That's the biggest myth about how we might behave during the end of the world, and pretty much everyone is pushing it, from Hollywood to government officials.

But, you ask, what about Condition Black, that catastrophic breakdown caused by stress hormones? If people are so freaked out they can't even dial 911, aren't those folks dangerous? What about dissociation? People can become animals then, right? It turns out that real Condition Black is extremely short-lived. It lasts for seconds, minutes at most.

If you had asked any New York City cop what would happen during a citywide blackout, he would have predicted chaos. What actually happened during the blackout of 2003? Gang members walked little old ladies home, and people checked on their neighbors.

Your fellow civilians might not be who you have to worry about. Cops live with the bad side every day. They're conditioned to see the worst, and "the public" is often part of their problem. Steve Rodriguez, a former SWAT sniper, writes, "Ninety-nine-point-something percent of police officers will never fire their weapon, yet we go through a lot of expense in training and equipping them. Even fewer are shot, but we issue body armor." Of course, we need to train and equip the police, but it can create an atmosphere where they do what they're trained to do, warranted or not. They see what they've been trained to see. Being prepared is expecting the worst. All this may play into what sociologists call elite panic, which, in a disaster, is something you *do* have to keep an eye out for. The elite, meaning government and law enforcement, sometimes overreact. They have the most to lose from the upending of order. "Elite panic in disaster, as identified by contemporary disaster scholars, is shaped by belief, belief that since human beings at large are bestial and dangerous, the believer must himself or herself act with savagery to ensure that individual safety or the safety of his interests. The elites that panic are, in times of crisis, the minority. . . ." writes Solnit.

A typical case of elite panic in a disaster is when police shoot to kill looters, out of the presumed need to protect property. In 1906, after the great quake in San Francisco, the National Guard came in and shot looters because the mayor was sure that all the poor folk were going to break into the taverns, get drunk, and start a rampage. Because, we have to assume, *that's what he would have done.* People got shot trying to clean up their own houses, or trying to pull neighbors from the rubble. And just in case you're thinking that was a long time ago, it also happened in New Orleans. The governor of Louisiana, Kathleen Blanco, said publicly of the National Guard coming in: "These troops are battle-tested. They have M16s and are locked and loaded. These troops know how to shoot and kill and I expect they will."

Katrina was a hotbed of elite panic, from Camp Greyhound (the first thing anyone built was a prison?) to police shootings to the mayor's decision, a couple days in, to reassign police officers from search and rescue to property protection while there were still thousands of citizens stranded and in need.

It's easy to judge, here at my desk, with the lights on. I know that. Most of those cops in New Orleans thought they were doing the right thing. They saw a city out of control. But I'm warning you about what the facts say happens in a disaster as opposed to what our fears say, or what Hollywood shows us. You may have to worry more about the police response than about your neighbors or the have-nots.

Terrence Des Pres begins his revelatory book *The Survivor* with a confounding idea: that survival in the Nazi concentration camps or the Soviet prisons was "neither random nor amoral." What can he mean by saying that *survival is moral*? Wouldn't a concentration camp be the definition of a dog-eat-dog world? You'd think that survival would be totally random, or that those that did make it were the most ruthless, remorseless, or conniving people. But you'd be dead wrong.

I began to understand this when I read, "Failure to wash was the iron law of the camps." The prisoners were filthy, often covered in excrement. They weren't allowed bathroom breaks. They had to work, eat, and sleep in soiled clothes. This was intentional policy on the part of the SS, which aimed not only to humiliate its prisoners, but also to dehumanize them. Turning the enemy into the *other,* into something less than human, is a crucial preparation for killing him.

For the prisoners, washing took energy, time, calories. It seemed to be contrary to survival needs. But here's the real iron law: those who stopped washing usually died within weeks. The failure to preserve *dignity* meant death. And by *dignity,* Des Pres doesn't mean "pomp or ritual pride," but "an inward resistance to determination by external forces . . . a sense of innocence and worth . . . one of the irreducible elements of selfhood . . . a self-conscious, self-determining faculty whose function is to insist upon recognition of itself *as such.* Certainly the SS recognized it, and their attempt to destroy it . . . was one of the worst aspects of the camp ordeal."

In short, what Des Pres gleaned from the interviews with survivors was that the "will to resist" and the need for dignity might be the same thing. Preserving your humanity and preserving your life are one and the same. Every survivor had a tale of being saved by a complete stranger, at one point or another, and every survivor helped someone else, often someone they didn't know.

The need to help is as great as the need to be helped.

When disaster does strike, retaining your humanity is the most important part of survival. There will be moments of chaos and confusion, but they won't last. Social order will reassert itself. Cooler heads will prevail. Working together with your neighbors will have a much higher success rate than going into paranoid bunker mode.

Over the years I spent talking to people about survival, I heard dozens of times, "I don't need supplies, I've got a gun. I'll just take what I need when the shit hits the fan." That sentiment, obviously, is part of the problem. Most likely, these people are going to be amazed at how quickly social order is restored and they are brought to justice.

Altruism is real, and it matters. It's not only what gives humanity a crack at the sublime, but also an essential survival trait. Just knowing this, and believing it, may be enough to mitigate elite panic. It seems to me that elite panic results from three causes: One, preparing for the worst. Two, being responsible for all outcomes, and for the health, safety, and property of others. And three, a misguided and overblown fear of people's degenerating into animals during a disaster. The first two are good things, it's the last one we need to work on.

"Okay, Pollyanna," you say. "Keep thinking that when the wolves are howling outside your door."

I get it. The sentiment that altruism is an essential survival trait seems opposed by pretty much all of human history. As the ancients said, *homo homini lupus est*—man is a wolf to man. And it's true, when the resources run low, when people are starving, they start eating each other. But it's just not true in the short term. Long-term, grid-down

TEOTWAWKI is different than a normal disaster, or even a catastrophe. But is it really going to happen?

Apocalyptic myths have been around as long as there has been writing. Ancient cultures including the Babylonian, Egyptian, Greek, and Roman all had stories that were precursors to the Bible's Book of Revelation. The word *Armageddon* comes from the Hebrew for Mount Megiddo, the location of the last battle.

If you want to talk about how far back apocalyptic thinking goes and how much it influences the way we see the world in the West, you could argue that the Crusades were in part fought because of belief in prophecy about the apocalypse. Richard the Lionheart was told by a leading scholar of his time that Saladin was the Antichrist. The Puritans coming to the New World carried with them intense apocalyptic fears. Scholars were convinced in 1758 that the return of Halley's comet was going to cause a massive, world-covering flood, just like Noah's.

More recently, Hitler was conceived as the Antichrist, but strangely it was Mussolini who fit the bill better for evangelicals during the Second World War, because the Bible foretold the restored Roman Empire (anybody still worried about that?). With the atom bomb and the threat of nuclear holocaust, now there really was a way the end could come in "fire and brimstone." President Ronald Reagan told *People* magazine in 1983, "[Theologians] have said that never, in the time between the prophecies up until now, has there ever been a time in which so many of the prophecies are coming together. . . ."

Religion aside, Thomas Malthus wrote in 1798 about the dangers of overpopulation, that "gigantic inevitable famine stalks in the rear," and this idea has sunk deep. So-called Malthusian theory has been with us ever since. Books like the 1968 best seller *The Population Bomb*—the race to feed humanity is already lost, by 1985 hundreds of millions will starve—have deeply influenced our collective thinking.

I could go on and on; when you start seeing how seriously people have been taking the end of the world—how close it's looked for basically all of human history—you start to wonder about your own fears. Whether it's man-made, divine retribution, or a cataclysmic natural disaster, the end has pretty much always been just around the corner.

In his 2005 book *Expert Political Judgment: How Good Is It? How Can We Know?* Philip Tetlock tracked "expert" predictions from political scientists, journalists, and pundits over twenty years and found that a coin flip would give you better predictions. In particular, the "doomsters" were way off—those who foresaw bad outcomes 70 percent of the time were right 12 percent of the time. *The Black Swan* makes this same point. Monkeys who bought stocks at random would outperform stockbrokers.

So be careful about selling the farm in preparation for sudden doom.

There is, however, an additional issue that informs all survivalist thinking. In 2008, 50 percent of people worldwide and 82.2 percent of the people in the United States lived in cities.

The dense populations of today's cities are only supportable through the functioning of the grid. That's it, end of story. Without the grid, population densities will find a new, much lower equilibrium. That is a reality of the world we live in. Survival writers talk about the ravaging hordes of starving people leaving the cities, looking for food. That is a possibility, but it's not inevitable. The grid is probably more durable and resilient than some people think. But the grid is also more fragile than many assume. This isn't science fiction, but a real vulnerability. You can ignore the system's fragility, but you can't say it doesn't exist.

Our world is completely dependent on the grid, and if it failed, we would either have to find very different ways to live or else die *en masse*.

That's a fact. Without the grid, the city is a time bomb. This vulnerability is what drove me into my quest to prepare.

The book *Collapse,* by Jared Diamond, analyzes the convulsions of societies that have failed. Cannibalism is a common thread—as communities crumble, and they do, the food runs out and the dead are eaten. Murder and warfare rage over vanishing resources. So Cormac McCarthy's *The Road* provides a possible scenario. People have behaved pretty badly to each other for most of human history. There is some argument as to how savage primitive societies actually were, but there is no argument at all about how savage they became. When competing for resources, man is capable of extraordinary ruthlessness.

If everyone in the country could become just a little more self-reliant, we could defuse this thing before it happens. If everyone lived with a few months' worth of food and water in their house or apartment, we could delay that competition for resources, and probably avoid a lot of the problems following something like an EMP attack, a solar flare, or even an economic crisis. Aliens or zombies are still gonna be tough, but that's a given.

So yes, get prepared, but don't "be first"—don't start talking about *us* and *them* already, because then you're making *them* into the *other,* and that's when the shooting starts. Far too many of the survival books I've read go there, way too early. You're becoming part of the problem; you're not the hero, you're the bad guy. It's all *us.*

Diamond looks at five societies that failed, including Easter Island, the Norse colony in Greenland, and the Maya, and notes that it was primarily environmental mismanagement and degradation of resources that doomed them: deforestation, overgrazing, and climate change. The Norse in Greenland survived for four hundred years before dying out. The societal values that allowed them to survive in a harsh environment, that gave them strength and cohesion, also doomed them as conditions changed. Sound familiar? Anybody seen a massive, heavily urbanized nation clinging to a two-hundred-year-old political system that was devised to govern a rural agrarian population 1/100th of the size it is now? Diamond makes the point that political leaders have to have the will to address environmental issues. The scapegoats, politicians and corporations, carry a responsibility for the damage they do; but the truth is, society as a whole is responsible. You and I are responsible.

As the world moves forward with seven billion souls, sustainability isn't something that only the granola-crunching hippies should be talking about. Seven billion narcissists is almost as frightening as a zombie apocalypse. But we can't be too scared to act. We have to be motivated.

Never in history has a people been so healthy and lived such long and free lives as we do now, here in the first world. And yet, in part because of the media and the twenty-four-hour news cycle, people are as afraid as ever. Humans are naturally drawn to scary stories for a variety of reasons. The government pushes fear through a combination of good intentions, cover-your-ass politics, litigation concerns, and Machiavellian manipulation (although much less of the latter, I suspect, than many believe). It's a bias inherent in humanity that we watch out for scary stuff and pay attention when it happens.

Anyone who thinks that right now is a particularly scary time in human history—that "things are getting really bad out there"—is a poor student of history. Really? Scarier than the Cold War, with thousands of Russian nukes pointed at us and Khrushchev yelling "We will bury you"? Scarier than the Black Death, when you watched one out of three of your friends and family die a horrible, utterly mysterious death, with strange swellings and black lumps, vomiting blood? The truth is, the past isn't scary to us, only the future is—the unknown.

There is some basis for fears of the end of the world, but there is also a lot of hype. Preparing for the apocalypse is essentially about walking the line between paranoia and self-reliance. To me, the definition of paranoia is a little like the definition of addiction. If something is destructive to your life—takes your job, alienates friends and loved ones—then it's an addiction (or paranoia). If it makes your life better, it's not.

By keeping my preparation mostly in the arena of self-reliance and knowledge (as opposed to the "my fallout shelter has four-and-a-half-foot-thick walls" arena), I have only made my life better. I've *enjoyed* learning new skills for dealing with new scenarios—and the confidence that comes with it.

But preparing for the end of the world is like being a parent—at some point, you have to let go. You can't control everything, you can't live in the bunker, you can't refuse to ever let your daughter go on a date. At some point, when you've done your best, you have to get on with your life and trust the universe not to fuck you. Some of the people I met over the course of this journey seem happy and content; for others, all their preparation seems to have made them more worried, more fearful.

I have hundreds of gallons of water. MREs for months. Antibiotics. A bug-out bag at home, SSB radios in the cars. Having a bulletproof vest and an AR-15 locked in a safe that I can get into in a minute or two relaxes me. The gun doesn't hurt anybody, I'm trained to use it, I'm responsible for it. And I've taken responsibility for the future. Maybe I've reassured a serious little boy that if the Indians do come over the wall in the dead of night, I'll be able to fight.

But the essential joy is in the space between my ears. I've broadened and deepened my understanding of the world, almost immeasurably—just by taking more responsibility for what happens to me and my family. That shift has resulted in a far deeper, more intuitive feel for the ebb and flow of life. I'm going to see Don Yeager again next year. I'm going to teach my son to hunt.

Maybe it's just part of maturity, fatherhood, being closer to forty than thirty, but I've finally managed to slow down. I'm no longer the boy who rushes through everything, desperate just to finish it and move on. I've internalized the idea that *slow is smooth and smooth is fast.* To go barefoot, to be deliberate and cautious, and to do things right the first time. That's not to say I never get it wrong; it's an eternal struggle.

All these new skills I've learned are perishable. Gunfighting, driving, making cordage, they all go away without practice. Just as with any skill, you have to keep grinding on it, make it all part of your routine. The idea of self-reliance is a complex and perhaps even foolish one, here in the twenty-first century. Maybe it always was—who in history was ever really completely self-reliant? I mean, they had parents, right? Hunting partners? *Homo sapiens* is not a solitary beast in the wild. I am not a bull elk.

But to me, the conceit of self-reliance has a critical relationship to understanding the fabric of reality, how the pieces fit together. Understand *how* things are done, because then you might truly begin to grasp the *whys* of the world. With the supreme good luck of being alive comes a duty, a requirement, to understand. You have to be curious. You have to try.

Acknowledgments

Anyone mentioned by name in the book, of course, *thank you* for your extreme generosity. The book was a delight to research.

But there are some I'd like to thank who served as an unofficial "brain trust" for the project, in particular Jon Rider and Steve Rodriguez. Jon was a retired colonel in the Marine Corps, a decorated Vietnam vet and security professional who enjoyed discussing some of these problems with me. He passed away in 2010 from pulmonary fibrosis, but even at the end, his enthusiasm and joyful spirit were an inspiration. He was one of those guys who had really learned how to live.

Steve Rodriguez, a veteran police sniper from Albuquerque, worked with Jon at a firm that consults with the Russians on how to keep nuclear material secure, and he was a tremendous resource for me and an engaging correspondent. Steve, as a sniper, deeply understands the value of life—he signs all his e-mails with "stay safe and enjoy everything." Amen. Thanks, Steve.

Hal Herring is an outdoorsman and a great writer, a friend of Tiger's, and a powerful, original thinker. His conversation and writing on hunting were great guides for me. Hal is a true gentleman, in the classic sense of the word.

ACKNOWLEDGMENTS

Roberto Juarez is a friend, a fellow boxer, and an ex-gang member who helped me understand the gang culture in East LA.

Colin Dickerman, my brilliant editor, thanks for putting up with me. At least when you edit me, you know you're earning your pay.

To David Kuhn, my agent, as always, thanks for the vision.

Thanks to my mother, Susan, and my father, C. Michael, who together taught me the most important rule of life: you are responsible.

And finally, thanks to my wife Patty Jenkins, for the support, for the belief, for the uncompromising purity of spirit.